NATIONAL INSTITUTE FOR SOCIAL WORK TRAINING
SERIES NO. 22

HUMAN DEVELOPMENT

Publications by the
National Institute for Social Work Training
Mary Ward House, London W.C.1

NO. 1 SOCIAL WORK AND SOCIAL CHANGE
by Eileen Younghusband

NO. 2 INTRODUCTION TO A SOCIAL WORKER
produced by the National Institute for Social Work Training

NO. 3 SOCIAL POLICY AND ADMINISTRATION
by D. V. Donnison, Valerie Chapman and others

NO. 4 SOCIAL WORK WITH FAMILIES
Readings in Social Work, Volume 1
compiled by Eileen Younghusband

NO. 5 PROFESSIONAL EDUCATION FOR SOCIAL WORK IN BRITAIN
by Marjorie J. Smith

NO. 6 NEW DEVELOPMENTS IN CASEWORK
Readings in Social Work, Volume 2
compiled by Eileen Younghusband

NO. 7 THE FIELD TRAINING OF SOCIAL WORKERS
by S. Clement Brown and E. R. Gloyne

NO. 8 DECISION IN CHILD CARE
A Study of Prediction in Fostering Children
by R. A. Parker

NO. 9 ADOPTION POLICY AND PRACTICE
by Iris Goodacre

NO. 10 SUPERVISION IN SOCIAL WORK
by Dorothy E. Pettes

NO. 11 CARING FOR PEOPLE
The 'Williams' Report
on the Staffing of Residential Homes

NO. 12 SOCIAL WORK AND SOCIAL VALUES
Readings in Social Work, Volume 3
compiled by Eileen Younghusband

NO. 14 EDUCATION FOR SOCIAL WORK
Readings in Social Work, Volume 4
compiled by Eileen Younghusband

NO. 15 CHILD CARE: NEEDS AND NUMBERS
by Jean Packman

NO. 16 THE VOLUNTARY WORKER IN THE SOCIAL SERVICES
Chairman of Committee: Geraldine M. Aves

NO. 17 A PLACE LIKE HOME: A PIONEER HOSTEL FOR BOYS
by David Wills

NO. 18 THE ADOPTION OF NON-WHITE CHILDREN
by Lois Raynor

NO. 19 HELPING THE AGED
by E. Matilda Goldberg with others

NO. 20 VOLUNTEERS IN PRISON AFTER-CARE
by Hugh Barr

NO. 21 HOMELESS NEAR A THOUSAND HOMES
by Bryan Glastonbury

HUMAN DEVELOPMENT

An Introduction to the Psychodynamics of
Growth, Maturity and Ageing

by

ERIC RAYNER
Ph.D.

London

GEORGE ALLEN & UNWIN LTD

RUSKIN HOUSE   MUSEUM STREET

ISBN 0 04 150936 9 *Cloth*
150037 7 *Paper*

Printed in Great Britain
in 11 point Fournier type
by Cox & Wyman Ltd, London, Fakenham and Reading

PREFACE

In writing this book I owe a great debt to what others have told and taught me. Much of this has come from books, but most has been learnt by word of mouth. First, I would like to thank my teachers in psychoanalysis, foremost amongst whom were Mrs Eva Rosenfeld and Dr Tom Main of the Cassel Hospital, but there were many others. In more recent years my patients have perhaps been my primary informants about the intimate and inner experience of living. I rarely get the opportunity to thank them even in private. To make amends for this I do so more publicly here.

This book has arisen directly out of my lectures on Human Development in the Department of Applied Social Studies at Croydon Technical College. In these I have always handed out duplicated lecture notes, so that the time of classes could be devoted to discussion with social work, nursing and health visitor students. This has given me the opportunity to increase the breadth of my knowledge of people in a way that would perhaps be difficult in any other place.

The distillation of ideas for the book has in many ways been an informal team effort by the staff at Croydon. I owe most to the encouragement of Florence Mitchell, who was abetted by all the social work and health visitor tutors. I owe a special debt to Mary Barker and Nano McCaughan, not only for their suggestions but also for spending many hours reading and criticizing the draft. My psychoanalytic colleagues Dr Alan Wilson and Dr Peter Lomas did the same. I should also like to thank Joan Willans for converting my nearly illegible writing into a readable manuscript.

The most intimate participants in writing have been my family. Although they are perhaps not old enough yet to realize it, my children Sarah, Will and Ben have done more to move me to develop the early chapters than anyone else. The actual writing itself was really a joint venture with my wife Mary. At the same time as looking after the household and suffering my irritability, she has given me ideas and arguments at every stage. Much of the writing was worked out between us, so that it is difficult to say whether it is hers or mine. Whatever grace of style the book might have is due to her.

E. H. R.

CONTENTS

Preface   *page* 7
1. Introduction   11
2. The Experience of Pregnancy and Childbirth   25
3. The First Six Months   40
4. The Second Six Months   55
5. One to Two Years Old   72
6. Childhood – Two to Three Years Old   87
7. The Pre-School Child – Three to Four Years Old   100
8. Four to Five Years Old   115
9. Five to Eleven: Early School Days   128
10. Puberty   140
11. Mid-Adolescence   150
12. Late Adolescence and Adulthood   158
13. Courtship and Being in Love   171
14. Being Married   186
15. Mothering   200
16. Being a Father   208
17. Mid-Life   220
18. Old Age   234
19. Dying, Grief and Mourning   244
References   259
Index   269

I

INTRODUCTION

I. THIS BOOK: ITS SCOPE AND LIMITS

We shall be concerned in this book with the experiences of people as they grow up, mature, age and die. Our attention will be upon the intimate or inner activities, feelings and thoughts, of the individual as he goes through life.

Each chapter will deal with a specific phase of life such as early infancy, going to school, puberty, mothering or middle age. In each there will be a discussion of some of the personal issues which assume importance for an individual going through the time of life in question.

Throughout the book we shall use a *psychodynamic* approach. We shall look at the person, whatever his age, as facing a multiplicity of problems which he attempts to solve in order to fulfil his needs. These needs may be felt as arising from inside his body, as with hunger, thirst, the need to breathe or sexual tension. Other needs may appear to be unrelated to physiology but none the less seem to stem predominantly from inside himself. This would be the case with someone who felt an urge to excel or to be a good person. On the other hand, problems may also arise from the environment, from other people's demands and from the necessities of the physical world.

This viewpoint may at first glance seem a gloomy one, as if a person is seen as burdened with difficulties. Perhaps this arises because we have introduced the notion of 'a problem' and this is often associated with seemingly insoluble emotional disturbances. We are not referring to these here, but pointing to a general characteristic of natural human thought and action. In this context problems may on occasion be burdensome, but it can also be a delight to be engrossed in them.

At any moment in time a person may solve a multiplicity of problems arising from many directions at once. Here is a simple example. A young woman may organize her morning's activities so that within a short space of time she washes up, makes the beds, sits back and has a cup of tea, looks out of the window to see the children in the garden, shouts to tell them to keep off the flower-beds and reads a letter from her mother whilst the washing-machine is going. She then goes out and has a game with the children, before starting to cook the dinner while she listens to the radio. If one attempts to clarify these activities into those which deal with inner problems or those arising from outside, it will be found that some are easy to define while others are more ambiguous.

It will be impossible in the course of this book to investigate every sort of problem situation likely to arise. We can only deal with a few in a rather arbitrary way. But the viewpoint will remain a psychodynamic one of seeing the person as continuously active in seeking and solving problems to meet his and others' needs.

We shall also be investigating how the individual *develops* psychologically. In other words we shall be concerned with how he learns from experience and how, as he grows older, his mind becomes capable of integrating the data of more and more complex problem situations.

This is a subject which will probably be new to the reader, and he may well be asking himself what use it will be to him. Naturally the book can be read for the sake of general interest, but it is mainly intended as a primer for students of the helping professions; social work, health visiting, mental nursing, teaching, counselling or medicine. It is part of the business of these professions to be concerned at times with the intimate private lives of individual people. In such work it is essential to learn afresh about each new person met, without resorting to prejudices and preconceptions. This applies to the process of getting to know anyone, be he friend, relative, client, pupil or patient. But fresh learning about each new person is aided by drawing upon a store of general background knowledge which has been picked up in the past and can be called upon when applicable. This book aims to be a preliminary exploration of some of the predominant personal problems which ordinary people face. Thus it is intended to serve as a starting-point for the professional person who wishes to develop a store of general background knowledge for later use when working with other people.

Having roughly described the book as one of general knowledge we can perhaps best go on to clarify its limits by describing what it is *not* about. It gives no information about how to help particular people with their problems: it is not about casework, medical, nursing or educational practice. Also, although we will be viewing the individual as facing problems throughout his life, it is not about personal predicaments which have become chronic. Thus it is not about psychopathology, psychiatry or abnormal psychology. However, there are many pointers to indicate where personal problems can become chronic. It should be fairly easy to integrate later learning about individual psychopathology within our elementary framework.

We shall not specifically be concerned with the physical processes of the body. But it is axiomatic to the approach of this book that a person cannot be understood if his physical functioning is ignored. There will be repeated references to this at every stage of life discussed. No very detailed understanding is necessary but an elementary knowledge of human physiology is essential. So if the reader has not done a course in this already, he should at least read one of the many simple textbooks that are now available on the subject (e.g. Green, 1969).

Since our focus of study will be upon individual inner experiences and not upon practices or beliefs common to groups of people, this is not a work of sociology. But, since an individual's experiences depend very much upon the groups to which he belongs, we shall be drawing upon the work and writing of sociologists and social psychologists. It is impossible to understand individual people without a sensitivity to the cultural background from which they come. Within the confines of this book it will not be possible to consider the nuances of experiences in a variety of cultural backgrounds. We have thus had to rest content with a book that is culturally biased. Its frame of reference is predominantly that of the British working and middle classes. The reader must bear in mind that developmental sequences and individual experiences are likely to be different for people with other backgrounds. He can use any insights gained from the book by applying them to people of other backgrounds, to explore how their experience compares with the narrow range discussed here.

There is little or no evaluation as to whether customs and practices are good or bad. It seems that every committed worker must eventually evaluate the practices of people with whom he comes into contact, but only after he has steeped himself in the subject.

Evaluation without prior exploration simply becomes an exercise in prejudiced thinking.

We now come to the last of our list of negatives. This is not a work that is primarily orientated towards either social surveys or experimental psychology. It is not a manual which evaluates research work. Such critical evaluation of scientific work is beyond its scope, but we shall give references to scientific texts where they highlight points of psychological importance to the study of the individual.

Some psychological concepts will be introduced in the text and summarized at the end of most chapters. These are concepts which are in everyday use particularly in social work, and the reader may find it useful to have them defined. Some of these theoretical concepts have been developed by academic psychologists, but many have been coined by psychoanalysts. I have placed stress on those concepts derived from the work of psychoanalysts, not because of a concern with psychoanalytic treatment, but because they seem useful to anyone interested in exploring the intimate processes of the individual as a single person. What is more, virtually all the concepts described in this book have become everyday jargon, so that it is part of general knowledge to be acquainted with them.

The book does not attempt a detailed criticism of various theoretical concepts, nor does it linger upon comparing various schools of thought. It attempts to provide a simple sketch map of some major features in phases of life in order to start the reader on his own explorations. If time were taken up with the theoretical exposition of various points of view, of argument and counter-argument, attention would be distracted from the primary subject of our study, which is investigating the experience of development and ageing. This is not to say that the author considers such comparison valueless, but rather that one should become acquainted with the raw material of the subject before useful comparisons can be made. It is to be hoped that the student will be sufficiently stimulated by the lines of inquiry started in this book to follow up the original work of other authors.

It is a common fate for writers on psychology to be ascribed a sort of mystic grandeur, as if they alone knew the secrets of life. Such an attitude can only hinder free exploration and learning. The reader should view this book as written by an intelligent fool who is himself exploring the subject in a half-blind way, attempting to draw attention to aspects of experience which seem to him to be important, yet missing many others. It would be best if writer and reader could talk to each other to clarify their ideas in argument and discussion. Instead, the reader will have to confine himself to argument with himself or with fellow-students and teachers.

When learning about human beings it seems that we must direct our exploratory thinking in several directions at once. First, we learn about human experience from our own inner feelings and ideas, by introspection. During the course of the book the reader will be invited to introspect on many occasions. Secondly, we learn by recognizing the experiences of those around us, our friends and acquaintances. Thirdly, these individual instances of experience may be summarized in the form of abstract psychological concepts. Lastly, these ideas are refined through reading or listening to the work of specialists. There will be further discussion of how we understand human beings in the next section of this chapter. Here we shall simply suggest that any abstract concept involving individual experience must have these four points of reference to be well understood. If the reader fails to exercise himself in all of them he is likely to find his ideas limited. For instance, if a student fails to make himself aware of the first two reference-points and confines himself only to the theoretical distillate, he may be able to sound clever but will probably be aridly academic. He will in short be devoid of common sense. On the other hand, if a student applies himself only to the first two reference-points, he will fail to distil his ideas into abstract form. He will then find it difficult to use his experiences in new situations and tend to be insular and narrow-minded.

In summary, the writer feels that this book can best be used as a stimulus to a personal exploration of the subject where the reader looks both into himself and thinks about his acquaintances around him. The book is not an encyclopaedia. It cannot be exhaustive of all the facets of different experiences of development and life. It merely scratches the surface, so that every reader will find important events in people's lives that are not even mentioned here. If the book arouses an enjoyable interest in the human experiences of development, the writer for one will be well satisfied.

II. ON UNDERSTANDING INDIVIDUALS

1. Listening and thinking

We have just attempted a definition of the viewpoint from which this book will explore a person's experiences. We suggested that the reader should exercise his ideas both practically and theoretically in order to develop the kind of understanding of people that will be useful to him. Let us now reflect a little further upon this subject, and discuss some of the forms thought takes when 'understanding people' is going on. In doing this we shall be turning in upon ourselves, thinking about thinking as it were. This can become a tiresome and sterile activity, a sort of 'contemplating the navel' if carried on too long. But the psychological questions which arise in this book often lead to confusion and misunderstanding and it is hoped that some clarification of the modes of thinking used will save trouble for the reader later on.

Let us consider what we are doing in a general way when we set about 'understanding' a person. Take a hypothetical encounter between two people. The first will be called the 'speaker', the second the 'listener'. The thought processes of the listener will be briefly investigated as he or she tries to understand the speaker. The listener could be almost anyone, and the speaker a client, patient, friend, acquaintance or relative.

A man comes into the listener's room. He seems to be in his thirties, and dressed in a suit which is clean but rather worn and old-fashioned. The visitor's face is deeply sun-tanned as if he has been on holiday. However, his hand has a slight tremor, his face is noticeably puckered, and his lips are trembling.

The listener is rather puzzled. The man's suit would suggest a badly paid clerk. But this does not tally with the deep sun-tan, which makes him think of Mediterranean holidays. The tremor of his hand also puzzles him; he wonders whether the man has some neurological disease, but then notices that his face is also trembling and puckered. The thought then comes to him that the man is probably very anxious about something. By the time these thoughts have rushed through the listener's mind the visitor begins to speak and blurts out the following story. 'I'm sorry to trouble you, but I wonder if you could help me because I don't know what to do. I'm worried because my wife is due to have a baby in a month's time, and they say she has to go into hospital till the baby arrives. They say there's something wrong with the position of the placenta. I can look after the other three children but I've got to go back next week to my ship, which is on the Cape Town run. If I don't, I'll break my contract and find it hard to get another ship. The trouble is we moved only a month ago from my mother-in-law's in the country and we don't know anyone here in town. If we had still been in the country my mother-in-law and all the people in the village would have looked after the children, but up here my wife feels at a loss and so do I. We moved up because my father-in-law had to move to a tied farm cottage which was too small for all of them, and my wife and I decided that it was time we set up on our own. We came here because it is close to where my ship usually docks.'

As this story is unfolding, thoughts are running through the listener's mind. He develops a geographical picture of where the seaman lives in town and previously in the country, also of his journeys across the sea. He forms an impression in his mind of the wife's pregnancy, and the possible trouble. He also forms ideas about the seaman's contract, and wonders whether compassionate leave is possible in the Merchant Service. He thinks of the children being left in a big city and compares this momentarily with the style of the small country village. He wonders whether the man is telling the truth, but then feels from his anxiety and conscientious tone of voice that he is anxious and responsible about his wife and children. The listener then thinks to himself that he has begun to get 'the feel' of the man who is talking. He has begun to understand both the problem situation and the sort of man who is speaking to him. He thus feels more ready to start talking himself and perhaps make helpful suggestions.

There is no need to go on with this hypothetical 'interview'. The further it went, the more it would be getting down to the specific question of interpersonal relations, helping interventions, casework and the like, and this is not our concern. Let us, rather, consider the listener's preliminary thoughts, for it will help to clarify what is meant by 'understanding people'. Our considerations here can only be brief, leaving many questions unanswered, but they may be sufficient to make several fundamental points clearer.

2. Mental representations
It can be seen that the listener was forming *representations* in his mind about the external events of the seaman and his situations. Any form of understanding involves mental representations. As impressions of a situation accumulate, we develop images in the mind to *fit* them. When the impressions are in accordance with our representations, we tend to feel that our understanding is sufficient. When on the other hand a representation is formed which does not fit our perceptions, we still feel puzzled (if we are sensible). In fact the process of understanding usually grows from preliminary ideas

which are not quite sufficient and give rise to puzzlement. This then spurs the thinker to create modified representations which may fit the situation better.

In an informal way, if we are being intelligent, often very quickly and subconsciously we *test hypotheses*. In the example, the listener was testing hypotheses when he had the idea from the tremor of the man's hand that he might be suffering from a neurological disease. But he found this hypothesis wanting when he noticed the sailor's trembling lips and worried expression. He formed the new hypothesis that he was very anxious, and this provisionally satisfied him more.

It seems that this quick, often subconscious hypothesis-testing occurs in any everyday intelligent activity. A mechanic tracing a fault in a car systematically tests out, 'Is it in the ignition, is it in the carburettor, is it in the fuel supply?' etc. Similarly, a mother woken up in the middle of the night by her baby crying will, doubtless in a fuddled way, test the hypotheses, 'Is he cold? No, he's got plenty of blankets. Is he wet? No, he's dry. Is it a tooth coming through?' She looks at his gums, feels them and sees one swollen. She thinks it is probably this, and sets about trying to soothe the gum.

Where the mental representations and hypothesis-testing refer to a specific everyday situation we talk about a person using his *common sense*. When this activity relates to specific processes in a person's work situation we talk of 'being technical' or technology. And when the process is one of forming *generally applicable representations* about things in the outside world and testing them we talk of 'theory construction' and validation, or scientific method. Thus there is a difference between common sense and science in that the latter is concerned with generally applicable theories. Professional practitioners and social workers will work near to the common-sense end of this spectrum. But any thoughtful person tests hypotheses in a way which has much in common with scientific method.

3. Modes of understanding

Let us now turn to the specific nature of the mental representations made by the listener as the story unfolded to him. Here again it is possible only to touch upon this question.

As the listener was thinking, he made representations for himself about various sorts of external events. He had thoughts about the geography (the positions in space) of the seaman, his ship and his family. He thought about the mechanics of the wife's pregnancy. He compared the social relationships in a village and town. And he also thought about the seaman's anxiety, concern, affection and sense of responsibility. You will notice that these representations, although interwoven in the listener's mind, are about different orders of events. His *mode of understanding* was shifting from moment to moment as he thought. Let us look a little closer at the modes of understanding he used. First of all, he was representing to himself the geography of the seaman and his family. Here he was making a picture to himself of them as objects relative to each other and other objects in space. Doubtless in doing this he was using his own past experiences of the external world of physical objects. In a very similar way he had thoughts about the wife's pregnancy, the position of the placenta in the uterus, the function of the blood system and the placenta as a permeable membrane. Here again his thinking was about physical objects 'out there' in the external world. You will notice that his understanding of the present situation was by means of relating it to other physical objects with which he was acquainted. Thus he may have understood the function of the wife's blood system in terms of the flow of fluids through pipes moved by the heart acting as a pump and so on. Putting it crudely he understood this bit of physiology by relating it to plumbing.

We can call this sort of thinking, where understanding external physical events occurs through relating them to other familiar external events, the *physical mode of understanding*.

The tradition of modern science has grown up using this physical mode of understanding. For example, astronomers have understood the movements of the stars as ball-like objects positioned relative to each other in various ways in space and time. For instance, for many years astronomers used to try and make sense of the movements of the sun, moon and planets as seen in the heavens by assuming that they all went round the earth. But this model did not fit observations very well until Copernicus over four hundred years ago proposed a new model or representation, which was that the earth and planets went round the sun. This fitted the observed phenomena much better, so that it has now become an obvious representation for us to make. Previously, however, it was not at all obvious. Medieval men, for instance, found it almost inconceivable.

We see the same construction of physical representations in biological thinking. Harvey's discovery of the circulation of the blood was a 'plumbing theory' which has fitted phenomena so well that it has become an obvious fact to us in the past three hundred and fifty years. Biological thinking is concerned with living organisms as objects of study, but the mode of understanding seems to be fundamentally the same as with the physical sciences.

When we turn to study *parts of the human being's* functioning and use the physical mode of understanding we talk of *physiology*. When we consider the human being relating to his environment with the mediation of his sense-organs we refer to the subject as *psychology*. And when our object of study is not the single human but groups or a plurality of humans relating to each other and their environment we usually call the subject *sociology* of one sort or another.

Some investigators prefer to use only the physical mode of understanding in psychology, as in the physical sciences. Here they would observe human behaviour as external physical events, and make models or representations in terms of other external physical events which seem to fit the phenomena. They might for example understand a person's behaviour in terms of patterns of firing of nerve impulses, as does the neurologist. The psychologist who confines himself to this physical mode of understanding human behaviour is usually referred to as a *behaviourist* psychologist.

In the everyday understanding of people we generally use, as well as physical thought, a mode of understanding which has a fundamental difference from what has been described so far. Returning to our seaman: it will be remembered how the listener understood about the man's anxiety, affection, concern and responsibility. Here he was making representations in his mind about the seaman's *inner experience*. This inner experience may be focally *conscious* or, as will be discussed later, it may only be vaguely felt and even quite unconscious. It seems that the representation of another person's ideas, feelings or experience is of a different order from the physical mode of understanding.

When someone is understood in this way it seems that a mental representation is made about them by reference to the observer's own inner experience. Thus our listener probably got the feeling of the seaman's anxiety and concern by referring to his own similar inner experiences. It could be said that the listener was 'putting himself in the seaman's shoes'. But he was not simply or grossly doing this, for he was forming a representation of the seaman's feelings while still being quite clear that he, the listener, was not himself going through the same emotions as the seaman at the same time. The listener was *identifying* something from his own inner experience with that of the seaman, but was at the same time maintaining his own sense of separateness from him.

This form of understanding, where representations of inner experiences are made, we shall call the *empathetic mode*. It will be noticed that, just as with the physical mode, testing of hypotheses can occur. Thus the listener wondered (made a brief hypothesis) whether the seaman was lying, but the worried expression, the anxiety, expression of concern and responsibility all tended to make him reject this hypothesis. This empathetic thinking or hypothesis-testing is very much the grist of our everyday relationships with people. For instance: a man comes home and sees his wife with a drawn face. He makes a representation that she is depressed and says, 'Oh dear! Are you feeling miserable?' She says, 'Oh no! I am just exhausted.' He then probably rejects or modifies his preliminary empathetic hypothesis.

It is in empathetic thinking that we find the essence of our feeling of 'being with' another person and of being understood in the personal sense. From babyhood onwards we seem to need assurance of such understanding for our sense of well-being, wherever and whoever we are. When such understanding is denied us we become cold inside, despairing, or angry, we tend to feel 'mad' with one another. It seems that a practitioner or social worker needs to exercise this empathy day in and day out if his patients or clients are to experience and use him as a helpful person. Without it they will perceive him as a thoughtless automaton and at best will feel miserable, at worst will naturally tend to hate him and be obstructive.

It does seem that, not only is it necessary to exercise this empathy in everyday and professional discourse with people, but it is also a valuable mode of understanding people in general. Social workers use this mode a very great deal; so do psychotherapists and psychoanalysts. This book will predominantly be concerned with using this empathetic mode of understanding interwoven with physical and sociological thinking. Incidentally, sociologists also use many empathetic ideas and concepts. The main difference between this book which is essentially psychological in nature, and sociology, is that here the primary object of study is the *single individual's personal experience*, whereas in sociology the ultimate focus of study is upon groups or pluralities of individuals.

This reflection upon modes of understanding will have to suffice here. There will be some further points to make before coming to the study of our individual person. But the last section of this chapter will bring us nearer to this focus. In it we shall outline the physiological and social background of the individual in very broad terms. In particular we shall consider some of the general factors which delimit a person's development and contribute towards his becoming similar to and also different from other people around him.

III. THE BIOLOGICAL AND PSYCHOLOGICAL FAMILY

1. Biological organism and environment

Having examined our own thoughts, let us now turn outwards and set the stage, as it were, for our exploration of the individual.

On looking carefully at any living thing, be it a plant, animal or human being, it is impossible not to be filled with wonder. It is an entity all of its own, similar to other things but separate from them. It has a *self-perpetuating organization*. This is particularly noticeable each spring when plants unfold their leaves according to their own pattern. Perhaps the most enthralling demonstration of organization is the sight of a baby just born. A limp messy bundle appears which suddenly springs to life. It changes colour as if by magic and cries with its own particular pattern of movements, when only moments before it had been a flaccid, almost inert thing.

This self-perpetuating organization continues from conception to death even though the substances of which a living being is made may change many times. We human beings, at least in normal and waking circumstances, have some conscious *awareness* of this organization and continuity in time. Broadly speaking, it is referred to as a *sense of self*. This is central to our thinking and will be referred to on many occasions.

We do not know what gives each organism its particular capacity for self-perpetuation. It is a mystery which is perhaps the secret of life. But research workers are rapidly learning about the nature of the *determinants* which delimit the structure, growth and functioning of an organism and which make it similar to or different from others.

2. Determinants of functioning

For our purposes we can distinguish between the *inherited* and *environmental* determinants of an organism's functioning. The inherited determinants or genes are passed from one generation to the next through the medium of the reproductive cells. An organism's genetic constitution is fixed from the time of fertilization. We will not dwell here upon the question of genetic delimitation of functioning and hence upon human experience. Our study requires no special acquaintance with genetics, but it is probably as important for the reader's general knowledge as is this book. Any elementary textbook of biology will give him an outline. For more detail see Carter (1962).

The first environmental delimitations of an organism's functioning come into play at conception. Here the reader should acquaint himself with the development of the foetus and the influence of the uterine environment upon it. An outline is given in many textbooks of child development (e.g. Stone and Church, 1957, or Chamberlain, 1969; for more detail see Gesell and Amatruda, 1945).

Physiological delimitation naturally continues after birth. Thus body growth and health depend upon the physical nature of the substances exchanged with environment (in feeding, breathing and excretion). But now we can also observe *psychological* determinants. By these we refer to those external events which are communicated to the individual organism through the sense organs of sight, hearing, touch, pain, taste, smell or body movement and which affect his activity.

The organism, or individual as we can now call him, is thus delimited by a combination of genetic, uterine and post-natal determinants. This determination does not exclude *free choice*; human beings frequently anticipate alternatives and choose between them. In doing this people experience freedom, but our cursory glance at the determinants of functioning make it plain that that freedom is inevitably limited.

3. The family[1]

The genetic and uterine determinants affecting an individual are carried exclusively by his two biological parents. In modern British society, these biological parents will also usually be the primary organizers of his immediate environment during the formative years of childhood. They provide the conditions for a child's exchange of substances (breathing, feeding, excretion). Interwoven with this they will present a continuing pattern of stimulation or a *psychological environment* in which the child develops.

There are wide differences of opinion about the importance of a child's early environment for his later development. It is perhaps

[1] See sociological works, e.g. Harris, 1969.

necessary for the author to state his own conviction here that early influences are vital in the formation of propensities for later life. It seems that the human's future more than that of any other animal is fated by his long period of childhood dependence upon adults in general and parents in particular. From this long dependency there probably arise both the human being's unique achievements and also his proneness to psychological disorders (Lidz, 1963).

The parents who organize a child's environment will themselves have developed modes of belief and behaviour derived from their own particular cultures. They provide their own idiosyncratic *network of relationships* between each other and towards the child, under the influence of which he grows (Lidz, 1963, 1968).

In Western culture today the *nuclear family* usually provides the fundamental unit for the early development of a child. This consists in principle of mother, father, child and siblings. In other cultures, and in some circumstances in Britain today, other forms of family pattern may provide the environmental unit. For instance, *extended family* networks involving grandparents, uncles, aunts and cousins may be as important a background to a child as his own mother and father. This being so, the pattern of psychological determinants would be somewhat different from that of the nuclear family. We would then expect the individual to develop in rather different ways.

This book will predominantly be considering the individual growing up in a nuclear family structure and then forming his own new nuclear family. We shall from time to time contrast this mode of life with extended family experiences, particularly in the later chapters on marriage and parenthood, but on the whole we assume a nuclear family background.

Having outlined the importance of the family as a physical and psychological environment, let us turn in the next chapter to how its members prepare themselves for a new individual, the baby.

2

THE EXPERIENCE OF PREGNANCY AND CHILDBIRTH

We shall now come closer to the individuals in a family, and focus upon the inner experiences of women during pregnancy and their husbands' reactions to it. Our main mode of understanding will be an empathetic one.

1. The interweaving of many different feelings in every human experience

Before we discuss pregnancy it is necessary to make one further point that is fundamental to the understanding of people's feelings in general. That is that at any moment in time a person may experience a complex mixture of many ideas, wishes and feelings within himself. A little introspection may make this plain. The reader's motives for going through this book will probably involve a complex mixture of personal wishes together with the necessity of external demands, such as being told to read it by a tutor. Likewise the reader's feelings are probably also a mixture of interest, satisfaction, puzzlement, irritation and anger.

It is obviously not possible to write or talk about the whole complex web of a person's feelings at any one time. Our modes of communication are just not capable of this. So by necessity a form of abstraction takes place where some particularly predominant wishes or feelings are focused upon. This may illustrate our understanding of someone's experience, but we over-simplify if we think that this one aspect is the whole story. For instance, one may look at a friend's gloomy face and say, 'Oh he is worried about the exams next week.' This might be true, and the friend may be glad of the sympathy, but in all likelihood the gloomy face has also a much wider complex of anxious feelings behind it.

In this and all the following chapters we shall be discussing some of the predominant feelings and ideas that occur to people during the phases of their lives. Such a procedure is necessarily an over-simplification. We refer to common experiences, but this does not imply that everyone going through each particular phase must have them. Nor does it mean that the experiences referred to will be the only ones felt.

2. Before pregnancy
From the moment a baby is born the nature of his environment, upon which he is totally dependent, will be determined by his family. Yet ten months before this they will have been going their ways with no cognizance of the human being who is going to change their lives. Thus the destiny of a child depends very much upon the changes and preparations which the family makes to accommodate him. This is why pregnancy is worthy of our study.

3. Conception
For us human beings sexual intercourse serves many purposes beyond simple procreation (J. Klein, 1965. Deutsch, 1945). Husbands and wives usually wish to enhance their intimacy with each other by making love far more frequently than would be necessary if procreation were its only aim. A young husband and wife's slow growth of trust and mutual knowledge, both physical and mental will partly have grown out of sexual love.

Men and women will, in their unguarded moments, tell you how making love in order to have a child often has a different quality to it from before. They may report about a lack of constraint, and that an animal reproductive urge is given its head. Perhaps phantasies of procreation occur more or less unconsciously in every act of making love. Certainly the dream of being reproductive can appeal quite consciously to us all. The realization which comes later of actually having started a child is a rather different experience from the irres-ponsible phantasy of procreation.

4. The first pregnancy, the mother's experience
Let us consider to begin with a mother who is pregnant with her first child. Her earliest indication will usually be the missing of a period. She may also feel 'different', hungry, tired, slightly 'fizzy', or her breasts may be tender. These will be signs of the metabolic changes taking place in her body to accommodate the newly-conceived child (Chamberlain, 1969. Stone and Church, 1957).

With experience, mothers usually recognize when they are preg-nant without any medical confirmation, but for the first child the mother and father usually have to wait for the doctor's word before they are certain. Until then they remain in a sort of suspended animation, but their confirmation gives them the cue to do two things. First, they turn outwards to people around them for recognition and acceptance, particularly from their own parents and family. This is the time of congratulations. A young woman is usually particularly sensitive to her own mother's reactions. You will often hear mention of bitterness because a mother did not seem pleased, or of relief and relaxation because she was glad. The same applies in a more muted way to the husband and his family. Secondly, a young couple tend to turn inwards towards themselves and anticipate the future. There is a quite conscious anticipation and organizing of finances, housing, rooms and so on. This is usually done rather vaguely in the first months but becomes more specific as time goes on. People naturally vary in this. Some couples who enjoy planning will go into great details. Others will leave everything till the last minute, but this does not necessarily reflect a profound reluctance to have the child. People just vary in their ways of preparation. For example, one young mother said, 'I expect I was in two minds somewhere about having Jane, but I loved being pregnant and very much wanted her. I wanted her so much that I was terrified something would go wrong. In a silly way I guarded against this by pretending to myself I wasn't pregnant. I made no preparations at all. As it happened this didn't work. About two weeks before she was due I just had to rearrange the house and go and buy things. In the end I decided on a daft compromise. I bought one of everything, until I was faced by buying one nappy. Then I gave in and bought everything in a rush.'

In the early months at least, bodily changes are the primary concern of most women. Nausea is frequent but usually subsides by about the third month. After this, most women feel very fit and full of well-being, particularly if they have no other worries on their minds. A first pregnancy is frequently an exciting new experience, quite as fundamental a change as, for example, adolescence though usually more private and less noisy. By about the fifth month the mother will become aware of the baby as a separate being inside her. She will feel him kicking, and from then on he will seem to grow and grow so that she becomes slower and more weary with the greatly added burden to carry around.

Throughout this time the young woman is slowly developing a relationship with her child inside her. This is going on physiologically and automatically, but at a conscious level she will be very aware of the creature which is part of her and yet separate.

One often overhears a mother making joking, half-affectionate, half-angry comments to the baby, particularly when he kicks. He is very often given a nickname. With the changes in herself the young woman usually becomes slightly dreamy or vague. There is an easy natural absorption in herself and the baby. She forgets things, walks along the road without her usual guarded alertness and is content to 'just be', feeling pleasure in immediate things around. Her concern for the distant future, the troubles of the world or things of the intellect are set aside in a preoccupation with the present and more immediate future. This has been referred to as *primary maternal preoccupation* (Winnicott, 1958, 1964). We can see this partly as a product of the physical state of pregnancy, but also as a necessary stage in the mother's change from her old ways of relating to the world towards absorption in relating to her child. We shall see in the next chapter how the young infant after birth seems to need this absorption in him if his physical requirements are going to be met.

This tendency towards absorption does not mean that the young woman has withdrawn from needing other people. On the contrary, her loose vagueness usually means she relies more than before on her husband, particularly to carry out the functions of watchful guardedness. If all goes well the husband will enjoy this, taking pleasure in being strong and protective. But as we shall see, this is not always so, and a woman deprived of protection at this time is extremely vulnerable and may well become disturbed and frantic in her attempts to cope.

Where a woman is living in an extended family she will probably have a network of relatives to act as watchers as well as her husband. This can give a sense of stability, but she may also be prey to the whims and prejudices of her elders (Willmott and Young, 1957. Newson, 1963). Most frequently nowadays in Britain a young woman will depend more upon her G.P., midwife, her friends and her husband. Between them they have to perform the functions of the extended family elsewhere. Let us consider the young woman's relationship with these helpers.

5. A pregnant woman and her professional helpers
We have suggested that a woman needs to be 'let be' to get on with her own private preoccupation. Yet she also needs to be watched over, and as such is very vulnerable to other people's influence

(Caplan, 1961. Winnicott, 1958. Deutsch, 1944). We shall consider in turn her relationship with her doctor and midwife, with her husband and lastly with herself.

Most young women want to get on with being pregnant with the minimum of interference from professionals. At the same time they anxiously rely on their examinations and advice, and often feel very sensitive to being in their power. Some women find it easy to be in such a state of helplessness, others are terrified and enraged that they are likely to be treated like cattle. This is not often experienced with a home confinement, but long waits and peremptory treatment by busy staff in hospitals has broken the calm peacefulness of many pregnant women. On a more personal level some district midwives have been felt as the terror of the neighbourhood, leaving young mothers weeping helplessly in fright, hating them yet not daring to say anything because they will be in the midwives' hands at the birth.

We have no way of estimating the lasting effects of these bad experiences. They are probably not very great, but the more time that is spent in angry, anxious feelings by a young woman the less time she has to relax and 'just be' with herself and baby inside her. If she has other personal anxieties which also impede her relaxation, this may be the straw which breaks the camel's back.

6. A woman and her husband

The person who is most important for the ease of her maternal preoccupation is a woman's husband. With him there is the obvious yet fundamental need for assurance of financial and physical security. A sense of intimacy and valuing each other is also wanted. Lost intimacy acts like a malignant thing within a young wife.

A woman will often say how sensitive she is to her husband's moods. It matters very much that he should want the child, for without this a woman is alone and often guilty both towards her husband and the baby. Even though he wants a child, it is not uncommon for a husband to be physically disgusted by his pregnant wife, and with this she is likely to become listless and depressed. When the baby is born, the husband's disgust may wear off and the wife's depression lift. Probably nearly all women worry that they will be sexually unattractive to their husbands during and after pregnancy. Lovemaking will inevitably be interrupted at the end of the pregnancy and immediately after birth. It may even be many months before easy intercourse is re-established. Husbands often find this abstinence difficult to bear and become impatient and bad-tempered, largely because they have not anticipated these difficulties. Quite a few men are at least tempted to be unfaithful in this situation.

The importance of the feeling of togetherness is reported so often by women that it is clearly one factor which can shatter the ease of a woman's maternal preoccupation. It is often quite sufficient for a woman to feel that her husband is with her in spirit. She can be quite happy if her husband is thousands of miles away if assured of his regard. Nevertheless pregnant women do repeatedly stress the value of day-to-day contact with their husbands. This has probably become more important in recent years where husbands and wives are expected to support each other rather than to turn to other members of an extended family (Young and Willmott, 1957. J. Klein, 1965).

One responsibility of a husband in day-to-day contact is to act as a receptor and container for his wife's anxiety-ridden phantasies, which are likely to arise in the dreamy stage of maternal preoccupation. This way of one person helping another with anxiety is not yet well understood. One instance of it would be when a wife worries that the baby will be deformed and her husband sympathizes with her, but points out that it is unlikely. Naturally enough, husbands can also increase anxiety both by panicking themselves or perhaps by being disdainful. In whatever way a husband responds, his wife is likely to be sensitive and easily stirred by him.

7. A woman's self-generated phantasies[1]

It is obvious that pregnancy is a time of change both physically, psychologically and socially for a woman. When faced by a changed situation she can only anticipate the future with uncertainty. When there is uncertainty, *phantasy* often comes vividly to consciousness. By phantasy we do not simply mean make-believe daydreams, but refer more generally to *impulsive imaginative mental activity*. This may be related to external events but is not a direct and organized representation of them, as is logical, common-sense or scientific thought. We shall discuss this in more detail later, particularly in chapters 4, 5 and 6. Here it is sufficient to say that phantasy seems to be active within us most of the time. Introspection will make it plain that, when one is absorbed in some external problem, then conscious phantasy recedes to a minimum. But when our attention wanders, all manner of ideas can flit across our awareness. Sometimes these ideas are pleasant or neutral, but as often as not they include vaguely

[1] Deutsch, 1944. Bibring, 1961.

anxious or slightly dread-toned anticipations of the future. This is referred to loosely as *anxiety*.

When a woman is relaxed, faced with inevitable changes in body functioning and style of life, her old ways of satisfying herself and others are threatened. With this there may arise floods of anxious phantasy. In pregnancy such a state is often followed quite unexpectedly by a happy, even joyous mood. Such fluctuations are common, and because of this a pregnant woman is often epitomized as being *labile* in mood.

Let us now consider a few quite commonly expressed anxious ideas.

A pregnant woman often feels that she will not be able to cope with her new life. There also comes rage at having to change her old ways. This is particularly so with a woman who has invested a great deal in a career, identified with it, and gained a unique sense of self-esteem from it. The coming of a child threatens this, and it is often possible to see how a woman cannot let herself relax into maternal pre-occupation because she needs to cling to her career and old sense of herself. This affects some women so deeply that they seem to deny their pregnancy for as long as they can. Then, when they can deny it no longer, they become angry, tense and depressed. This is a problem that has been particularly noted among women isolated in the suburbs from friends, relatives and old pursuits (Gavron, 1966).

Less tied to external circumstances, and hence more difficult for the outsider to comprehend, is the problem of lack of self-esteem which all people experience to some degree and some feel chronically. Some women seem, as an underlying characteristic, to doubt themselves as having any value, so that when they become pregnant they have not got the self-confidence to say to themselves, as it were. 'Now I can relax, I am good enough to be a mother and I shall know intuitively what is right.' They continuously seek reassurance and support from others. Midwives will often be familiar with women who are nervous like this, for it is often the midwife as well as husband and friends to whom such an anxious person will cling.

It is sometimes possible to relate these doubts, at least in part, to a woman's own earlier experiences. For instance:

(i) A very self-doubting woman confessed when pregnant that she herself was conceived as a replacement for a brother who had died. She said she always felt she was not quite what her mother wanted in the things she did as a child. When pregnant she was a great worrier about doing the right thing, and consulted health visitors and the midwife persistently. Incidentally, as her children grew older she thoroughly enjoyed them, but was noted throughout the neighbourhood as being unduly apologetic for them.

(ii) Another woman was convinced her own conception had been a mistake. Her parents spent all their time running a shop, so she lodged with her grandparents or aunts throughout most of her childhood. She was swept by anxieties during all her pregnancies, obsessed by the thought that it was all a mistake, that she didn't want the baby and couldn't cope.

Such illustrations cannot be a convincing general proof of the importance of early childhood experience, but they perhaps suffice to alert one to their importance. That they are important is given added support by the observation that most women who felt predominantly at ease with their parents as children feel more or less serene about their own maternality as long as they are happy with their husbands. It must be added that the author knows of no formal survey that confirms or denies this, but it is a common enough experience of those working with pregnant women.

For most outsiders a pregnant woman's internal preoccupations must remain hidden. Delving into a woman's past is usually the last thing she wants, and serves no purpose. The best we can do when confronted by her anxieties is to reply to them honestly and realistically. Phoney reassurance seldom convinces. Doctors and nurses who say too soothingly, 'Don't worry my dear, nothing will go wrong,' leave women feeling uneasy. They know only too well that things can go wrong.

8. Anticipations of the birth and having a child
During all this time the young woman will probably be anticipating the birth and after. Most women are frightened of the pain of birth and of the shame of losing control if it hurts too much. A lot is done by midwives, clinics and classes to prepare mothers for childbirth, and drugs are also available. Nevertheless many women still worry a great deal about what it is going to be like. In many ways they have good cause to worry, for childbirth itself is pleasant to only a few. Why some women worry more than others, and why for some it is more painful than others must remain undiscussed here (Deutsch, 1944. Bibring, 1961. Caplan, 1961).

Perhaps of more long-lasting importance is anticipation of later mothering. Thinking about coping with children must be a private preoccupation of most young women. Such anticipation no doubt carries a great deal of anxious phantasy, but may also be necessary as a realistic problem-solving activity.

Many pregnant women express doubts such as the following:

(i) I am sure I shall not have enough patience to stand a child.

(ii) I have never really liked other people's children. I hope to goodness I shall like my own.

(iii) I don't know how I shall stand the mess. Keeping things beautiful around me has always been important.

(iv) It is getting up at night that frightens me and I am sure I shall lose my temper.

(v) To be a really good mother surely one has to surrender everything, but what is going to happen to me then?

In some of these quotations one sees the working of phantasies that may seem unrealistic, but are none the less deeply meaningful to the mothers who express them.

Perhaps the most commonly felt anxiety about mothering is concerned with aggressiveness in one form or another. Often this is expressed as a fear of losing one's temper, or that the mother will not be able to stand up to her child's demands. Many women feel they should show no aggressiveness towards their children and suffer agonies when, out of frustration, they quite naturally find it rising up in themselves. This fear of aggressiveness seems to vary from person to person, from family to family, and from one culture to another. Probably in Britain, where social norms are more fluid than in traditional societies, a woman is more or less allowed the freedom to find her own way with the children. But this freedom of choice means that a great burden of responsibility and hence guilt is likely to rest upon her shoulders. The burden has increased if anything with greater understanding of the needs of children. To many young mothers the professional adviser, G.P., midwife, health visitor or paediatrician has something of the aura of the priest of old who purveys knowledge of what is right and wrong. We shall have more to say about this problem for parents in later chapters, as it is a serious one today. No responsible parents can ignore our technical understanding of the needs of children. But if parents blindly obey the pronouncements of every expert on the subject they are likely to be driven crazy with doubt.

We may mention another anticipated worry in passing. Some women feel they must not cuddle their babies because it will be too sexy. It seems quite natural to some mothers that they should have enjoyable sensuous feelings about their babies, but for others such sensuousness has the quality of a guilt-ridden sexiness.

9. The pregnant woman's feelings about her own mother

One common trend which runs through many mothers' doubts about themselves is an implicit comparison and rivalry with their own mothers. Such feelings are not often consciously expressed, but when they are they have a poignancy which rings true. For instance:

(i) My mother believed that childhood was the golden age and a mother must surrender everything to the children. I don't want to do that, but I am terrified not to.

(ii) Mother never lost her temper with us. I am sure I shall. I am awful, aren't I?

(iii) Mother always made us go to the lavatory every few hours; I am determined that my children shall not suffer such agony and indignity.

It seems that pregnancy, like so many other things, involves a complex of feelings of conflict, rivalry and conformity between the generations. It is usually very important to a young woman that her own mother is pleased and appreciative of the pregnancy. For instance, a young woman who was a very active and convinced rebel against the absurdities of the older generation said some months after her baby was born, 'My mother is a crazy idiot, but I forgive her everything and love her dearly because she dotes on Ann, the baby. I could murder my mother-in-law because she has just blatantly ignored us since I got pregnant.'

It is possible to detect a thread of anticipatory thinking in most of these comments about mothers. The young women seem to be forming resolves about how they will behave and comparing them with their own, perhaps distorted memories of childhood. This, incidentally, can be a most enjoyable activity. It also seems likely that such anticipatory thinking serves very definite preparatory functions. It helps the young woman to form a preliminary attitude towards handling the baby. This in itself is valuable because it helps her to be certain of what she feels to begin with. Then, as things turn out later, she can alter her ideas to match her experience without too much floundering. If she does not have any preliminary attitude she is much more likely to feel lost and helpless. Of course such attitudes can, with some women, solidify into prejudices unchangeable by circumstances and the baby's needs. But we shall wait till the next chapter to discuss this.

10. The father's experience

So far we have been identifying with the young, pregnant woman and have only mentioned her husband as being important to her, but not discussed how he may feel about the matter (Winnicott, 1964).

We have already mentioned that several sociologists have pointed to an increased intimacy and sharing of function between husband and wife in Britain today (Young and Willmott, 1957). This seems to be related to the mobility of families in our industrial society so that, as the extended family network dissolves, it tends to be replaced by an increased sharing of responsibilities between a wife and husband. This being so, a husband's personal feelings about having a child are likely to play an increasingly important part in the progress of a child's rearing and development.

It is perhaps not the tradition among many Englishmen to elaborate upon their private feelings. However, it does not take much exploration to discover that pregnancy usually brings a husband to a sense of fulfilment and passionate pride, the feeling that 'this is what life is all about'. This is very close to the emotions of his wife, so they can intimately share in them. Such deep feelings of shared pleasure probably help them both through the doubts and anxieties that assail them.

Just as with his wife, pregnancy calls him to change his old ways of life and thought, though to a less obvious degree. Here are a couple of examples:

(i) After that first feeling of 'Ah, we've done it', I began to feel scared. Would my wife be all right? What would I be like as a father? And then all sorts of worries about whether our housing would be all right, would I earn enough money to keep the family, came upon me.

(ii) Money seemed my main worry. My wife had worked before and now it was up to me – quite exciting in its way but scaring all the same.

A very common anxiety for a man is that his wife will withdraw from him and not dote on him as before. Probably every man wants to be mothered, and looks to his wife to meet this need. With a real baby as rival this satisfaction is threatened. Here is an extreme example:

I know I feel an outsider. My wife says I make myself one. But I know something disappeared for me when the first child was born which has never returned. And the second child seemed to finish things. I am very fond of both children but something went dead between me and my wife.

For most men such alienation is hardly felt at all. They shift happily enough to sharing. But it is rare that a man never feels afraid of being left out, if not in the first pregnancy then in later ones. In some ways it is inevitable, because a wife turns into herself and it would be an insensitive man who does not feel it. Thus in pregnancy the wife needs her husband's concern perhaps more than on any other occasion, yet this is the time when he is very likely to feel alienated.

Just as with their wives, pregnancy stirs many men to phantasy. Often we can trace them reaching back to their own childhoods just as their wives do.

(i) My parents counted up our misdeeds until the end of the week, when we were beaten for them. I am determined never to lay hands on my children.

(ii) I find it easy to look after children. I suppose I got it from my mother, who was always a nice warm person.

(iii) My father enjoyed playing with us and I am looking forward to doing the same.

But, just as with the wife, such ideas must usually remain private to himself. The listener or onlooker would be interfering if he tried to do more than understand what was being said.

11. Second and further pregnancies

Much of what has been said about the first pregnancy applies equally to later ones. The joy and anxiety will be there, but in a more muted way. There are not the extremes of pleasure and fear that are experienced with any event for the first time. Both parents will probably be surer of themselves, at least if all has gone well with the first child. In a sense the first child, by doing well, contributes to the parents' confidence. He gives them something by just being all right. This will not be by any conscious intention of unselfishness or kindness on the child's part. But it is communicated in a very real sense none the less. Winnicott (1964) has called this a child's *contribution*.

Just as the parents had to change when they had the first baby, so now the first child also will have to accept a change with the second child on the way. Most children are very aware of the changes that take place in their mothers in pregnancy. This will be perceived in her changed body shape and also in her tiredness and withdrawal. One can usually see signs of anxiety about this if one listens and watches. It is not something a child can easily speak about directly, and being unable to communicate makes it all the worse for him. The child tends to be in the same position as the husband whom we described above, alienated from his mother, who because of her pregnancy, is not able to respond to him as sensitively as before. It is noticeable that many very kind and devoted parents ignore this pregnancy anxiety of the child. It is often thought that the child will be jealous of the baby after the birth. This may be so, but anxiety before birth, related to the mother's withdrawal, seems also to be very common. Many parents think that, because a child is too young to understand the facts of life, he will not be frightened about the changes in his mother. Such an idea seems to be misplaced; in fact rather the reverse is true. The younger a child is, the less he understands, and hence the more puzzled and frightened he can be by the mysterious differences in his mother.

Often a father and the first child draw closer together in their sense of being left out, they feel sorry for themselves and hence for each other. A subtle shift in relationships takes place which, if continued chronically can be a source of anger and mistrust in the whole fabric of the future family. Usually such shifts are transient and benign in that the father helps the child by his attention and vice versa. The child is helped over a difficult patch, and later closeness with mother is re-established.

Each child that comes into the family will, to a greater or lesser degree, mean different things and satisfy different phantasies in the parents. These phantasies will be only dimly known but are very real. Examples of such ideas would be a mother's passionate wish to have a son, a father's need to have a son like or better than himself, or to have a daughter to whom he can be tender and flirtatious. These yearnings are primitive, mysterious and very various. They can be disturbing to parents and children alike, especially when the need is felt to be rigid and all-consuming. Instances of this would be when a mother never forgives a child for being a boy when she wanted a girl, or when a parent desperately needs a child to be brilliantly clever. There are many variations of these imperious ideals and phantasies.

It often seems to happen that a family becomes set or fixated upon one particular phantasy about an ideal child. This can become a torment for the real child, because he is then growing up in an atmosphere where an impossible criterion is demanded of him. On the other hand, it must not be thought that these irrational phantasies are all bad and valueless. Such phantasies seem to provide a substratum of interest, excitement and meaningfulness for the parents. When a child grows, parents literally see their dreams coming true, and having children is felt as deeply worth while. Such pleasure seems only to occur where parents are flexible about their yearning and have a sense of humour, so that when a child does not conform to their wishes they can still enjoy him for what he is.

12. Labour

The last weeks of pregnancy are usually spent in hanging about apprehensively waiting. Weak contractions or 'labour pains' are common, so that it is often uncertain when labour has really begun.

Labour itself falls into three stages. During the first, muscles around the neck of the uterus contract to create a passage into the vagina. This stage is usually the most prolonged and unpleasant part of childbirth. The second stage is the actual passage of the baby from the uterus into the outside. The third takes place some minutes after this, and involves the expulsion of the placenta from the uterus. This is the afterbirth.

The birth has involved a fundamental change of bodily organization for the baby. *In utero*, oxygenation and nutrition took place through the placenta and umbilical cord. At birth, ventilation commences suddenly with the first breath through the lungs. Thus a whole organization of breathing reflexes comes into play which has not been exercised before. Likewise with nutrition, he will not feed for a day or so, but when he does nutrition will be through the sucking reflexes of the mouth and digestive functions of the stomach and intestines. Excretion will be through the bowels.

A new person has been born, and from now on he will be breathing, feeding, sleeping, seeing and hearing; relating to his environment with pleasure and pain until the day he dies.

3

THE FIRST SIX MONTHS

We now turn from the mother and father to the baby himself. The main body of the chapter is concerned with this, but at the end there will be a brief introduction to some general theoretical concepts which have arisen out of the text. These concepts are applicable both to young babies, and later phases of life. This will be done in many of the chapters of this book; theoretical concepts will be introduced as they arise in the text which are of application to individual psycho-dynamic processes at any age.

1. Just after birth

The last chapter ended at the point of birth of a baby, and emphas-ized the remarkable shift in physiological functioning that takes place at that time. We need not be concerned here with this in detail, but it is important to recognize the extent of the change that takes place in the activity of the body – particularly in neurological functioning, which mediates the responses of breathing, feeding and excretion. There is an afflux of new stimuli and responses to them with which the baby's system has to cope.

Soon after birth it is possible to see that the young baby has a variety of *reflexes* at his disposal (Stone and Church, 1957. Piaget, 1953. Werner, 1957. Carmichael, 1954). By reflex we mean an innate pattern of behaviour which is mediated by the nervous system. Many of these reflexes are invisible, being concerned with inner metabolism. Others are plain to see and hear, e.g. breathing, crying, excretion. Sucking appears within a few hours. This reflex is more complex than might appear. When a baby is stroked on one side of the cheek, he will automatically turn his head in that direction, his tongue will come out and mouth-sucking movements will commence. These become vigorous when a nipple, teat or even a finger is placed between the lips.

There are other reflex patterns which are apparent at birth, for instance the 'startle reflex' – a splaying of arms and legs, accompanied by crying, at loud noises or sudden loss of support. With the 'grasp reflex' the baby will automatically close his hands round an object that touches the palm of his hand. There are many others. The reflexes that the observer can see have the defining characteristic that they are automatic and innate patterns of response to the environment. Some sort of exercise may have taken place *in utero*, but they appear in their new environment in a form which could not have been completely enacted before. In addition to these it is likely that many reflexes appear only long after birth, but by then it is difficult to detect what is pure reflex and what is a *learned* accommodation to the environment.

Thus the newborn baby comes into the world equipped with a variety of as yet unco-ordinated, automatic reflexes. His nervous system is also not fully developed even anatomically. Nerve fibres for many parts of the body may be functioning in a rudimentary way, but maturation of structure has still to take place in the coming months. Perhaps to allow for this structural growth, as well as to accommodate to changed environmental conditions, the little baby sleeps nearly all the time in his early weeks.

Except for feeding he seems to need to be 'let be' as much as possible. The optimal condition for this is that he be kept warm and usually quite tightly wrapped. A baby who has not got the *support* and *touch* of something encompassing him gets distressed. Perhaps being unwrapped is too different from the uterine state for his nervous system to cope with. Some parents often think an infant should be given freedom of movement and that such archaic habits as using swaddling clothes are detestable. This may well be so for an older baby, but it does not seem to be the case for the very young.

2. *The baby's experience as we know it*

We shall pause for a moment before going on to discuss the developments of the first few months and reflect about the newborn baby. With his puckered face he often looks like a wise old man or woman. However, one thing we can be certain of is that he is not wise. He may have immense potentiality for learning, unless he is malformed, but his capacity to relate to the world at present is confined to his reflexes. These are automatic and as yet unintegrated with each other. When awake he must in some sense be conscious, but ideas can have no *meaning* for him. This is because meaning seems to develop by forming associations between perceptions and memories, the baby has had no time to do this (Hebb, 1949. Carmichael, 1954. Piaget, 1953. Werner, 1957. Spitz, 1965). He has a generalized capacity to feel distress. This is evident when he cries and his whole body becomes active in an unco-ordinated way. How much pain he feels it is not possible to tell. We adults often identify with him when he is distressed, and in doing this we imagine how we would feel distressed if we were crying like him. But we have only the most generalized communication from him of his inner experience. It is doubtful whether we can say he feels 'happy' – perhaps contented or satisfied is a better word – when he is dozy and quiescent after a feed (A. Freud, 1953).

In general the young baby's emotions seem to be confined to gross psycho-physiological responses of 'distress' and satisfaction. It is only with maturation and learning that he comes to articulate his feeling-life in the complex experiences of love, hate, joy, sorrow, affection, bitterness, envy, pride and so on that we know as adults.

From this it is possible to infer that such phrases as 'He's a good baby', 'naughty', 'bad', 'helpful', are not appropriate when referring to a baby's state. He has not yet differentiated self from others, so has not articulated any intentions towards other people, and without this the terms 'good' or 'bad' are meaningless. When people use such phrases they seem to be putting their own inner feelings about the baby into him in an inappropriate way. Thus when a mother says 'he is a good baby', she really means 'he is contented and his behaviour satisfies me'. Parents often start by attributing moral qualities to a baby. This probably does not matter unless they get stuck or *fixated* upon doing it in a set emotional pattern. For example, a mother, for some inner reason of her own, may decide her baby is 'bad' and continue for months and years to feel this. When this happens, he will grow up with the most important person in his environment attributing badness to him. This can be chronically depressing to a child, just as it is to adults when surrounded by people who do not like them.

3. The baby and his mother in the early weeks

Undoubtedly the activities that are most important to the young infant are feeding and sleeping. It is the function of a mother or her substitute to organize her baby's environment so that these can occur with a minimum of disruption.

Within two or three days he will be put to the breast or bottle.

and for the first few weeks the mother's concern will be directed towards establishing a satisfactory feeding pattern. He has his innate sucking reflexes and, if all goes well, as the weeks progress he will, within limits, adapt himself, that is learn, so that his sucking becomes progressively more efficient. Babies differ very considerably in their rhythm of hunger and sucking. Some are voracious and take in more than their stomachs can cope with. Some swallow a lot of air and suffer agonies from wind. Others are slow and sleepy (Winnicott, 1964, 1965. Spitz, 1965. Brody, 1956).

The mother's task here is to adapt herself to the baby, for he can hardly adapt to her. Some babies are by nature easy to start with. Others, who cannot suck well and are unco-ordinated test their mother's patience and adaptability to the limits. These early days of feeding are nearly always an anxious time for a mother. Even though she has experience from other babies, each one is new and different. With the first child a mother will naturally not be very confident and will be groping for a way that suits the baby and herself.

Feeding is not simply a question of nourishment. The breast or bottle and milk is the baby's most important contact and communication with the world. The sensations of the mouth together with the eyes provide information which constitutes the substratum of his first 'awareness' of outside things. As we shall see, much primitive intellectual activity is focused around the mouth and eyes (Piaget, 1952). If the baby's feeding is badly disturbed, he will in all likelihood be a generally discontented baby. This is not just a matter of getting enough milk inside him, but also involves the satisfactory play of his sucking reflexes and hence of his early awareness of outside things.

In this a mother's handling of her baby seems to play a vital part. If her movements are gentle and smooth he will tend to remain relaxed and able to concentrate on sucking. But if she is jerky, tense, or continually changing her pattern of handling, he will respond to these with startled activity. In this way his attention upon sucking will be disturbed. When this occurs he becomes frantic, only too often making the mother frantic too, which usually makes things worse.

We can now see the importance of what was referred to in the last chapter as 'primary maternal preoccupation' (Winnicott, 1958). A mother's relaxed awareness allows her to be ready to adapt to her baby's style and also provides those smooth gentle movements which provide no startling stimuli for the baby.

With feeding and holding goes cuddling. It has already been noted how a baby needs to be held all round by being wrapped. The same applies when feeding. He seems to be most satisfied when supported, even encompassed, so that there is body contact round most of him. Later he will want to be freer in his movements. It is of note that for several years a child will want to re-establish this situation of *holding* when he is distressed. He will run to his mother to be kissed and hugged to be made better. Later in life, lovers do the same. This primitive need to be held has been stressed not only by people working with babies, but also those concerned with physically or mentally distressed adults (Winnicott, 1965). It probably comprises an important part of any sort of nursing.

Body contact also perhaps provides the physical substrate for the awareness of affection. Sensations of this sort may also be elements in the development of awareness of the existence of other people. It seems likely that it is largely from the sensations of warmth, move-ment, heart-beat and breathing of another person that we become aware of other people's feelings and their inner worlds. Cuddling is primarily concerned with the skin sensations of touch and body movement. It is thus *erotic* or sensual. Being erotic it often arouses anxiety in some mothers. But this sensuality seems to be important to the life of young babies and children. Evidence suggests that babies who are *deprived* of cuddling tend to become inert, prone to illness, lethargic and even to wither away and die (Bowlby, 1953. Spitz, 1965).

Mothers vary, both individually and from culture to culture in the patterning of their sensuous stimulation. Such differences may con-tribute towards later differences in the responsiveness of their children. But from the baby's point of view his mother is 'good enough' if distress and pain are kept to a minimum.

Although many other functions are taking place for the baby, this time of life is often referred to as the early *oral phase* of development. This is a conception coined mainly by psychoanalysts (Freud, 1905, 1917. M. Klein, 1958, 1960. Abraham, 1921. Erikson, 1950. Cameron, 1963) to emphasize the importance of the mouth and digestive tract in the child's primitive relationship with his environment.

4. Muscular and intellectual development in the early months
So far we have been discussing the bodily well-being of a baby, particularly with regard to his digestive system. We have also noted how these physiological processes probably form a substrate for

later emotional development in relation to people around him. At the same time as the weeks and months go by, we can readily observe that this muscular activity develops new co-ordinations arising out of his innate reflex patterns. This could be called the origins of a child's intellectual activity (Piaget, 1953. Werner, 1957. Sluckin, 1970. Boyle, 1969). Now more complex patterns of visual, auditory and muscular activity emerge. Integration or assimilation is taking place (Hoffer, 1949).

When some new integration forms itself we say that the baby has passed a *milestone*. These milestones seem to take place in a fairly definite maturational sequence for most babies. Because of this, various observers have made summaries of the average ages at which milestones are passed by statistical samples of babies. These are called *developmental schedules* (Gèsell, 1940. Griffiths, 1954). A very useful brief schedule for the early months is that of Sheridan (1968).

It is important for parents and people working with children to have a background understanding of such milestones. For instance, it is useful to know when a child is likely to focus his eyes, turn to a sound, smile, sit up and so on. If several functions do not seem to have developed normally in a baby then there is cause to worry, and early diagnosis may save a great deal of trouble later. But these schedules are only general indicators. Babies are very variable in their development. Rigid adherence to them only causes parents unnecessary anxiety.

Turning now to the baby's early learning activity, if a baby is observed very closely it is possible to detect active spontaneous exploration even within the first few weeks (Piaget, 1953. Spitz, 1965). For instance, he will probably by chance lick his lips, seemingly get pleasure from the sensation and try to repeat it. On subsequent days he will repeat the licking with greater sureness, simply enjoying the activity. He seems to have initiated a motor pattern with his tongue to get a sensation. This repetition of motor patterns is referred to as a *circular reaction* (Piaget, 1953. Boyle, 1969). As the weeks and months go by, and as the baby spends more and more time awake, these explorations will be tried out in all sorts of ways. One can see that in them *active learning* is taking place. An example is the way a baby 'finds his thumb or fingers'. There is no innate thumb-sucking reflex pattern, but very early a child gets his hand to his mouth, and keeps on repeating it until he is very adept. It has the function of providing a self-generated comforter. Incidentally, there is no evidence to show that this is a harmful activity in the early months, and preventing it is quite unnecessary in ordinary circumstances.

At the same time a form of *passive learning* also seems to take place. A baby's adaptation to a mother's particular rhythm of breast- or bottle-feeding has already been mentioned. Here there seems to be little sign of self-generated exploratory activity. Rather it is an automatic passive adaptation to external conditions. There is no doubt that this occurs widely in children and adults. It is perhaps an everyday counterpart of the conditioned reflexes observed by many experimental psychologists. It is not possible here to investigate these different learning functions in more detail. A great deal of work has been done upon general theories of learning by academic psychologists, and if the reader is interested he should consult their work (see Sluckin, 1970).

Returning to the baby's active explorations, within a few weeks his eyes begin to focus, and slowly it is possible to see the baby begin to *look* actively rather than just 'vaguely contemplate'. Sounds too are responded to, and he will turn to look at the source of a sound by two or three months old. By three months or so he will smile in recognition of familiar sights such as his mother or favourite toy. The baby is beginning to *recognize*, things seen are recalled as famil- iar, *memory* is coming into play. And by means of memory, things and people are gaining meaning in the child's mind. This develop- ment of recognition and meaning is usually a joyful experience. He chortles and laughs with zest and pleasure. It might well be that the earliest laughter is associated with this gaining of meaning.

It is not just a question of looking and listening. Motor activities are co-ordinated with visual percepts. For instance, at about four months a baby will form his mouth differently at the sight of a spoon from when he sees a breast or bottle. Thus the spoon must mean something different from the bottle to him. This is not simply that the food is different, but also that a different active motor pattern is necessary to bring satisfaction.

During these first six months the baby will be lying prone most of the time, and his spontaneous visual-motor explorations will largely involve his eyes, ears, mouth, head and hands. To the casual observer he will not be doing very much, but close attention shows how spontaneously active he is in learning to gain meanings, repeating and repeating motor activities. This is very predominantly focused around the mouth and is the basis of thinking and intel- lectual activity (Hoffer, 1949).

5. A baby and his environment in the early months

We have already suggested how a baby's mother is important as the organizer of his environment, in providing for his exchange of substances and in stimulating him. We have also discussed the beginnings of his intellectual development. Now we shall briefly integrate these two aspects by introducing two general theoretical conceptions about psychological functioning which are helpful when thinking about older people as well as infants.

If the environment is prone to frustrate a baby or if it is contradictory, then something of the rudiments of *mistrust* or suspicion seem to develop in the baby's mind. For instance, if a mother makes to feed him, the baby, as we have discussed, will respond by anticipatory activity, he will 'expect' to be fed. But if she then does not feed him he will become frantic, and when the pattern is repeated he will begin to mistrust the signs of feeding the mother gives. On the other hand, if his mother is consistent and the signs of feeding are in fact followed by satisfaction, then he will tend to *trust* both the environment and his own anticipations. When the environment is felt to be predominantly satisfactory, so that development continues unimpeded, we say that it is 'good enough' (Winnicott, 1966) and that the baby has formed the foundations of *basic trust* (Erikson, 1950).

Developing trust in the environment also means that a baby is forming some of the rudiments of trust in himself. For example, if expectations of pleasure are confirmed, not only is the environment felt to be trustworthy, but so also is the baby's own capacity to anticipate future events correctly. In a primitive way, his mental representations will be 'correct', or trustworthy to him. If on the other hand his environment is patchy and contradictory, he will tend to mistrust both his environment and his own expectations.

It will be noted that both physiological processes and intellectual functioning are involved in the development of these feelings of trust and mistrust. The reader might well object that activity such as this is too complex to be achieved by a very young infant. Naturally our description is too clear-cut for what actually happens in a baby's experience. His awareness will be vague, sporadic and unintegrated. But close acquaintance with babies does make one realize that some show themselves quite characteristically as full of something akin to mistrustful trepidation when relating to things around them. Others become inert and uninterested very early in life (Spitz, 1965). Most 'normal' babies have become eager, trusting,

chuckling people by a few months old. For many centuries this
happy state has been called innocence.

The question of the consequences of infantile experiences such as
these for later life must remain open. Many workers have demon-
strated how very severe mishandling, or deprivation, has lasting,
even irreversible effects (Bowlby, 1953. Spitz, 1965). But in many
ordinary home environments where parents are devoted, a child
who has difficulties seems to 'grow out of them'. Probably the
experience has some after-effects for the child's feeling about things,
but these may become the grist of his ordinary experience of life
and will not be catastrophic.

The evidence that has been accumulated so far that specific
problems in infancy must inevitably lead to specific difficulties in
later life seems to be quite inconclusive, at least for children growing
in a consistent home environment (J. Klein, 1965). But emotional
difficulties in adulthood can often be seen to have a history going
back to early infancy. When this occurs something of the following
sequence seems to take place. In early life a pattern of stimulation
disorganizes (or traumatizes) the infant. This pattern is then
repeated again and again in the family's ways of relating to the child.
It may continue for many years so that the child is not afforded
the opportunity for creative reorganizations to take place in his
mind. Different mental activities thus remain unco-ordinated or
disintegrated and he is ill-equipped to deal with problems of living
later in life. This is a highly condensed statement doing no justice
to individual subtlety; the question is both fascinating and important
but at present full of uncertainties (see also Lidz, 1968).

6. The mother's experience

After the birth of her baby a young mother will usually be exhausted.
For nine months her physiology has been attuned to the baby inside
her. Now it is outside her, her physiology must shift to this and she
needs to get to know the baby outside her. The days after pregnancy
are thus times of very great physiological and psychological change.
Because of this she is usually rather disorganized in herself. She is
labile, often with the swift swings of mood which accompany any
time of great change. One moment she is very happy, the next,
weeping bitterly. Most people recognize this and expect 'the blues'
a few days after birth. Occasionally this depression becomes
entrenched so that a woman continues in a *puerperal depression* for
months and even years (Lomas, 1967. Deutsch, 1944).

A day or so after birth a mother usually finds her breasts filling with milk. Breast-feeding has natural advantages; there is no fuss with bottles, the mixture is usually just right for the baby and the situation provides that sensuousness which is important to the baby. However, bottle-fed babies who get the right mixture of milk and cuddling seem to have no difficulty in thriving. In fact very many mothers find breast-feeding most unsatisfactory, and gratefully turn to the bottle. Even though they have probably been encouraged to breast-feed by their hospital or midwife, they turn to the bottle when they get home (Newson, 1963). This may be because the milk is insufficient or because they find such feeding difficult for personal reasons.

Perhaps many doctors and health visitors have been alienated from mothers for insisting too authoritatively that they ought to breast-feed their babies. Mothers are very various in the ways they handle their babies (Newson, 1963. Brody, 1956. Douglas and Blomfield, 1958) and as long as mother and baby enjoy the business it would seem that interference does more harm than good. A woman who is commanded to go against her inclinations is prone to become tense, anxious and irritable, which is not likely to be much good for the baby. The necessity of 'letting the mother be' to find her own way has been much stressed in recent years (Spock, 1957. Winnicott, 1964. Fraiberg, 1959).

During the first few weeks the mother will be attuning herself to the baby. If it is her first she will usually be anxious, feel he is fragile and that she is sure to drop him or let him choke. But as the weeks go by she usually slowly discovers he is tougher than she feared. She will find ways of soothing him, the easiest way to feed him, how to bring up wind and recognize the different reasons for his crying; his tired cry, hungry cry, windy cry, etc.

In all this the mother will be discovering her baby as a real person separate from herself. This is an enthralling experience for most mothers, and makes all the weariness of broken nights and being tied to him worth while.

Getting to know a baby involves *identifying* with him, that is, feeling along with him. You will hear mothers doing this when they say, 'Poor fellow he's hungry', or, 'Oh, she does hate a wet nappy so', or comments like these. Most mothers absorb themselves in their babies and identify themselves with them, while still maintaining a sense of themselves and their own needs (empathy). In some mothers this process gets unbalanced. Some *over-identify* with the baby and tend to lose all sense of themselves and their own needs. One mother expressed her anxiety about this when she said, 'He was a big fine baby, and as he grew I seemed to get smaller and smaller. I seemed to be drained with the milk that went into him. I felt I died as he lived.'

Other mothers find it hard to identify at all with their babies. They feel sickened, bored and irritated with them. They are just a nuisance impinging upon them. These mothers usually come in for a lot of moral censure because of their 'heartlessness' or selfishness. Certainly it is hard to sympathize with mothers who have no insight into themselves, but just seem unwilling to change their ways for their own children. It is easier to feel sorry for mothers who recognize their own problem and are disturbed by it, as for example the mother who said sadly, 'I just can't feel for babies in the way I can for kittens,' or, 'I can't believe that babies are anything but things.'

We cannot here go into the inner dynamics and causes behind women who feel disturbed in these ways (Deutsch, 1944. Lomas, 1967). But it is valuable to recognize that these are extremes of over- and under-identification which all mothers have to cope with to some extent. The optimal state of identifying with a baby, yet also being able to look after herself, is something towards which a mother has to find her own way as she goes through the early months. And the pain of the baby's impingements upon herself usually brings spates of rage and despair. Mothers frequently feel profoundly guilty about such feelings, yet it is probably as natural for a mother to feel angry when overstressed as it is for her baby to be angry when disturbed or frustrated.

7. Fathering

Mothers are usually surrounded by a network of helpers. In some societies it is even normal for other members of the extended family to take over all mothering functions. In Britain today a mother often finds herself at the other extreme, alone with her baby with few relatives near. Under such circumstances a network of friendships with other women often replaces many of the functions of relatives. But more than any other person the husband is placed in a position of special responsibility. A distinctly noticeable social change has occurred in the past twenty years, whereby fathers take an active part in nursing young babies (J. Klein, 1965. Young and Willmott, 1957. Newson, 1963).

In doing this a father acts as an auxiliary mother in bathing, feeding, changing or getting up at night. This performs two functions. It gives the mother a chance to rest, but also it provides an opportunity for a father to get to know his baby and vice versa. This is important in the nuclear family because, if the father knows how to handle the child, then the family can feel assured that he is ready to take over in emergencies. Furthermore, handling a baby means that a relationship has been established from the beginning, so that a closeness has already developed by the time a father will be of more focal importance in his own right later in childhood.

Many fathers think that their time will come later when their children want to be shown things in the world, and meanwhile they need do little. But if they are indifferent in the early years, their children will be strangers to them when the time comes. This is not necessarily catastrophic, but it may sow the seeds of later difficulty. For instance, children who never know their fathers in their early years for one reason or another will often report how difficult it was both for themselves and their fathers to get to know and trust each other.

Just as important is the father's relationship with his wife. His main function seems to be to watch over her and see that she is free to let herself be relaxed, even chaotic, in her preoccupation with the baby. This has already been discussed with regard to pregnancy and the same holds true in infancy. This watching involves 'standing at the door of the cave' – seeing that all is safe from the outside world. It also involves a husband in watching over his wife, seeing that she is all right inside herself; to do this he must necessarily remain in intimate communication with her. Perhaps we could say that, if all goes well, just as the baby is cared for primarily by his mother, so the mother is primarily cared for by her husband.

8. Introduction to theory: the concepts of id and ego
It is now necessary to introduce some theoretical concepts. Although the theory given in this book will be brief and elementary, it may be puzzling, at least to the beginner. It is not difficult to grasp immediate perception and feeling. But when theorizing, the mind has to engage in pure thought, ranging wide over a general host of memories of phenomena and then *abstracting* certain common features which seem to be significant. A distillate of these features has to be formed and named as a theoretical concept.

Some people find that such intellectual exercises are easy and perhaps more enjoyable than personal emotional contact and the immediate perceiving and feeling that goes with it. Others, particularly those in the helping professions tend to find abstract thought tedious, even arrogant and cold, especially in large doses. Psychological concepts have an added irritation in that they are usually vague with none of the precision of pure mathematics. There are actually good reasons for this vagueness. It is particularly important for those of us who work with people and use psychological concepts to be tentative and speculative in our thought. If we are not we allow neither ourselves nor our patients or clients to be free in thought and imagination. If background concepts are too precise this freedom is likely to be lost in preoccupation with correctness.

Even so, for all the puzzlement aroused by theory, it is important to conceptualize because in this way real communication can be facilitated. Concepts are a shorthand or code condensing a network of ideas into single words or phrases which speed up discussion (if concepts are understood alike by all concerned).

As it is likely that the reader will find the theoretical sections puzzling, it may be easier to read them over quickly, to get a feel of them as it were, with a view to returning to them later when more attuned to the form of thinking presented in the book. There are also many more detailed texts to consult, e.g. Freud (1923) or Cameron (1963). Very clear and concise definitions are also given by Rycroft (1968 a).

Let us now begin by considering two concepts originating from psychoanalysis but also in common usage today. These are *id* and *ego*. It is necessary here to start from a physiological standpoint.

We have noticed among other things in this chapter how feeding, breathing and excretion are naturally of vital importance to the baby and that a mother's life is centred about seeing to their harmonious functioning. The baby is like any living organism in being continuously active in balancing the excesses or deficits in its body. This maintenance of physiological balance is termed *homeostasis*. Take, for example, an infant's breathing. Here an optimal level of oxygen and carbon dioxide is maintained in the blood system by the activity of lung ventilation. Homeostasis is also evident in sucking when hungry, or when sphincters open to excrete waste matter; and there are many others which can be detected.

These homeostatic body processes, or physiological needs to use another phrase, are highly complex and many states of need can only be brought to quiescence through the mediation of the external environment, as in (say) feeding. This environment is itself usually organized by the mother during infancy. The *brain* and central nervous system act as an *organizing agency* for, or intermediary between, specific physiological processes and the environment. In other words, the brain acts as a *control system*, receiving information or signals from the body on the one hand and from the environment, through the sense organs, on the other. As a control system or organizing agency, the brain can be seen as analogous to a computer controlling a complex chemical plant, or to one which directs the movement of a space rocket.

So far this discussion has been confined to the physical mode of understanding; our thinking has been physiological. We have viewed the infant's brain as a control system, and of course the brain of any person can, until death, be equally considered as a control system. We now turn towards the idea of an individual being *conscious* and hence experiencing things. The concept of the brain is then transformed into the psychological idea of the mind. This consciousness is what a computer lacks. Although the mind can still be seen as a control system, it has the additional quality of experiencing and feeling, which must be taken into account when considering its activity.

The individual's mind (that of the baby or the adult) can now be seen as a control system receiving information or signals both from organs of the body and from the environment. The *signals* or representations of body needs (homeostatic processes) in the experience of the mind are often referred to as *id-functions* (Freud, 1923).

We do not know exactly how an infant experiences these body-function signals. They are probably very acute and intense, because his mind is unlikely yet to be filled with other more intellectual ideas. The strength of his crying when hungry tends to confirm that the signals are acute. In the older person body-function signals are sometimes clear, but mostly they are only dimly perceived consciously, and always clothed, as it were, by an interwoven pattern of other ideas. The raw direct signals always seem to be *unconscious*. The only time the signals reach consciousness in anything like a raw state is perhaps in the extremity of exhaustion, madness, or under drugs when we hallucinate. Putting this in other terms, under ordinary circumstances *id-functioning* is always unconscious. It must be added that our definition of id given here is not the only one in use. There are many other subtleties of meaning but ours contains many fundamental ideas which will serve as an introduction.

The mind also receives signals from the environment and co-ordinates these with information from the body organs to act as a control system. We have seen in the preceding chapter how the young infant develops, through maturation and memory, an increasing capacity to co-ordinate and control his body in relation to his environment.

The general term used to refer to this co-ordination and control by the mind of the body is that of *ego-function* (Freud, 1923). In terms of experience we say that ego-functions mediate between outer reality on the one hand and inner impulse life on the other. It will be evident that the infant's ego-functioning is quite rudiment-ary; it is focused and intimately dependent upon a mother's activity. The baby has not yet developed highly organized modes of thought and feeling, but as we investigate childhood we will trace the growth of an individual's ego-functioning.

It is common practice to refer to these organized mental activities as a 'thing' and to speak of an individual's *ego*. This should not be confused with the idea of *self*, which will be introduced in the next chapter. The ego refers very generally (and loosely) to the organiz-ing of activity with the body on the one hand and the environment on the other. The self refers to the experience of 'being', as separate from other people. The concepts are related but not identical.

4

THE SECOND SIX MONTHS[1]

These months are usually remembered by parents with special delight. The early days of worry and drudgery have passed and routines have been established. The time has yet to come when the child is really mobile, 'into everything', provoking clashes of will and fears for his safety. During these intermediate months parents often have time to be relatively idle. There is plenty to enjoy. The baby will usually be eagerly interested in all things that come into his orbit be they human, animal or simply shapes, colours or movements. Incidentally, this is the age which classical painters often chose for the Christ Child when painting the Madonna and Child. At a more mundane level it is still a favourite for photographs of babyhood.

This is a time of enormous thrusts in intellectual and muscular developments. These in turn lead to crucial emotional developments, so it behoves us to investigate them quite carefully. We shall start with a brief survey of observable behavioural developments. We shall then go on to analyse some of the changes that must have taken place in the child's mind to allow these behavioural developments to take place.

1. Observable behaviour developments[2]
During the first six months the baby will have been progressively awake for longer periods during the day. He will probably have dropped his night feeds, much to his parents' relief. By the middle of the first year he will usually still be feeding from breast or bottle but will also be using spoon and cup. He will be kicking and wriggling, and probably sitting up for long periods, at least when supported. Sitting up means that he has a much wider scope of vision and use of his hands. He will continually be examining things, not only by

[1] For general discussion see Fraiberg, 1959.
[2] See Sheridan, 1968.

looking but also by manipulating things with his hands, and often with his feet. He will take things to his mouth, suck and chew them, twist them round and look at them. This chewing also gives him relief with teething pains. His first teeth will be coming through by about now. He will be listening to sounds, turning towards them and singing and babbling to himself. He will also probably be beginning to play with his parents, both with things and in cuddling, tickling and babbling, usually to the delight of all concerned.

In the latter months of the first year he will be sitting up unsupported, and later start moving of his own initiative. This is usually by crawling, but babies find their own modes of progression. Some never crawl but move on one arm or by sitting up and propelling themselves with their hands. By one year a child will probably be able to stand and may be walking. In this again babies are very variable. Some quite normal children do not walk until they are getting on for two years old. Having found another means of progression, they do not seem to bother to learn to walk.

When he has learnt to sit up, and then to move, a new range of experience is open to him. He can actively explore new places. He throws things away and looks to see where they have gone. He bangs things together to make noises and manipulates toys in relation to each other, not just towards himself and his mouth. Towards the end of the first year he will use *instruments* in his play. For instance, he will have learned to grasp strings to get hold of toys out of his reach, and so on.

Most gratifying of all, perhaps, to his parents, he will be getting more and more interest in other human beings. He will usually actively seek their attention, chortle with pleasure at their company and begin to *show off* to them. He will copy or *imitate* other people's actions with increasing coherence (Sluckin, 1970. Millar, 1968). Playing with sounds is enjoyed by babbling and repeating intonations to himself which are seemingly meaningless. These sounds will later be refined to become recognizable imitations. Probably by about one year or a little older the first recognizable words for objects will be developed. We shall discuss this development of language in greater detail in the next chapter. (For developmental scales and milestones see Sheridan, 1968. Gesell, 1940. Griffiths, 1954.)

2. The development of meaning

From observations such as these we can make some hypotheses

about, or interpret, what is going on in the baby's mind intellectually. In the previous chapter we drew attention to the *assimilation* of visual impressions with motor and tactile sensations (Piaget, 1953. Boyle, 1969. Werner, 1957). In the second six months this is even more striking.

With spontaneous exploration the child is bringing more information into the realm of his awareness. This is aided by his capacity to sit up and crawl. Things take on enhanced *meaning*. By meaning we refer to all the associations attached to a perception. Thus, a rattle to begin with probably only has a vague 'meaning', that it is hard, can be picked up, sucked, and makes a sound. It will gain further meaning, however, when the baby finds out that it can be thrown away, picked up or used to push things and make them move. This simple illustration emphasizes how assimilation of meaning is dependent upon the child's memory. The central importance of the *mouth* (orality) in these early intellectual explorations is also evident. Objects are eagerly taken into the mouth, smelled, chewed, looked at and handled. Thus the meaning of a much-sucked rattle must involve the recall of memories of sensations of sucking, chewing and swallowing. Evaluation of objects is also beginning to take place. This involves tasting and sucking objects, licking them with pleasure or alternatively spitting them out with an 'ugh' sound if they are distasteful (Hoffer, 1949. Spitz, 1965).

As his dexterity increases and perceptions become assimilated by memory, the baby actively tries to bring about situations that he must have anticipated in his mind. We can see this: for instance, in his efforts to retrieve a toy. He will perhaps fail on the first attempt, but try again and again until he succeeds. The baby's thought and action has begun to be overtly *intentional* (Piaget, 1953. Boyle, 1969).

For such intentional activity to occur the child must be forming mental representations not only of the present stimulus but also of some anticipated future situation which he is trying to bring about.

3. Mental representations of reality and phantasy

We have seen so far how the baby slowly develops mental representations of the immediate world about him. These form the origins of his intelligence. However, it seems likely that other mental activity which is less tied to the external environment is also going on. We might infer that the precursors to phantasy and imagination are taking place (Sandler, 1962. Isaacs, 1952).

If we listen to children or adults who can talk, it becomes obvious that large parts of their mental lives are concerned not so much with the immediate environment as with imaginings and phantasy. Since a young baby cannot talk we have little direct evidence about his imaginative activity. However, since imagination is manifestly present as soon as a child is able to talk (see chapters 5 and 6) it is probably valid to assume that a baby's mind is full of unspoken phantasies before this.

The phantasies of older children and adults are inspired not only by the social situations around them but also by their *bodily urges*, particularly from the viscera. The part played by some of these urges is evident from excited imaginings about lavatorial or sexual fun. Oral and digestive phantasy is also manifest in children's talk of biting, swallowing and spitting. Since the infant is very preoccupied with his viscera, particularly digestion, it is probably safe to assume that he too forms imaginative representations from bodily functions like older children, but in a vaguer form.

It seems most likely, as some authorities suggest, that a phantasy arises in the mind whenever a physiological need is present (id function). A phantasy is thus primarily the representation of a visceral impulse (M. Klein, 1960. Segal, 1964. Isaacs, 1952). Since an infant is continuously activated by digestive needs, so his mind is repeatedly filled with phantasy, particularly of an oral kind.

Other authorities emphasize the *wish-fulfilling* nature of phantasy (Cameron, 1963). According to this theory, when a bodily urge is frustrated a *hallucination* of satisfaction takes place which temporarily assuages the urge. It is said for instance that a starving man dreams of or even hallucinates food. It is suggested that a baby has not yet learnt to differentiate between phantasy and reality, so that for him there is no difference between hallucination and imagined reality. Only later by repeated experience does he inhibit hallucination and turn it into realistic imagination.

If we actually observe young babies, it is very hard to say how often this hallucinatory wish-fulfilment takes place. Later in life wish-fulfilment of a non-hallucinatory kind obviously plays a very large part in adult and older children's make-believe and phantasy life. Hallucination itself is perhaps most evident in older children's sleeping dreams. These often spill over into waking life so that, for instance, the child is frightened and wants to come in his parents' bed for reassurance. Lack of differentiation of phantasy and reality also occurs of course in the adult disturbances of mental functioning known as psychoses. Since we tend to hallucinate in later life when our more developed faculties break down, so it seems possible that a baby frequently hallucinates when these differentiating faculties have not yet developed.

There is little point at this stage in arguing further about these theories. Basing their ideas on the intimate investigation of young children, psychoanalysts have gone into very considerable detail in their hypotheses about the phantasy life of young infants in their first year (M. Klein, 1953. Winnicott, 1958, 1965 *b*. Spitz, 1965). I myself on the whole agree with these writers, but cannot expect the reader to go further with me in this without more evidence, which lies outside the scope of this book.

4. Irradiation of pleasure

We have already mentioned the deep pleasure a child experiences when, after all his exploration and searching, he achieves something to his satisfaction. This occurs when, physically satiated with breast or bottle, he relapses into a drunken contentment. A milder and more transient delight occurs when a child has achieved a physical feat, like reaching a sought-after toy. He is similarly delighted after achieving something intellectually, as when an activity or percept has gained meaning. For instance, when he successfully imitates a sound, he will chortle with joy and want to keep repeating the performance.

We could call such joy at achievements 'little ecstasies' – and perhaps the satisfaction of early feeding a 'grand ecstasy'. In these ecstasies there seems to be a discharge of excitement that irradiates throughout the body. This has been but little studied. However, its proper functioning seems vital. Some people quite consciously complain of being unable to feel pleasure in this way and are very distressed by it.

Incidentally, another word for these ecstasies is *orgasm*. This term is usually reserved for the irradiation of pleasure from the genitals. The physiological functions involved in this particular ecstasy have been well studied (Masters and Johnson, 1966). Whether other ecstasies are physiologically similar remains for further research to explore.

For the present we need simply to recognize the importance of ecstasies in healthy and enjoyable living. These ecstasies probably play a vital role in gaining meaning, of integrating ideas and feelings and retaining them in memory. Recapitulating so far, we have seen how the young child, if allowed the opportunity to do so, spontaneously explores and, from previously unstructured 'thought' and phantasy, slowly develops mentally structured and meaningful representations and actions in relation to the world around him. Also, when things gain meaning or in other ways give him satisfaction, he experiences ecstasies of pleasure, which seem to play some part in further integrating experiences for him. With this enhanced mental structuring come the beginnings of differentiation of *self* and *outer reality*. This is of fundamental importance to the individual of any age.

5. *Differentiation of self and outer reality*

During the second half of the first year various subtle changes can be observed. We have mentioned most of them already. In his crying and babbling a note comes into a baby's voice which can best be described as 'calling' – a sort of 'hey, come here, I want you'. This presupposes that he has got some sense that, 'what I want is not present but can be recalled.' We can also see something similar occurring in relation to inanimate objects, as for instance when he looks for objects that have gone out of the field of vision. Later, we see the child actively searching for hidden things and also repetitively throwing things away in order to have them back. At this time also he will begin to get enormous pleasure from playing peep-bo.

These observations suggest that the young child is beginning to be aware, to represent to himself that a world exists outside himself. So the child is beginning to come out of his original state of undifferentiation. The first glimmering of the conception of *self* and *not-self* seems to be occurring. We adults usually differentiate between our bodies, our *selves* (situated somewhere in our bodies) and the outside world. It is not plain how far this differentiation has gone with the infant. We cannot yet ask him, but it is probably vague and unstable (Winnicott, 1958, 1965 *b*. Cameron, 1963). We ourselves as adults sometimes in weird moments lose something of this differentiation between self and not-self when, for instance, we cannot remember whether it was we or someone else who said something in a conversation. Perhaps the most vivid experience for us is when we wake up from a dream, and in the dark room are not sure whether the dream happenings were real or not. This breakdown in differentiation, which can happen to anyone at least transiently, occurs chronically in psychotic illnesses like schizophrenia. In such illnesses delusions and hallucinations often occur when the differentiation between imagination and external reality breaks down.

With regard to one side of this differentiation, that of *outer reality* or the non-self, it seems very likely that the development of awareness of this is intimately bound up with *frustration* of wishes or needs and the rage and *aggressive impulses* that are its consequences. (Spitz, 1965. Winnicott, 1958. Freud, 1915. A. Freud, 1949.) If we introspect, we can detect that the non-self is that which can frustrate us; it is not entirely under our control. We can infer that, when a child cries to call his mother, he is beginning to recognize that she is not entirely under his control and can thus frustrate him. Indeed, if she does not respond quickly he will often burst out into rage, kicking and grinding his mouth aggressively. It seems that in this frustration she has become a 'bad' thing to him, at least momentarily. That frustration and aggression are a basis of the sense of external reality is evident also in ordinary parlance when we speak of 'hard facts' or 'bitter truth'. If this is so, then it becomes plain that frustration and aggressive impulses *per se* are not to be considered simply as bad experiences to be got rid of. Without some frustration and play of aggressive feelings it is doubtful whether we would have a sense of external reality. It is a strange paradox of life that frustrations feel bad, so that we continually wish to rid ourselves of them. Yet to do so, even if it were possible, would stunt our reality sense.

A mother who tries to satisfy her child in everything is not only attempting the impossible, she is also doing her child a disservice, for he is literally being spoilt. On the other hand, continuous frustration of impulses and needs, as we shall see, leads to withdrawal and grave disturbances in children. Usually a mother does not need to try to invent frustrations for a child. There will be enough arising in the ordinary course of events. Somewhere a blend of uncontrived frustration with warm attention seems to be optimal for the development of a firm sense of the self as differentiated from outer reality. Needless to say, none of us as parents ever achieve this all the time.

6. Helplessness and omnipotence

With the differentiation of self and not-self must come the first glimmerings in a child's mind of his *helplessness* or *impotence*. Here he wants to do things but cannot. This sense of helplessness is not consciously spoken about very much by children, but it seems to be a very pervasive feeling. We only have to recall our own early lives to remember how very big things seemed, how out of our control and frightening they were. In fact a child's urge to grow up often seems to be driven by the feeling of 'I can't do it yet, but will when I grow up.' The converse is the phantasy that one can do anything; nothing is too much for us. We can see older children and adults often resorting to the *phantasy of omnipotence* when they are frustrated and helpless. In the first year of life there is no direct evidence of such phantasies, but they probably occur.

It is likely that a baby derives a sense of his own power from willing things and seeming to make them happen. For instance, when he demands to be fed and his mother actually comes to feed him, it must seem that he has control over her. As with the case of aggression, we cannot say that this sense of power or omnipotence is a bad thing *per se*. Without any sense of power within us, we are unlikely to have a feeling of effectiveness at all. Somehow, by a blend of frustration and attention coming from parents' ordinary behaviour, the child gets a feeling of *potency*. This is a sense of omnipotence that has been refined and differentiated so that the child feels power only when he has really got it.

7. Parent–child communication

In the previous chapter we described how a mother provides an environment for a baby, optimally one that is fairly quiet and warm and free of shocks. Although he does not know it, he is in a state of dependence upon her, and his whole childhood will be taken up with developing out of this dependence. In theoretical terminology, the baby's ego functioning is rudimentary, so that his mother carries out many of the functions for him. Only slowly, with the growth of ego functioning, does independence come to the child.

Looking closely at a mother with her baby we can see how complex a patterning of activities mothering is. She feeds and cuddles him and thus acts as an *object of gratification*. Probably based upon this physical gratification, but with a subtle tracery of other ecstasies interwoven, she becomes his first, and hence deepest object of love. We have already described how, since she cannot meet his every need she must often frustrate him and thus also become his first *object of hatred*.

It must be recognized here that these frustrations are not only concerned with physical needs. Much more frequently a mother is likely to frustrate his explorations, curiosity or wish for cuddles and caresses. These are more subtle requirements than feeding, and hence the more likely to go unnoticed. There will be more about this later.

If a mother has the time and enjoys mothering she will play with him, talk and sing, as well as providing stimulation from her movements about the house as she goes about her business.

In all these functions a great deal of *communication* is likely to go on. To begin with this will be entirely non-verbal. At first in feeding, and later in playing, the little child probably becomes aware of his mother's moods as expressed by her movements, the smooth or jerky play of her body, the movement of her hands, the curve of her shoulders and the expressions on her face. From these it seems that the basis of communication arises (Spitz, 1965).

If one sees a mother and infant playing happily together with a lot of body contact, it is very obvious how the mother's pleasure can communicate itself to her baby. She will give him a big warm hug and say, 'Oh, I love you so much I could eat you.' He will wriggle with pleasure and ecstasy, grin toothlessly and start crowing 'Ga ga ga ga'. The mother will probably then repeat this back to him with another hug of pride and pleasure. The observer usually feels a bit embarrassed at how silly the mother is being, but he perhaps knows too that this is what love and the good things of life are about. It seems likely that experiences like these give the young child something of the idea that he himself is 'all right', worth while or good. They give him *self-esteem*. Conversely, the baby's smiling, his 'clever' talking and affectionate cuddling back give the mother the feeling of herself being all right as a mother. The baby is 'contributing in', as we have mentioned. Incidentally, adults yearn to refind this intimacy when they fall in love and say equally silly but just as important things to each other.

On the other hand, as we have said, the mother acts as a frustrator. The tensing of her body, pursing of the lips, withdrawal of the breast or bottle, are some of many signs of freezing up or showing anger. At quite an early age the baby clearly becomes distressed by these. They are what can be called the pre-verbal communications of the mother saying 'No' or *negation* (Spitz, 1965). We have referred several times to the distress, then rage, hatred and despair that these expressions of the mother's negation evoke in the child. Where continually repeated they probably set in gross deforming mental processes in the child. But without them he is spoilt. Perhaps most ordinary mothers find a mean between the extremes. It is likely that the common mother's game of shaking her head and saying 'No' affectionately to a child is an intuitive way of helping a child to integrate the 'Yes' of affectionate cuddling with the 'No' as signalled by head-shaking. Such an integration seems to be most important in the development of an individual's *sense of other people's feelings*.

It need hardly be emphasized that such a sense of other people's feelings is as important a development in the individual's conception of external reality as is the intellectual recognition of external physical objects. It is of interest to note how frequently the latter more 'intellectual' aspects of reality are emphasized in educational systems, often to the exclusion of the former 'feeling' aspects. Certainly the feeling aspects of our reality sense seem to be more prone to disturbance than those concerned with the physical world. Disturbance of feeling in relation to other people is much more common than distortion of the sense of physical reality.

8. Primitive anxiety

We have just been considering the disturbance of a child when his mother negates him. Let us now turn to his feeling of disturbance in a wider context.

We have already stressed the child's growing sense of helplessness as he begins to differentiate himself from the outside world. When he is enjoying himself and feels good, this impotence obviously does not worry him much. But when he is frustrated, angry or feels bad, it is likely that his helplessness is often of catastrophic proportions. His screams and misery indicate this. A convenient term for this sense of helplessness in the face of forces that are too 'big' is *persecution* (M. Klein, 1953. Segal, 1964). As adults we can easily feel the same. When things are experienced as getting on top of us, they are often felt as getting *at* us. A baby's misery seems to match this, so we are probably justified in assuming that he also is feeling persecuted. In theoretical terms, the sense of persecution arises when ego-functioning is inadequate to cope with a situation.

This brings us to the question of *anxiety* (Rycroft, 1968 *a* and *b*. Cameron, 1963. Mayer-Gross, 1960). In the first months of life we noted that a generalized distress occurred. This was not yet anxiety since there were no indications of anticipation which is intrinsic to anxiety. By the latter half of the first year things have changed. For instance, a baby of this age may look frightened when a stranger comes into the room. Further, he may burst into tears and clutch his mother when she goes to hand him to the stranger. Or again he may start screaming on seeing mother getting her coat to go out, leaving him with the stranger.

Here we see that the intellectual development of anticipation has become assimilated with the sense of helplessness in distress or of persecution to produce anxiety. Anxiety can become very complex later in life, but in these early days it seems to be concerned primarily with ideas of being overwhelmed by mysterious and hence bad forces.

9. Primitive modes of alleviating distress and anxiety

We have just been discussing the infant's experience of distress when everything seems to persecute him. In such a state his mother also is felt as absolutely bad. At other times she is probably dearly loved. The infant seems to hate completely or love whole-heartedly. Loving and hating the same person has not yet become integrated in the baby's mind. Rather a primitive mode of dividing feelings towards people into two, good ones and bad, takes place. This occurs particularly towards his mother, so that a child not only feels in two separate extreme ways but also has two different images of the same person, his mother. One is felt to be completely good and loved, the other absolutely bad and hated. The occurrence of this is not immediately obvious to the observer of early childhood. Much of our evidence for it is derived from the close study of older children and adults. Perhaps the most clear indication of its occurrence in the early months is the way infants will readily change their mood. One moment they will be raging, kicking, screaming, and then with a kiss or cuddle they will suddenly change. The rage vanishes, they will be all smiles and hugs, and behave towards their mother as if the bitter rage of a few moments ago had never occurred. As children get older and the good and bad feelings are experienced in a more integrated way, the transition from one to the other is more subtle.

This tendency to feel in extremes of good and bad, or affirmation and negation, is referred to as *splitting* (M. Klein, 1947, 1932. Segal, 1964). For any individual, be he child or adult, such underlying splitting processes seem to have many aspects and can reach great complexity. It must be stressed that the splitting takes place quite automatically and is outside conscious control. Such a process probably saves a child from intolerable confusion, for to hate a person whom one also loves is a most unpleasant experience even for a knowledgeable adult. To a child who is much less clear about

E

the consequences of his hatred, the pain of this ambivalence must be worse.

The childhood proneness to split into good and bad seems to carry on into adult thought also. It seems to occur wherever prejudice is played out in social relations; in this context it is often referred to as dichotomization. Young children seek to dichotomize when they play at 'goodies and baddies'. Adults do the same when they over-simplify into 'black–white', 'free world–communist', 'worker–boss', or 'us–them'; the reader can easily continue this list for himself. The social consequences of the untrammelled play of such splitting mechanisms in groups of adults often seem to be catastrophic. They can be seen occurring before and during wars for instance. This is obviously a vital subject deserving of more attention than can be given here.

10. The parent's part in integrating good and bad feelings

There is little doubt that some mothers make a mess of helping the subtle integration of good and bad feelings in their children, and probably everyone flounders over it. It seems that chronic problems arise when a parent and child get entrenched in a particular attitude for a long time, perhaps throughout childhood. For instance, one mother nurtured and adored her son as if he was the most marvellous person on earth throughout his childhood. She went out of her way to protect him against all the disturbances of the outside world and marvelled at his every achievement. However, at times her patience would give way and she would burst out in violent rages at him. It is not surprising that part of him grew up convinced that he was the most wonderful person on earth, a genius. This was shattered when he first went to school and found that he was treated as just another child. He feared that everything in the outside world was all bad, full of violent rages at him, just as his mother in angry moments had been.

Another mother was convinced that one of her daughters was psychotic, and went out of her way to allocate the role of the mad, bad child to her. Not surprisingly perhaps, this girl was deeply convinced that she must be insane. These are just a couple of examples, but studies of the families of disturbed people are full of accounts like these (Lidz, 1963. Lidz and Fleck, 1965. Laing, 1959).

As mentioned before, all parents, however competent, probably muddle along trying to find an optimal balance of good and bad, of gratification and frustration for their child. This being so, elements of disturbance and ill feeling are probably present in everyone. It seems very likely that the character of each one of us is in part dependent upon the particular pattern of good and bad, of gratification and frustration that has been meted out to us by the style of our parents, particularly our mothers.

Cultural studies have suggested how some attributes are affirmed and others negated in subtle ways from very early ages in differing ways in different societies (Erikson, 1950. J. Klein, 1965. Newson, 1963). In any one culture or class it seems that parents differ from family to family in the unspoken ways by which they express pleasure or dislike, affirm or negate the things their children do. Furthermore, in any one family different children are responded to in slightly different ways. For instance, in our second example just given, the mother grossly affirmed the activities of two of her daughters and negated the third.

11. Separation anxiety and loss of mother

Perhaps the most emphatic work to show how important mothering is, has been the studies of children who have been deprived or lost their mothers for long periods for one reason or another. Spitz and Goldfarb in America and Bowlby in Britain have been pioneers in this field. We shall not go into details here. The evidence is well known and easily available (Bowlby, 1953. Spitz, 1965). There have been critical studies of this work, but the main contention of Spitz and Bowlby that a child needs a continuity of attention, stimulation and affection from, at most, a very few well-known individuals seems to stand. Generally, it is observed that when a child is parted from his mother and placed in a strange environment he is at first distraught, screaming and extremely anxious. After some days he quietens down and seems to be better behaved. If the deprivation continues for long he becomes apathetic, depressed and unresponsive. We can understand this if we consider the infant's point of view. Previously the most important aspects of gratification, excitation and organization of his world came through his mother. Now she is gone, he is in a sort of vacuum. He has not got this familiar person to attach his feelings to. They can only be directed at mid-air, as it were. From the intellectual point of view all his previous experience led him to expect certain things. Now none of these occur. The easy flow he has known before is interrupted, internal psychological chaos reigns, and he is distraught. If he is very young, he has no way of being able to anticipate whether his mother will ever return – she is as good as dead. When this is prolonged for many months, the child does not seem to let bygones be bygones and start things afresh with no ill effects. He may seem to get on easily with people, but depth of feeling is very often lost. This can be understood by recognizing that the young child has been developing vital processes in relation to his mother. These are at the same time both physical and mental and hence involve deep feelings. When mother disappears all his expectations and hence trust are shattered. He is left with a primitive deep-seated mistrust of his environment which cannot easily be dispelled. His deep and passionate feelings have been shattered. It seems likely that, within limits, a very young infant can adapt to a change from one mother to another, as in adoption. But for babies over six months and up to four or five years or beyond, such changes can be catastrophic. This is understandable when we realize that the very young baby has not yet organized himself psychologically and physically in relation to his mother. But by six months he has begun to organize his expectations and to differentiate himself from the external world. When he loses his mother this organization goes to pieces. Certainly in the years from, say, six months to three years old the ordinary child is very demanding of his mother's presence. It seems that this is the crucial phase of developing the sense of self as separate from the outer world. When this is taking place the child can very easily become terrified of his mother's disappearance. He is not yet sure that when she disappears she will return. For the child whose mother does not reappear the experience feels catastrophic – and does become internally really catastrophic if the separation continues for months.

There is, for instance, evidence that infants brought up in some large institutions, where they may be kept in their cots all day and are thus grossly deprived of affection and stimulation, tend to be stunted in physical growth. In extreme cases of such emotional deprivation, the death-rate of such infants is very high, even though they are kept clean and plenty of food is available. Intellectual development is also impaired. Of equal importance, institutionalized children's ability to *feel* about themselves and others is often stunted (Spitz, 1965. Bowlby, 1952, 1953). This sort of observation and argument gives rise to a great deal of anxiety in parents. The more conscientious ones may feel they must never leave their children, and hence become tied to and oppressed by them.

This brings us to the other side of the argument. If a child experiences no separation, he gets no exercise in learning to be alone. He is also likely to be surrounded by parents who are burdened with him. Some separation is necessary for both child and parents. But if the separations and deprivations are prolonged, they may become malignant for the child. Bowlby gives the rough guide that the effects of separation of a week or so up to four years old are usually easily resolvable, and of a month or so from age four to seven. Other writers suggest that longer separations are tolerable.

The effects of separation depend very much on the child's state before separation, and of course upon the conditions when separated. If he stays in his own house in familiar surroundings with a familiar person whom he trusts, the effects are minimal. They may be valuable to him, for he learns to get on with someone else. If on the other hand he goes to a completely strange place with unfamiliar routines, the effects will be more traumatic. Likewise when a child returns to his mother; if she expects him to behave as if nothing has happened, she will probably be in for a nasty surprise. He is likely to be very cross for some time to come. What is more, if a child feels that his mother does not recognize his distress, he is going to feel just about as lonely and alienated from her as he did when she was actually away.

We have mentioned that parents and others often find these observations about separation very disturbing. This no doubt is because they emphasize the importance of parents, and hence their very great responsibility to their children. Thus parents intuitively feel frightened, not only of neglecting their children, but of the consequences for their children if they themselves die or are ill. This is perhaps an anxiety that just has to be faced and lived through. If the worst does happen, we can only see that a child is provided with as much that is familiar as possible, and try to understand and respond to his distress. For parents who have to leave their children, it is perhaps possible to help them bear their pain and misery. This is a task that doctors, nurses and social workers, particularly child care officers, have to face repeatedly.

It must also be stressed that this separation anxiety occurs not only when a mother is physically separated from her child. Something more muted but similar occurs when mothers 'withdraw' or do not respond emotionally to their children. This in some way occurs, no doubt, in any emotionally disturbed family. To a degree it also happens in any 'normal' family. We have noted already that some degree of frustration and separation seems to be necessary for development. But again, as with long physical separations, the problem of withdrawal becomes malignant if it continues through many developmental phases of a child's life.

12. Theoretical summary: object relations, feelings, physiology and illness

At the end of the last chapter we introduced the concept of ego functions to designate those mental processes which sort out information from the environment on the one hand and representations of bodily processes (or id) on the other. We shall now proceed from this preliminary model.

In the early sections of this chapter we described how there is evidence to suggest that the infant is slowly developing *mental representations* as he explores his environment. In particular we noted how he is just beginning to differentiate *self* from the outside world or not-self. He is also forming representations in his mind of external *objects* in the world around him and getting some notions about the relations between them. He is beginning to form a personal *representational world* (Sandler, 1962) or *inner world* (M. Klein, 1960. Segal, 1964).

We can recognize various aspects of this representational world. First, there are representations of the physical *inanimate objects* which he has explored and about which he has begun to organize a network of meanings. The aura of meaning around those objects will contain not only memories of impressions derived from his external senses but also representations of his physiological responses from muscles, mouth, stomach and intestines. These responses will have occurred when he was playing with the objects. In other words, his ideas about external things are probably infused with meanings, literally, from his viscera. This would lead us to suspect that when a child or adult views an object that 'means a lot' to him, then there will also be considerable physiological reaction to the object. Recent psychosomatic research seems to bear this out (Alexander, 1952).

When an object 'means a lot' to a person we usually infer that he experiences strong *feelings* about the thing. Thus feelings involve physiological responses. They involve two aspects at least, first the intellectual representations of the perceived object and secondly the representation of bodily reactions to it.

So far we have discussed, for simplicity's sake, representations of inanimate objects. Something very similar seems to occur in relation to animate and human external objects. Representations are formed with a tracery of meaning from memory and from bodily reactions around the visual and tactile image of the object. In the case of human objects, and a child's mother in particular, the attendant meaning will usually be fraught with passionate reactions and memories of ecstasies and frustrations.

When we refer to what a mother and child actually do with each other we speak about their *here and now* relationship. When, on the other hand we are referring to what is going on *inside* a child's mind about his representation of his mother, we use the term *internal object relation* with his maternal image. The phrase *internal object* is used to refer to the mental or internal representations of a human being. This is perhaps an infelicitous term, but it has come into technical usage, and so long as we recognize its meaning there need be no difficulty (M. Klein, 1960. Segal, 1964).

At this early phase of life it will be recognized that internal object representations are probably very vague and transient. We have noted how little children are prone to split their feelings about their parents, so that they tend to dichotomize their good representations from the bad ones. Furthermore, we have also noted how, with only a rudimentary sense of self as distinct from external objects, the child is likely to confuse his representation of himself with that of his external objects. With time and experience the differentiation becomes more distinct and structured.

We have discussed persecutory experiences and the effects of separation and maternal deprivation. In this we mentioned some of the repercussions from these disorganizing experiences. This raises the question of illness. We say that a person is *ill* when some part of his functioning is disorganized for any length of time. When the integrated organization of some *part of his body* becomes disorganized for whatever reason, we say that he is *physically ill*. When mental representations and capacity to relate to the environment are disorganized we say the individual is *mentally ill*.

It must be recognized that states of mental or physical disorganization occur in the normal course of events for everyone. Thus obviously illness, both mental and physical, is part of normal living. However, for most of our lives these illnesses are experienced as minimal and require no special care. For others, illnesses of physical or mental disorganization may become chronic (as with the deprived children) and irreversible.

5

ONE TO TWO YEARS OLD

1. Observable behaviour[1]

At the beginning of his second year a child will just about be taking his first floundering steps: by the end of that year he will usually be moving with assurance. At the beginning there is a slightly anxious pleasure in discovering his movements: at the end of the year, and on into the third, he usually shows a sheer joy in progression, and the discoveries that come with it. A young child's life is all movement. He absorbs himself in exploration, finding new things and then manipulating them, thus discovering what can be done with them, what they will fit into, what noise they make, and so on. *Play is sensory and manipulative.* For instance, sand is ladled from one cup to another and run through the hands, water is splashed about, not only to see what happens to it, but also for its feel. Primitive tools are used to prod things, draw them closer and, of course, to make noises. He will be feeding himself with a spoon, and incidentally using this to ladle food into other places as well as his mouth partly through clumsiness but also, it seems, to discover the relation of food to other things as well as to himself. The first primitive scribbles will be attempted, not to represent things, but for the pleasure of movement and to see that marks are made on the paper (and floor and walls if he is not stopped). Although he cannot draw representational pictures, he will recognize photos or pictures of familiar objects. Probably by the end of his second year he will attempt to be clean and dry, at least during the day (for milestones see Sheridan, 1968. Griffiths, 1954. Gesell, 1940. See also Millar, 1968).

The child will be understanding more and more words and increasing his spoken vocabulary almost daily. At the beginning of the year he may be using a few approximations. By the end of it he will probably have refined a vocabulary of many words, all clearly

[1] For more detailed discussion see Fraiberg, 1959.

recognizable. What is more, these will not just be isolated words, but articulated into simple sentences. This is an immense achievement and most important to his life as a sociable human.

2. Trust in self

As a child explores and goes through ecstasies of pleasure at his new-found powers of progression, investigation and manipulation, he is very much concerned with growing a *trust in himself* and his ego-functioning (Erikson, 1950). This is never entirely smooth. He may try too much for instance, and fall over and burst into tears, not only because he has hurt himself but because confidence in himself is dashed. Tears of frustration and anger at his own inability are very common at this age.

Consider this trust from the point of view of the child's inner or representational world for a moment. By his explorations he must be developing a representation of his self as someone who can do some things and not others in relation to reality. We are drawn to make such inferences when we observe his anticipatory activities. He may for instance become quite happy about clambering upstairs but, with trepidation on his face, will refuse to go down after having come a tumble on one or two occasions.

Let us consider the possible link between the trust in the environment, mentioned in chapter 3, and trust in self. Where a child feels at ease trusting his environment, he is free to explore spontaneously and develop his own skills, hence trust himself. He will also find it easy to learn from such an environment, to imitate his parents for instance, and hence again develop the skills that lie behind trust in himself.

If his parents tend to ignore him or are hostile, he may be able to discover a lot about his environment for himself, but he will not be encouraged to imitate and then *identify* with other people with ease. With the possibility of easy identification denied him, many short cuts to learning still tend to be lost (for discussion of imitation see Millar, 1968. Sluckin, 1970).

If on the other hand his parents provide a *confusing* environment for him, he may imitate his parents readily but not be able to trust what his parents do or say. For instance, a mother says, 'Get out from under my feet. Go and play in the garden where there's lots to do.' The child then goes out into the mud and gets dirty, at which mother says, 'Look at you, those nice clean clothes all ruined. Come out of that filthy garden.' More will be said about the confusing effect of parents later. We shall simply note here that most parents will tell you, if they are honest, how difficult it is, especially when tired and over-worked, to maintain consistency with their children.

3. Parent–child communication and language

We have already stressed the importance of non-verbal communication. In the first year of life, communication by gesture alone is paramount. After this, words come into play, but even later in life the meanings of words to an individual person must have a web of non-verbal memories and experiences attached to them.

Let us consider communication in general to begin with (for detail see Lewis, 1963. Sluckin, 1970. McCarthy, 1954). For communication to take place, there must be a *transmitter* and *receiver* of messages. A transmitter can send out messages for ever but, if there is no receiver, there will be no communication. Thus a baby crying unheard cannot be said to be communicating until his mother responds.

Communication messages consist of *signs* used to represent a state of affairs. The state of affairs itself is never directly communicated. Thus the baby's crying is a sign of his internal state of affairs, his distress. When heard by his mother the crying becomes a message. Communication like this can easily become garbled. It can particularly happen in the earliest months, when the mother has very little to go on to decide what the baby's messages are about. For instance, he may be crying, so that she is at her wit's end to recognize the state of affairs behind the noise. She will wonder, 'Has he got colic?' 'Is he wet?' 'Is he hungry or thirsty?' 'Is he just tired?' On the other hand a baby's message may be clear to others, but his mother may twist the meaning for reasons of her own. Thus she may interpret his crying as, 'He's not wanting to be alone in the pram,' when in fact the sun is glaring in his eyes. The stage is set for all sorts of failures and misunderstanding in the vital area of communication. We have suggested that perhaps the baby's first communications come through the medium of his crying, to express distress. On the other hand bodily movements give messages of satisfaction to his mother (Spitz, 1965). A mother will usually respond to crying by a certain sense of anxiety which alerts her to discovering its cause. By a slow process of learning she will probably begin to interpret what lies behind the infant's crying, and meaningful communications about distress will then have been established. Such learning to interpret involves a deal of common-sense intelligence on the mother's part. She must recognize when he is likely to be hungry or tired and so on, as well as to discriminate between his various cries.

With regard to communication from mother to infant, we have mentioned that her body movements are probably the first messages to the child about her inner state. Of course in the early months he is not likely to recognize these as messages coming from some other person 'out there' in reality. Her movements simply either distress him or relax him. But slowly he will begin to get some vague sense of her existence as separate from him, so that her movements, smiles, facial expressions and vocalization will begin to take on 'real' meaning (Spitz, 1965).

Proceeding now to *verbal* communication, the growth of language is fascinating and mysterious. We can here only highlight a few aspects. *Understanding the meaning* of words spoken by others clearly comes from repetition for the child of a conjunction between the sound of the word and the object or act to which the word refers. The child's first understanding of words usually refers to some easily discriminated external object which is spoken about frequently like milk, bed, daddy, car, bus, pram, dolly, etc.

The child's own *speaking* of words is refined from a welter of babbling. He proceeds by a series of approximations, using *imitation*, until he gets it right. It can be said that learning to speak is a genuinely *creative* process. One gets the sense of this when listening to a child's first approximations in speech. They have a freshness and inventiveness that is a delight to hear. For instance, 'bissica' for biscuit, 'blabbi' for blanket, 'wowies' for trousers, 'toon' for spoon, 'coddispeeper' for compost-heap! These are just a few. They tend to be individual creations of the child, determined no doubt by his difficulty in forming some consonants, but are very individual none the less.

Perhaps adults delight in these approximations largely because they reflect a searching, discovery and creativeness that is very much alive in a child and which the adult feels he has lost.

Each new word used is a triumph of *abstraction* of various elements from the whole sensory field. The result of this is the formation of simple verbal concepts. To begin with, these concepts will be approximations until the child has actively sorted out the generally accepted meanings of a word. For instance 'Dada' may first be applied by a child to every grown-up male before he refines his understanding down to the fact that he has only one Dada. Only later still will he generalize this verbal concept and apply the term 'daddy' to other children's fathers. To begin with, the child learns about immediate *sensory* data. His abstraction is only partial in that he uses concepts only in the immediate proximity of the actual objects or events. It is only much later that he will be able to think and speak coherently (use truly abstract concepts) about things that neither are present nor apply directly to the child himself (Boyle, 1969. Piaget, 1932).

The process of verbal concept formation is a slow discovery, enthralling and baffling to the child. By using words he begins to be able to communicate precisely what his inner wishes and feelings are. To say 'drink' when he is thirsty is much more economical and peaceful than the crying and shouting he had to resort to before speech. With development, he will be able to communicate much more than simple wishes; he will be able to speak about his inner state. For instance, 'I feel unhappy because Jenny wouldn't play with me,' or, 'We had a super picnic in the park.' Also, with language the child is brought into a clearer apprehension of other people's wishes and feelings. He will recognize his parents' wishes – 'Don't do that, it is very annoying,' or, 'Mum feels tired now,' or, 'Well done, that is a lovely sand-pie.' Later still, the vastly moving and intricate web of other people's inner feelings will be opened to him through everyday speech, novels, biographies, poetry and drama.

It is not only in the communication of feelings and wishes that language has such value. The realm of physical facts is widened immeasurably. By attaching known words to a new object, that object immediately gains meaning. For instance, walking down a strange road, mother points to one building and says, 'That is where they bake bread,' and points to another, 'That is where the milk van has its garage.' With this, unknown buildings are brought into contact with familiar things and, in a flash, gain meaning for the child.

Language can, of course, in certain circumstances, be condensed into signs and symbols to such a degree that they seem to be unrelated to ordinary words. This occurs in mathematics, where symbols condense what may take pages to write in ordinary language. It is perhaps a good exercise to imagine what the world would seem like before we learnt the meaning of words. Deaf people can perhaps tell us something of what it is like. A little imagination can give us the impression of an inner and outer world where sound is only noise, where there are no sure signs to indicate hidden connections, and which is thus full of mysteries and terrors.

Returning to the meanings of words themselves: there is of course a common agreement about the meaning of words among members of any one linguistic culture. However, each word and sentence has grown its meaning slightly differently for each individual person. These meanings will have been derived from each person's idiosyncratic experience. For instance, the word 'mother' has commonly the meaning of warmth, protectiveness, and sympathy. But for some people the word 'mother' evokes very little of this, but rather coldness, blame, and spite. The meaning of 'mother' will very largely depend on one's experience of one's own mother. So also for many words.

Commonly accepted language often gets detached from inner feelings. One often hears 'parroting' by some people who may speak fluently, but seem to have no emotion behind their words. Other people do not seem to be meaning what they are saying. Feelings may be attached to their words, but one gets the impression that these are 'acted' or put on either consciously or unconsciously so that there is a 'phoniness' about their speech.

Lastly, we may mention that a child usually learns his first words from his mother. His knowledge of the world is first given to him by her. He has no other way of knowing to begin with. Her view of the world is true as far as he is concerned. A mother with a warped view gives the child a representation of the outside world that is warped. Only later may he have a chance to learn otherwise.

4. Parents, toddler and socialization

Parents will often tell you that the times between one and three years old are the most exhausting years of childhood. On gaining confidence in his movements, a toddler is into and on to everything. And since his awareness of danger is as yet rudimentary, a mother has to keep an eye open continuously. Fires, electric plugs, cookers, open windows and gates on to the road all have to be watched. Modern machines may help with many domestic chores, but they have added greatly to the responsibilities of mothers of young children. The motor-car has for instance stunted the freedom of movement of young children and greatly increased the burden of worry that a mother bears. At the same time she needs to keep an eye open for the safety of her own precious things about the house, to save them from small, destructive hands.

Furthermore, the child himself usually demands his mother's presence continually. He wants to wander everywhere at will, but expects her to follow in case he gets too anxious. This demand to be independent and yet clinging is infuriating, and mothers often say how overwrought and exasperated they get. Toddlers probably have no wish to be naughty. On the contrary, they are usually innocently affectionate and want to be 'good' in that they are repeatedly copying and imitating their parents. However, self-determination must inevitably annoy parents who have their own set habits.

This is the time that 'Don't do that,' 'Come along now,' 'If you do that I shall be very cross,' and so on, echo around the house. The clash of wills and ill feeling between parent and child probably begins now if it has not done so before. The child tries to control his mother, while she for her part attempts to instil some controls into him. *Socialization* of the child has become explicit. Attempts at socialization come forcibly into play when the child can *turn away* from his mother. Here he is using his independence, but his turning away can be experienced by him and his mother as an aggressive act. The degree to which this is felt to be 'badly' aggressive will depend very much on the mother's ideas. Some mothers, for instance, tend to think that any show of independence is a hostile act.

At all events this 'no, no, no' from his mother certainly upsets the child. A 'no' or negation rather sharply given most often evokes a look of pain upon a child's face, which then dissolves into miserable tears. We have already discussed this in the previous chapter.

Unlike the infant, a toddler has now some explicit power to revenge himself. When still in his cradle he may have felt all sorts of hostile ideas about his mother, but he had few means of expressing his negativism except by grizzling. But now he has power, he can move and hence drive his mother to distraction. Previously he was forced to accept persecutory experiences from his parents. Now with greater intellectual awareness and muscular control he can turn the tables and become a provocative persecutor himself. With a conscious intention to annoy, the term 'naughty' is now meaningful.

Even though it involves conflict, a child needs to incorporate controls into himself for his own and others' safety and comfort. What is more, he will need many controls later in life in order to perceive the world and its people realistically. A child can hardly be expected to incorporate controls into himself if he is not presented with them by his parents in the first place. Parents who fail to make their own wishes clear seem to confuse a child. He never quite knows what is right or wrong, so that he becomes prone to a dim but very pervasive sense of anxiety and guilt. It is common to see such children far from feeling free, but rather slipping into a depressed listlessness.

As well as consciously thought-out controls, all parents seem to impose controls upon their children which are based upon their own unspoken phantasies. These can drive a child to distraction because they are often contradictory. A child usually wants to please and be at peace with his parents, but their contradictoriness may make this impossible. Here are a couple of examples.

(i) In a restaurant a mother says, 'Don't use a spoon for the peas, behave properly, sit up and use your fork.' The child sits up straight, picks up his fork, and with quivering hand lets the peas fall as he tries to get them up to his mouth. Mother then shouts, 'Oh you hopeless boy.' The child breaks into tears which evoke the words, 'Stop that immediately, you are disgracing me and ruining everyone's dinner.'

(ii) A father, very proud of his pretty little daughter, takes her around with him in his car when visiting for his work. He is delighted by the attention both of them receive, but becomes irritable and scornful when she herself shows signs of being a flirtatious show-off.

It will be noted that such paternal contradictions as these involve intellectual confusion for the child. The parent's communications first mean one thing, then another. They also involve confusion of feeling and mistrust. Such behaviour may sow some early seeds of the child's experience of *disillusionment* with his parents.

Other parents may not be contradictory in this fashion, but create mistrust in a different way. They systematically set out to socialize their children by intentionally inflicting pain to dissuade them from unsociable or dangerous acts. For instance, they may intentionally make a child burn his hand slightly on an electric iron to acquaint him with its heat. Such procedures may be well-intentioned, but a little child is unlikely to be able to understand this. Rather, he will only become aware that his parents are people who coolly intend to inflict pain upon him. They will then be profoundly mistrusted. Similar mistrust is likely to be engendered by other systematic 'conditioning' procedures such as graded or organized punishments.

Individual families seem to vary greatly in the patterns of unconscious and irrational controls used upon their children. Some parents break out in scorn when their children displease them. Others never explain why they are cross, but just belt their children when annoyed. Others never appear to get cross, but moralize to a child who is too young to grasp the intellectual complexities of such abstract ideas. An uncommitted observer is likely to be shocked by such absurd behaviour. Perhaps many years hence, when our descendants have learnt more about themselves than we know today, such absurdities will be rare. But as things are now, it seems that unspoken controls driven by unconscious forces are in the background of every child's family life.

On some issues the average parent is probably quite clear and consistent both in what is expected of his children and in how he communicates these wishes. If we picture ordinary parents as floundering over many things by trial and error, by entreaties, threats, bribes and smacks to get their children to do what they want, we shall not be far from the truth. Slowly the child *internalizes* these commands so that he conforms to ordinary standards without having to be told about them. Conformity has become automatic. (For social studies of socialization see Douglas and Blomfield, 1958. Goldberg, 1959. J. Klein, 1965. Newson, 1963.)

5. Bowel and bladder control

One instance of internalization of control is toilet training. It is of particular importance, because it concerns a vital part of every human being's physiological functioning and is central to social life. There is no need to say that this is a much-discussed subject both by parents and experts. Everyone has opinions about it, but there seems to have been very little systematic study and observation of the subject (see Newson, 1963. J. Klein, 1965).

We know that the nervous system is neither structurally developed nor functionally organized at birth to cope with the complex organization that has to come into play to achieve sphincter control. Let us look at the sequence of thought that must take place in the child for control to take place.

He must first be aware that he *has* wetted or soiled himself. He must then become aware of the sensations *just before* he wets or soils himself. He must then become aware that other people want him to *communicate* this inner state of affairs to them. He must also *inhibit* the relaxation of his sphincters long enough for him to be brought to a pot. Lastly he must learn to relax his sphincters when over the pot.

Clearly a child does not necessarily learn this sequence in the order presented here. Many children for instance quickly learn the last part, opening the sphincters over the pot, long before they master the first part of the sequence.

One suspects that there are as many methods of achieving the sequence as there are mothers in the world. And more: because there are children's experts too who are willing to pronounce upon the subject without ever having gone through the business. Perhaps we could distinguish two main schools of thought, first the 'start it early and repeat it often' school. They advocate potting from the earliest months to get the child used to the situation. Some mothers of this persuasion emphasize routine, and will have their children on the pot for half an hour or more after meals to establish a routine and a habit.

The other philosophy could be called the 'wait till he wants to' school of thought. These people emphasize that a child will learn quickly and easily when the situation of potting means something to him so that he himself wants, for his own as well as other people's sakes, to control his bladder and bowels. Those who wait for this usually have to put up with nappies for eighteen months at least. But they may find that learning to control himself has an element of fun and pleasure for the child as well as the parent.

It is an open question which school of thought is best. I know of no statistics on the subject. My recollections suggest that there is not much in it as far as the final age of being clean and dry is concerned. However, it is likely that children brought up by the two methods will have rather different underlying feelings about their bowels and bladders, but here again very little has been studied in real depth in this field.

Because bladder and bowel control is an important milestone, this stage of life is often referred to as the anal phase of development (Freud, 1905, 1916. Abraham, 1921. Erikson, 1950. Cameron, 1963). We have already noted that controls in many other spheres are coming into play at this time, so to consider that excretion is the only important mode of control is too narrow a view. However, it seems that when faced with problems of control in almost any area, stronger

F

phantasies arise in the individual which involve sensations from the penis, vagina, bladder, anus or rectum and intestines. The young toddler is not old enough to verbalize these phantasies, but they sometimes appear in behaviour. For instance, a boy of two, who had already achieved sphincter control with ease, became chronically constipated soon after a baby sister was born, and his mother doted on her rather than on him, while insisting that he keep quiet and not disturb her.

The later pervasiveness of anal phantasy is evident to anyone overhearing children talking in unguarded ways. Children usually have dirty minds. For instance:

(i) A five-year-old girl sings, 'God made little children on this earth to dwell' – three-year-old brother, 'Pah, God made little poo-poos.'

(ii) Two five-year-old girls talking. 'She was of course a very great duchess, a queen, so great a queen that when she went to the lavatory her sausages went right round the whole world.'

The infusion of anal impulses into adult phantasy life is seen in swearing and dirty jokes. The reader can exercise himself in recalling other instances. In the neuroses, obsessional ideas are often closely linked to anal phantasy (Cameron, 1963).

6. Shame and guilt

Earlier in this chapter we stressed the toddler's eagerness to excel and achieve mastery of new skills. When he succeeds and is recognized for his success, he often struts about with glowing face exhibiting what must be rudimentary feelings of *pride*. We have already described a child's experience of helplessness. Observation of toddlers' drives to achieve draws us to the inference that they must experience a pervasive sense of smallness and incapacity.

When a child achieves a new mastery, his underlying trepidation is assuaged with welling pride. When he thinks he can do something but fails, he is overcome by misery and often breaks into sobs, not of fear but *shame*.

The toddler is extremely sensitive to shame. When he is a little older and can talk, a child can often be heard to shout, 'Don't laugh at me, don't laugh at me,' as he dashes away in rage and tears. A toddler cannot be so vocal, but there is little doubt that his crumpled face and bitter tears reflect shame when he has made a mess of something. Bladder and bowel mistakes are very sensitive subjects for such shame. Some parents are very prone to shame their children actively. For instance, a mother spoke to a neighbour in front of her two-year-old daughter, 'I hear Jenny is dry every night now, not like this filthy brat of mine. I go into her in the morning and the stink is fit to make you sick.' Shaming such as this is often never forgotten or forgiven.

In shaming, an invidious comparison is made so that the child feels himself to be useless or uncontrolled compared with some better or *idealized* person. With such an experience of uselessness his persecutory anxiety is raised and he usually has few means of soothing himself, except to deny his shame or vow revenge. Some cultures seem to use shame as a systematic mode of social control. With us it is perhaps not systematically used, but it is pervasively present both in children and in discourse between adults.

More explicit in our culture is the evocation of guilt. In the early months, the child's response to negative reactions by his parents is likely to be a diffuse distress. But as he gets older and begins to differentiate a sense of himself from the outside world, he develops something of the idea, 'I have done something which has made mummy angry.' This primitive sense of guilt is usually quite clear in the one to two-year-old. It can be seen in the crumpled-up, rather startled expression on the face and the hiding of the head away from the mother. We can also see it in the way children test out and provoke their parents.

At this stage there seems to be little sign of an internally organized or systematic sense of guilt, let alone of conscience. These require a highly articulated sense of self, the world, and people. Rather, at this young age, guilt is tied to specific concrete personal situations for the child and his parents. However, quite young children do often seem to be overwhelmed by phantasies of guilt, so that their general behaviour becomes stilted. Here the sense of guilt, of the child himself as 'bad', seems to have become entrenched and can spread to many and various situations.

At this point it is important to distinguish two different forms of guilt that are experienced throughout life. We have described how the young child seems to feel great distress when his parents are angry. It seems that in some ways he feels 'attacked' by his mother's anger. It comes at him from 'outside' as it were, invades him so that he feels pain and anxiety. This is a form of persecutory anxiety. With this the child's experience of guilt seems to take something of the following nature: 'I had better not do this because mother will be angry and that is unpleasant for me.'

Closely linked to persecutory anxieties is the formation of *paranoid* attitudes. When an individual slips into a paranoid position with regard to a situation, he denies any sense of blame or badness in himself and feels that outside forces are malignantly persecuting. The phrase 'It is not me, it's his fault' epitomizes the paranoid attitude. The most obvious examples of relapsing into this position come from individuals suffering from paranoid psychoses. But the stance is very frequently adopted in the normal course of events by children and adults (Klein, 1953, 1960. Segal, 1964).

As a child grows older and begins to see his mother and others as real people with feelings of their own, he begins to get the sense that he can hurt them, or cause distress. When this occurs he seems to begin to have ideas such as 'Oh dear, what I have done has hurt my dear mother.' We can see that this has a subtle but very important difference of tone from the guilt mentioned above. The first glimmerings of a child's *concern* for his mother can be seen when he goes and kisses or hugs her better when she is distressed. This can be seen in quite young children, often by the end of the second year.

When a child feels that it is he who has caused mother's distress and wants to make amends, we refer to *depressive* guilt (M. Klein, 1947, 1953. Segal, 1964. Winnicott, 1958, 1965 *b*). For a young child this sense of guilt can be very painful indeed and, since he is still small and weak, there is often little he can do to make things better. Depressive guilt is often very strong in children whose mothers are chronically miserable or ill. In a dim way children often seem to feel that it is their fault and yet that they can do nothing about it. Close understanding of such children often shows how very pervasive are their imaginative phantasies of guilt.

The discrimination between persecutory and depressive guilt is important. It has wide implications for the understanding of the disturbed phantasy life of both individual children and adults. Reflection will also suggest that the discrimination is valuable in understanding social processes as well. We have already mentioned how persecutory and paranoid feelings come to the fore when class, national or racial prejudices are holding sway. It may also be noted that social control by the threat of force evokes predominantly paranoid anxiety and guilt. If this is so, then it would seem that those seeking to understand these social processes should also acquaint themselves with the individual's paranoid processes.

On the other hand our living together peacefully with mutual recognition relies upon our capacity to feel concern for others. Such functioning is dependent upon the development, in each individual, of depressive guilt. For instance, historically, the development of Christian ethics seems to have been concerned with forming a social way of life based upon depressive concern and guilt rather than paranoid dread and retaliatory revenge. The chequered history of Christianity suggests how complex and tortuous is the resolution of these sets of feelings, both for individuals and for mankind in general.

7. Theoretical summary[1]

We have seen in this chapter how with locomotion and growth of speech the child's ego-functioning has become greatly broadened and enhanced. This articulation of function is reflected in his representational world by a growing sense of trust in self.

At the same time his maturing ego-functioning, as for instance in locomotion, brings more frequent verbal admonitions or negations from his parents. This must have its effect in his representational world, so that his internal parental objects begin to take on more definite qualities of reproof than previously. The child then forms internal representations of reproof and accusation. This is experienced as guilt.

The term used for these aspects of internal parental objects which scrutinize the self and accuse if the child transgresses their criteria, is *super-ego* functioning (Freud, 1923. Cameron, 1963). This is a conception coined by Freud to refer to the individual's self-critical faculties which evoke the experience of guilt. At the young age we are discussing, these self-critical functions do not yet seem to be organized into any integrated or consistent whole. This does not mean, however, that the child's guilt is painless, or that self-criticisms are less severe than later. Rather the reverse occurs if anything. At any moment he may be overwhelmed with guilt. However, by using such mechanisms as splitting he can often quickly deny and forget his bad feeling, so that a few minutes after feeling remorse he is smiling as if nothing had happened. We shall have more to say in later chapters about modes of warding off painful feelings.

[1] For detailed definitions see Rycroft, 1968 *a*.

Finally, we may briefly recapitulate how, in the first two years of life, the little child has enhanced the complexity of his feelings. At the start we recognized simply gross distress and satisfaction. Now his inner world has become sufficiently articulated to evoke such feelings as ecstasy, love, pride, self-esteem, persecutory anxiety, revenge, hatred, anger, shame, depressive guilt and concern. These are just a few emotions which have been mentioned, but they suffice to show how complex the inner life of a child is becoming.

6

CHILDHOOD – TWO TO THREE YEARS OLD

The period of toddlerhood is epitomized by the discovery of a rudimentary sense of self-trust in physical movement. With this fundamentally established, our child moves into the pre-school years. Vitality, full-blooded feeling and phantasy are the hallmarks of this period. In discussing this time of life we would be wrong to separate out each year and discuss it apart from the others. Many things that apply to a two-year-old can equally be said of a four-year-old, and vice versa. Developments are taking place at a rapid speed, but one child will develop in one direction but not in another till later, whereas with another child it will be the other way round (for a discussion of developmental lines see A. Freud, 1965). However, we shall stick to our age differentiation and highlight some functions which are particularly important at each phase, while remembering that they apply to the whole pre-school period and have consequences in later life.

This chapter will be particularly concerned with make-believe or symbolic play. The next will focus upon the group play of children and also upon feelings about adults. The chapter on the four-year-old will draw our considerations together.

1. Motor and intellectual development of the two-year-old
With the firm knowledge that automatic movement is possible, the two-year-old will delightedly be seeking out new and more refined movements to achieve. From toddling the child goes on to walking steadily but, not content to rest at that, will want to run everywhere, practise climbing, jumping and skipping. Perhaps the most immediate impression one gets of pre-school children together is one of continuous flowing movement, eager excited running, bouncing up and down from dawn till dusk.

This sense of physical autonomy is perhaps reflected in the child's conception of himself. As a toddler he will have referred to himself by his first name, which has been given to him by others. Now, less passively, he uses the word 'I'.

The young child's vitality is seen not only in gross bodily movement but also in his flow of talk, play and ideas. With the two-year-old his chatter is predominantly a stream of observations, 'There's a bus', 'Ooh, a train', 'Look, a pram', 'I saw a cow today'. Later, at three and four, these simple observations give way to complex stories of events, and to questions, 'Why?', 'How?' and 'What?'

In both movement and ideas, the young child throws himself into one activity and then switches, often without warning, to something quite different. This free flow of imagination and shifting from one activity to another is exhausting to an adult as well as a delight (Fraiberg, 1959. Isaacs, 1930, 1933). It is tiring not only because of the physical movement involved, but also because the adult, to keep up with the child, must allow his own imagination to range freely at the same speed as that of the child. He must give up his well-tried modes of thought and action and allow free play to his own 'childish' phantasies. To do this, and at the same time remain a realistic responsible adult, is no mean task. Many people are clearly frightened of letting themselves go in this childlike way, and remain stiffly adult. However, to many parents the pre-school years of their children are unforgettable. There is enough drama of joy, pain, anguish and violence from one family to fill a hundred theatres.

The two-year-old's capacity to speak gives us the opportunity to understand his point of view with a precision that was not possible in the earlier years. We see that while most two-year-olds are zestfully interested in the world, it is a puzzling place which often frightens him. He still rushes back to his mother when it gets too much for him.

As he goes about the place he often seems to be talking all the time. His speech may be about what he feels – 'I want a biscuit.' 'Don't want to go to bed.' 'You are horrid,' – but most often it communicates an observation. 'We did go to the swings today.' 'We did see an elephant.' 'There's the moon,' and so on. Although stated as observations, these require an answer and a child will become very angry if there is no reply. He is not only making an observation, but he is also asking for confirmation that his conceptualization is correct.

If we listen to a child, it becomes plain why confirmation of his observations is required. He is trying, as we have mentioned before, to build up coherent and meaningful representations of the host of impressions that impinge upon him (Piaget, 1955. Werner, 1957). A lot of his observations sound silly but are perfectly sensible from his rudimentary point of view. For instance, many children search behind a television set or look under a telephone to 'find the people'. Or when told, 'We are going to post a letter to Granny,' he may burst into tears at the pillar-box because 'Granny locked in box'. Again, on seeing a chimney smoking, he puzzles and says, 'Bonfire on the roof.' Such observations indicate the feats of learning which every child must accomplish.

2. The child learning from others

The child is usually quite content to have his observation simply confirmed by his adult companion. But he also relies on the adult to explain and fill out his direct perceptions. Obviously it would be a very careless person who just said 'yes' to the observation about bonfires on the roof. A child's parents and siblings are asked continuously to correct, fill in and expand the child's knowledge of the world. It seems that his intellectual grasp is very dependent upon these parental explanations (and lack of them). Thus a child when drinking says 'milk', and his mother may reply 'yes' and no more – in which case his concept of milk is confirmed but not expanded. On the other hand she may say, 'Yes – do you remember the cows we saw yesterday? Well, milk comes from cows.' The child usually readily picks this up, and may speculate with quite vivid approximations or phantasies as to how milk comes from a cow. He says, 'Cut cow open and milk comes out.' 'Milk in cow's tummy.' This would be refined perhaps when mother and child again see a cow, and she points to the udder and say that is where the cow makes the milk, and that it is sucked out through the teats by a machine and then put in bottles.

A child brought up in a family where complex ideas are conveyed by words will have plenty of opportunity to exercise himself in this form of functioning. It has been suggested that there are marked social class differences in this. Middle-class families tend to use highly articulated verbal ideas, whereas manual workers' families on the whole do not. Conversely, it is likely that manual workers stimulate their children in other non-verbal ways which the middle-class parent may not (Bernstein, 1970).

The young child is continuously trying to make sense of the things around him in the world, to make connections and hence give his percepts meaning. On the positive side parents explain and hence give added meanings for the child to assimilate. On the negative side they most commonly ignore the child's puzzlement. All parents have to do this to a greater or lesser degree. They cannot cope with everything. More than this, parents can actively confuse a child and this will make him frantic. Here is one example:

(i) A father given to enjoying his own phantasies told dramatic stories of how the woods were filled with wild wolves around the house. He refused to tell the children that this was 'just pretend'. Later, when his children discovered that his stories were untrue, they clubbed together in loathing him.

(ii) Another father loved to pretend, and insisted that Father Christmas and fairies were real. His son said in later years, 'I still have a lurking feeling that I can't ever quite believe what he says.'

These are just two simple instances of how parental phantasy-systems affect the next generation. Many other more gross and vivid examples of confusion abound in modern psychiatric literature (see Lidz, 1963, 1968. Laing, 1964).

3. Concept formation

We are reiterating in this chapter what we have described earlier, that is, that the child has to make sense of his world, his body functions, himself, and the external world. Fundamentally he must feel baffled and helpless, and he is *continuously building up representations out of his spontaneous phantasy*, and then testing them to give ordered meaning to what he feels, sees and hears. The very development of language is a sign of forming *concepts*. In the formation of concepts the child's mind seems to range widely over a host of perceptions and memories and then *abstracts* certain common features which seem significant to him. Lastly a distillate of these features is formed and a word is attached to the common characteristic. He then uses his mental representations of the abstracted characteristic to understand new perceptions as they arise. For instance, he may begin by thinking that all four-legged animals are dogs. But soon he will notice that some heavy four-legged creatures eating grass are called cows. After this he may see a similar creature in a yard and know it also as a cow. Thus he has begun to recognize an actual cow as belonging to the class 'cows'. The beginning of abstraction has taken place. But it will be several years before he can think consistently in the abstract without the concrete objects being present (Piaget, 1935. Werner, 1957). For instance, he will not be able to answer, 'What makes a cow different from a dog?' probably until he is six or so. This requires a comparison of the two classes of animal in thought without the animal's being present, and is more than a two-year-old can manage.

4. Symbolic or make-believe play

Towards the end of the second year the toddler will begin to state explicitly that such-and-such is something else, and then play with it *as if* it were the real thing. For instance, he will pick up a stick and gleefully say 'saw', and start a sawing movement with it. Then in the third year (when he is two, that is), he will probably multiply his instances of make-believe. Here are just a few instances. A stick can be a saw, a screwdriver, fishing-rod, sword, gun, crane, hose-pipe, wireless aerial, telescope, kerb to a road, aeroplane wing, or knife. (You can think of other uses, no doubt.) A grocer's box can be a cot, a bath, a seat, car, train, aeroplane, boat, pig-sty, oven, table, cage, or house.

Make-believe takes place in two directions as it were. First, the stick or box is made to stand for something imagined. The visually recognizable similarity between a toy and the thing for which it stands makes this possible. It is here that the child is using his capacity for abstraction. But also the child pretends that *he* is somebody other than himself. Thus when he uses a stick to saw he is perhaps 'being Dad', or at least himself as a person who can use a saw. Again, in using the box as an oven he is being 'Mum cooking'.

In make-believe there is thus an 'as if' activity or suspension of reality (Fraiberg, 1959. Millar, 1968. Erikson, 1950). This is naturally only partial. Children usually know very well that they are playing. We have already mentioned how both children and adults may on occasions doubt whether their phantasy is real or not. When this occurs, anxiety is experienced and play usually ceases.

There is little doubt that make-believe has origins much earlier than two-years-old. We discussed this in chapter 4 when considering hallucinatory wish-fulfilment. A similar process is again being described now, but this time it is plain that hallucination is not involved. The child is quite clear that he is pretending.

Primitive make-believe is probably taking place when the child

sucks his thumb instead of his mother's breast, or chews and sucks
an old blanket, sheet, or teddy bear, when he is going off to sleep,
instead of clinging to the body of his mother (Winnicott, 1945).
Imaginative play is more flexible and less compulsive than this.

It would be a mistake to think that all a young child's activity is
make-believe. Much play is manipulative – sorting out and getting
to know the world as it really is. This is play in so far as the child is
going at his own pace. He is not essentially obeying any rules except
those that immediate reality presents. His spontaneous activity and
interest has freedom. We call this play, just as an adult inventor
'plays' with an idea before it is crystallized. With make-believe play
there is the added element of pretending or 'as if'. Naturally these
two forms of play are interwoven, so that the child is also getting to
know the world when he is pretending (Millar, 1968).

A child's activity is also at times definitely not play. He is not
playing, for instance, when he is doing what he has been told to do,
or when he gets down to a clear-cut task. For example, when eating
he is not usually playing, and if make-believe begins to intrude, he
gets into a thorough mess, wasting food, and angering his mother.

5. Motives for make-believe play

In discussing the manipulative play of the baby and toddler we
recognized his spontaneous activity as a means of making sense of
the world. We saw the baby as having few structured representations
of the world, and as being rather mystified by it. It seems likely that
as a response to this helplessness he begins to play, and through it
develops understanding and mental organization. We could call the
child's underlying sense of bafflement *normal anxiety* or trepidation.
If this is so, then a child is motivated to play (in its widest meaning)
by an experience of normal anxiety. However, in order for play to be
free and enjoyable such anxiety must be minimal. If bafflement and
helplessness become too great, the child is flooded with fear and is
unable to do anything constructive. He has been traumatized.

Turning now to the specific case of make-believe play, what states
of normal anxiety lie behind the child's choice of a particular game?
Naturally it is pointless to try and specify one overriding condition.
The forms of play that a child chooses are very many and various,
so we would conclude that the states of normal anxiety that motivate
his play must also be very various. What is more, a child's choice is
restricted to the materials and ideas for games that are available to
him.

We can usefully consider a few instances to acquaint ourselves better with the complex motivation or psychodynamics of a child's play (Fraiberg, 1959. Isaacs, 1933). Here are some where the connection between underlying normal anxiety and the form of overt play is quite clear.

(i) A family car, in which two young children were travelling, was involved in a slight collision. Even several weeks later the children's favourite game was still playing at crashing cars. The same happened with my own family after we narrowly avoided a crash. All the way home, and later, the children gaily played at crashes. We parents on the other hand wanted to forget the appalling possibilities of what could have happened. It might be added that if the crashes had been severe the children would perhaps have been terrified — or traumatized — and been unable to play over the experience.

(ii) A child was given a severe smacking by his mother — for the rest of the morning he viciously scolded and punished his teddy bear, cars, and a host of imaginary and real children around him.

Another very common example is the way a child will play vigorously at doting upon, feeding, nursing and scolding dolls when a baby brother or sister is born. Here is such an incident.

A three-year-old girl copied her father very frequently in her games. He was a carpenter, and the girl was most often away from her mother in the garden or another room playing at carpentry. However, her mother gave birth to a son, and when he was three weeks old the little girl saw her mother and the health visitor changing his nappy. On seeing his penis she was amazed and asked, 'What's that, why haven't I got one like that?' Her mother was dumbfounded. But the health visitor and mother together there and then gave her a lesson in sexual anatomy, explaining that her brother would grow up like Daddy and she would grow up like Mummy. The day after that, she began to play with her dolls which had been untouched till then, feeding, cuddling and changing them like babies. In the following weeks she spent her time switching, rather anxiously, between playing dolls and doing carpentry.

Another game where we see young children enjoying anxious ideas is nursery rhymes. Consider the themes of Little Bo-Peep, Rock-a-bye Baby, Jack and Jill, Tom Tom the Piper's Son, Ding Dong Bell, Sing a Song of Sixpence, Three Little Pigs, Georgie Porgie, Oranges and Lemons. Nursery rhymes are often the first playful verbal communications between adult and child around themes that have an element of anxiety in them, and are meaningful to old and young alike. In them the adult communicates with the child on the simple level that a child can understand. The same applies to the classic stories by Beatrix Potter. These are very simple, yet the themes evoke anxiety, and are just frightening enough to fascinate a child. Later of course, fairy stories are often full of terror. They are more articulated, but seem to hold a child's attention for just the same reason.

Returning to make-believe play, what do children pretend to be? They usually become adults such as mothers, fathers, car drivers, doctors, nurses, cowboys, soldiers, tractor drivers, engine drivers, sailors, policemen, queens, kings, princesses. All these are adults. If we ask what sort of anxiety in general lies behind these games, we would naturally come back to our earlier suggestion that the sense of *not* being an adult is a somewhat anxious one. The child, seeing around him people doing things which he cannot yet do, has a dim feeling of childhood helplessness. So in play he says to himself, 'I cannot do that yet, but at least I can pretend.'

In play, we see again the function of wish-fulfilment in phantasy where frustration in reality occurs. There must be many other functions involved in a child's choice of games but, incomplete as this discussion is, we must let it rest here.

6. Boys and girls – gender differentiation

No mention has been made so far of differences between the sexes. Let us consider the child's awareness of his or her own masculinity or femininity. The term 'gender' is used to apply to this aspect of self-recognition.

In the course of a young child's explorations he almost inevitably becomes aware, however dimly, of differences between the sexes and that he belongs to one gender or the other. To begin with this differentiation will be vague, but probably by two he will be saying 'boy' and 'girl', 'man' and 'lady' and usually getting it right. He will also be making it plain that he knows which gender he is. To the two-year-old this is often a matter of very great importance. He will

assert that he is a boy or girl in no uncertain terms and, if expected
to do something which seems improper to his gender, he will get
very touchy. At two and three, boys and girls usually display a great
deal of curiosity about their differences in a matter-of-fact way (if
allowed to). They will examine each other's genitals, and discuss
the differences between sitting on a potty to 'do a wee' rather than
standing. In families where there are children of both sexes, differentiation will usually be clearly understood anatomically in relation
to the genitals. Boys and girls see each other naked. But in families
with children of only one sex, this difference is not necessarily so
apparent. Whether children are aware of anatomical differences or
not, they usually begin to act and feel according to their gender at
quite an early age. Boys and girls do seem to have a different 'shape'.
Apart from the genitals this shape is not very obvious from super-
ficial anatomy until puberty. However, observation of young children usually brings one to the conclusion that boys and girls tend to
use their muscles and bodies generally in rather different ways from
quite early on. One has only to be involved in a birthday party for
children over the age of, say, three to notice this. One or two adults
can quite easily cope with an indoor party of twenty or more little
girls. With boys, five or six is the limit inside an ordinary house.

Gross bodily activity is also matched by differences in the natural
'shape' of boys' and girls' modes of phantasy. Boys tend to turn their
phantasy games towards external spaces, girls towards internal or
enclosed spaces. For instance, given the same set of toys, boys will
tend to play with objects outside and between toy houses; girls will
make up games and stories for activities inside the houses (Erikson,
1968).

It has been suggested that these differences are determined primarily by a child's culture. Thus a boy is encouraged to *imitate*, then
incorporate into the image of himself the actions of men like his
father, and hence *identify* himself with his gender. Likewise a girl is
encouraged to identify herself with members of her sex. An extreme
position in this point of view would be that all differences in gender
preferences are the result of social encouragement. It is difficult to
decide upon this question, because it is not possible to rear a human
being in controlled conditions as an experimentalist might do with
laboratory animals. But several lines of evidence make such an
extreme social view implausible.

As we have mentioned, it is evident quite early that boys and girls
tend to use their muscles differently. It is also noticeable that boys

and girls actively seize upon different games as if differing inner impulses are being met. Just as Erikson (1968) has suggested, boys tend to throw themselves into games which have a similar form or shape to their genital awareness. Thus they are concerned with the *outside of things* and with thrust, push and collision of objects. Girls on the other hand are interested in *inner spaces*, just like the form of their genitals. This is seen particularly in their domestic house play. We cannot pretend that the shape of genitals is socially conditioned.

There are also instances where humans have been brought up to be of the opposite gender to what they are biologically, and these people invariably turn out to be very confused and disturbed people. None of these lines of evidence can be absolutely convincing when considered on its own. But the extreme social conditioning viewpoint ignores the importance of biological determinants.

On the other hand, parents' underlying attitudes must play a large part in children's differing activities. They do this partly by giving 'boys' toys' to boys and 'girls' toys' to girls. Also they encourage their children to differentiate. For instance, a parent is usually delighted for his son to play with a ball, but often gets worried if he plays with dolls. The child must notice such reactions. A similar pattern applies also to the girl.

7. Feelings about body functions as motives for play

Young children are unsure of control over their body functions. This gives rise to normal anxiety which acts as a spur to play with representatives of such functioning. For instance, one favourite form of game, particularly with boys, is playing with cars. A boy running round the lawn will buzz to himself and comment as he passes, 'I am a very fast racing car,' or 'I am a diesel engine.' The very physical power of these machines seems to impress children. Perhaps this is because boys particularly seem to attach importance to their own physical musculature and strength. As little children they realize their own smallness, and wish to emulate the machines which have so much more power and speed even than adult men. This was clearly in the mind of a two-year-old boy playing in the bath. He looked down at his feet rather sadly and said, 'I wish I had wheels,' and then a little later, 'When I grow up I'm not going to be a man I'm going to be a car, a Rolls-Royce.'

Normal anxiety about other body functions, particularly visceral ones, can be seen in play as well. Games about being wild animals are very popular; for instance, 'I am a very fierce wolf (tiger, lion) and going to eat you up,' or, 'Be a terrible tiger, Daddy, and I'll shoot you.' Pleasure in such games as these points to concern with phantasy about *eating* (Klein, 1960. Segal, 1964) and being eaten. This is echoed in favourite stories which abound the world over about tigers, wolves, lions, foxes and ogres. The Three Little Pigs, Red Riding Hood, Jack and the Beanstalk and Puss in Boots are just a few.

Turning now to anxiety about anality and bladder control (Abraham, 1921), it is often observed that at about two, when toilet training is in full swing, a child goes through a phase of playing at being tidy. This usually involves things being 'put away' in all sorts of odd places – so it cannot be said that the child is really being tidy. But he is playing at hoarding, hiding and neatness. Later in the third year a child usually makes his first dirty jokes. They are very simple, nearly always about urine or faeces, but they have all the effect and naughty laughter of the more sophisticated dirty joke. A child looking at chocolate pudding will chortle, 'I've a poo-poo in my plate, ugh.' He will repeat it with glee and relish till all the other children at table are rocking with dirty laughter too.

In the first year of life, the third sensitive zone of the body, the genital, seems very often to be ignored by the child. But, usually the time of potty training, when his nappies are removed, he discovers its particularly sensitive and gratifying qualities. This is most obvious with little boys, who quickly discover the pleasures and excitation of playing with their penises. With girls it is sometimes less obvious, but they usually find out how to tickle themselves quite soon. Active stimulation of his body quickly becomes a 'fact of life' for a child. For all sorts of reasons, good and bad, this masturbation is met with by a taboo of more or less strictness from parents (Freud, 1905, 1913, 1917. Cameron, 1963).

We shall see later that this inhibition of sexuality is important to achieve. But to the two-year-old, it seems to present an unnecessary and incomprehensible prohibition. So the genitals become a particular source of anxiety. It is exciting, but the pleasure is to a greater or lesser degree disapproved of – and the child has no direct means of discharging his excitement without guilt or fear.

As we would expect with an anxious situation, representations of this part of the body enter into play. This seems to be evident in boys' love of sticks. A stick which in the space of an hour has been a sword, a hose-pipe, a fishing-rod, a gun, a spear – will finally be held sticking out from the boy's trousers as he says, 'I've got the biggest willy in the whole world, bigger than a king's, who's got one much bigger than any other daddy.'

Such stick play usually presents little interest to a girl – she will turn to dressing and undressing dolls, arranging flowers, making houses, moving doll's-house furniture, dressing up as a fairy or a princess. All of these more directly match the shape of female genital sensations.

Over and above this normal anxiety as a motive for play, it seems possible that the genitals may have an even more central part to play in the physiological functions that lie behind the very process of imagination itself, though our understanding of this is by no means clear yet. You will recall how important oral sensations seem to be in the process of thinking. Something similar seems likely to be true also about genital sensations and the process of imagination and phantasy. Recent experiments and observations on sleep and dreaming (see Luce and Segal, 1966) have shown fairly conclusively that dreaming occurs consistently for periods during the sleep of all mammals, including humans, from birth onwards. At the times of dreaming there are various consistent changes in physiological activity, changes in brain rhythm, rapid movements of the eyes, changes in breathing, mouth-sucking actions and also, in males, erection or partial erection of the penis. This occurs consistently from, a few days old onwards. Observation about excitation of the female genitals is of course not so easy. It is likely to be somewhat similar. It is clear then that excitation of the genitals takes place strongly in night dreaming. It is probable that some, more muted, excitation of the genitals may also play a part in daydreaming and all imaginative activity. This however remains speculative.

8. The function of make-believe play

What value has make-believe to the developing child? We have seen it so far as a response to anxiety; feeling helpless and small he pretends to be competent, and so on. This wish-fulfilment is certainly fundamental. It gives him a chance to have a 'rest' from the anxieties of reality. Life without this would probably be intolerable. However, many secondary values are achieved in development through the medium of play. Probably most activities could not be mastered until played at first. Thus in play one exercises many of the functions required for the real thing. For instance, a child wants to drive a car. He is too small, so he pretends with his tricycle. On his tricycle he learns to steer and stop, avoid obstacles and keep to the left. From the tricycle he graduates to a bicycle and ventures out on to the road. He learns to judge speed and distance, the rules of the road, movements of vehicles and so on. When he grows up and learns to drive a real car, half of the task has been accomplished already. The same applies to doll play and looking after children. With dolls or teddies the child learns how to dress, pin and tuck up, how to cuddle and be gentle. She also learns how to 'put her feelings' in the dolls, in ways which are very similar to those of nurses, teachers and mothers of young children. It is an interesting exercise to list the functions learnt in each sort of play activity of a child.

More than this, the very act of make-believe itself is of central importance in intelligent foresight for both children and adults. If one acts with intelligence one thinks something out in advance. This is planning. It is a pretence that it is happening. Thus architects make model houses, and imagine themselves or others in them. Traffic engineers play at traffic jams. Soldiers play war games. Students of all sorts anticipate the real things to come by various forms of make-believe. Proficiency in such make-believe does not mean that one can do the real thing, but it exercises various essential functions (Erikson, 1950, 1968).

9. Theoretical summary[1]

We need dwell upon theory only briefly in this chapter as no new concepts have been introduced. We have been stressing how the child's ego-functioning, using his body in relation to his environment, is enhanced by phantasy in play. We have also indicated how sensations from the most sensitive parts of the body, the oral, anal and genital zones, act as instigators of phantasy (id-functions). Then, through phantasy and play, the child is able, if all goes well, to integrate data or sensations from his sensitive zones, his musculature and from the external world (ego-functioning). With this growth of mental integration the child is able to experience himself more as a whole unique individual in the real world.

[1] See Cameron, 1963.

7

THE PRE-SCHOOL CHILD – THREE TO FOUR
YEARS OLD

In this chapter we shall again be discussing aspects of a child's life
which are common to the whole pre-school period, but which are
particularly noticeable in the three-year-old.

1. Observable behaviour of the three-year-old
As a toddler, even as a baby, a child will have been interested in other
children but without knowing what to do with them. His play was
egocentric (Piaget, 1932. Boyle, 1969). Around two, he will begin to
seek out the company of other children but his games will still
essentially be private. This has been called 'parallel play' or 'collect-
ive monologue' (Piaget, 1932. Isaacs, 1930, 1933). At this stage
there is usually a lot of squabbling and fighting over toys, interspersed with quiet periods while children go separately about their
own business.

At about the age of three the first group games emerge. Here
children share ideas, and help each other. It is social in the real sense
with comradeship and friendliness. We shall see later in the chapter
that a child's social play depends upon his growing capacity to feel
himself as a coherent person in a world of other people, and that this
in turn is dependent upon his intellectual development.

In this intellectual sphere, bafflement about the world is still in
the forefront of his mind. But now, having organized mental structures which take in more and more experience, he is beginning to be
able to pinpoint puzzles in his mind and hence ask questions, which
often go on from morning till night.

His skills broaden and become articulated. He will be able to ride
a tricycle, probably actively keep a swing going. He begins to make
recognizable drawings, scrawl 'pretend' writing and even write some
recognizable letters. He will get absorbed in simple constructional
toys.

Play becomes less concerned with learning how to manipulate objects. A child now enjoys things more for their ideational content. Thus he enjoys drawing for the things he can reproduce rather than the pleasure of the feel of pencil on paper and the sense of control that he is achieving.

2. Conceptual development

We have already stressed the importance of recognizing the child's efforts to create coherent representations for himself of the world about him. Now, with his ability to talk, he can make plain to us the nature of his puzzlements. At the start of life the child has no coherent ideas about the nature of the physical and social world, and with great pains he slowly creates, tests and articulates his conceptions.

The questions asked by a three-year-old make it plain how far he has got, and yet how uncertain are his concepts. To quote a few examples of three-year-olds' questions – taking representations and concepts of *space* first of all (see also Boyle, 1969);

(i) How big is a ship? Is it as big as the moon?

(ii) Can you hold a star in your hand? It isn't as big as an electric light, is it?

(iii) Could I touch the sky if I stood on the roof?

(iv) Are clouds as big as a house?

He has a similar puzzlement over time (see Boyle, 1969). For instance, 'We did see Father Christmas yesterday' (said in late spring). It seems that 'yesterday' is often used for any time in the past, just as 'tomorrow' is used for the future in general. If you are a parent you have to be on guard not to promise a treat too long in advance. When you say 'next week' the child may expect it the next day and be bitterly disappointed.

Number is similarly undifferentiated to begin with. The three-year-old can usually count up to two or more correctly if the objects are placed in front of him. Later if he can, say, count up to ten in speech he may nevertheless be unable to count this number of objects placed in front of him. He will forget which ones have already been counted and end up with a wild guess. There are great variations in this ability. Some children can enumerate quite young, but many are unable to count up to more than three by the time they go to school at five.

The statistical norms or average ages at which these intellectual skills are developed have, of course, been studied by *intelligence testing*. (Those interested should consult Butcher, 1968 or Wiseman, 1967.)

The importance of representing the physical world for himself is seen in a child's delight in drawing. If encouraged he will draw with great vigour and liveliness. He undoubtedly gets great pleasure in 'expressing his imagination' in drawings. Much about a child's interests and preoccupations can often be learnt from these. Even so, a child wants to re-create actual visible things. He wants to represent people, animals, houses, aeroplanes, flowers, trees, hills and roads. Children are satisfied when someone recognizes what they have drawn and they are very disappointed when people fail to do this. 'Oh, what a lovely tree,' says mother. 'But it's not a tree, it's a flower,' sobs the young artist.

At some time in the fourth year a child usually gets the idea that written words stand for speech and hence for things, actions or ideas. A few children can read and write by this age, but most content themselves with scrawling 'pretend' writing. They usually recognize a few letters, and may be writing them in an unsteady way. This recognition of written signs is a great step forward. For a long time the child will have recognized pictures, but these are of the same visual form as the objects represented. Written words bear no resemblance to the sounds they represent; they are conventions.

At the same time as developing conceptions of the physical world he is also becoming more articulate in his representation of his own inner feelings and those of others. A few examples will show how intellectual and emotional developments are interwoven:

(i) I don't like you, Mummy, when you are angry.

(ii) This Little Pig, that is a sad rhyme.

(iii) David is cross because his Mum smacked him.

These are all about inner feelings, but it will be recognized that their conceptualization and communication involve highly articulated intellectual processes.

Here the child is becoming coherent in his *empathy*. This is dependent upon the child's ability to recognize, on the one hand, that he himself is a coherent individual who has a physical place in time and space and has inner feelings as well. On the other hand, he is recognizing that other people also have their places in time and space together with their feelings. Intellectual development has played its part in the articulation of feelings.

Optimally, intellectual and emotional development go hand in hand. However it is plain that the two can become separated. For instance, some clever adults and children are highly articulate in physical thinking, yet remain emotionally and empathetically stupid. This can be seen from the difficulties they have in getting on with other people. Likewise others can be very articulate and mature in their feelings, yet intellectually ignorant.

3. Children playing together[1]

Even quite young babies under a year show great interest in others of their age. They may even be carried away in imitation of them, for instance, when they burst into tears at another baby's distress. We have noted how little children are vulnerable to other people's moods, not only their parents' but also strangers' and particularly other children's.

Toddlers are more coherently interested in fellows of their own age. They often greet each other and want to be together. There seems to be a pleasure and relief in being with another person who is of the same size, whose face is on a level with theirs, whose hands are as small as theirs and who is puzzling about the same problems as themselves. But play is in parallel. When paths cross there is usually a fight – often because both children want the same toy. Towards the age of three, however, children begin to want to play at the same game together. 'Let's play at houses,' 'You be ill and I'll be the doctor,' 'I'll drive and you be the conductor' – begin to be heard.

Games still often end in tears. After a brief spell of peace, a battle breaks out for possession because one child will not do what the others want. Parents or elder children intervene to stop bloodshed, and then within a few minutes the two are playing together as if nothing had happened.

By four or five, children will disappear from the company of adults and may play for hours together in peaceful contentment. Deep bonds of comradeship and friendship grow. The importance for later life of a child's learning to play with others can hardly be overstressed. It seems to provide the foundation for social-mindedness and the ability to work and sympathize with others. The

[1] See Isaacs, 1933. Millar, 1968. Fraiberg, 1969.

steady functioning of these qualities is not only necessary for the individual but also for the very fabric of a society, wherever it may be in the world.

What mental functions are involved in this social play? The most obvious is language, and clearly a child cannot play with others until he has developed a conceptual framework that allows him to speak freely, to know the meanings of words used by other children and also to voice his own ideas. Incidentally, it is easy to recognize the disadvantages of a deaf or blind child here, though often they and other children are remarkably ingenious in finding ways to communicate.

As well as using language a child must empathize with other children. He must be aware of them as human beings like himself, whose needs are recognized and accommodated. He must inhibit his own wishes for the sake of other children and for the game. *Sacrifice of egocentricity* has to be achieved for a child to play easily with others. One can hear this taking place in children's conversations. 'Oh all right, you get the water this time and I'll get it next.' 'You can have the blonde dolly if you want it. I can have her later.' A child will usually console himself with a substitute gratification or postponement. If no such substitute is available he will often fight for what he wants and be unable to make any sacrifice.

It is now possible to summarize why true social play does not occur until about three. Until then the child has not developed intellectually or emotionally enough to conceive of delay or substitute satisfactions. Nor has he developed the capacity to be coherent about other children's needs and wishes. And without these, contented inhibition and sacrifice are impossible.

When social play has been achieved the child quickly sees its advantages, he learns a great deal from other children, he can use their toys as well as his own. He no longer has to rely on his mother for ideas. And greatest of all, he has friends – he belongs to the society of children.

Playing with other children is a discipline that has to be learnt, often painfully. Many mothers and fathers make the rules of play easier by seeing that they themselves have provided an environment where sympathy and empathy have marked their own relations with children. Many parents are also aware of the importance of children playing together, and will discipline their children to share toys and patiently explain other children's points of view. Such efforts usually pay dividends both for the children and their mothers' later peace of mind. In larger families and close-knit communities the mother herself is often spared this task. Elder children, particularly sisters, provide much of the tuition. Many parents on the other hand are unable or unwilling to tackle this important aspect of socialization and make little provision for their child's companionship.

It is evident that a child needs for his own sake to get on with others of his own age, quite apart from the value of socialization to others. For instance, it has been suggested to me that children who create their own imaginative 'little friends' are usually only children with few close playmates or ones whose siblings are much older or younger. They lack the day-to-day company of real friends of their own age. I know of no statistical survey on this question but informal investigation has so far revealed few exceptions to this rule. If this is so, then it seems likely that lonely children, feeling disturbed by the lack of company of their peers, create them in imagination instead. Other children deprived of human companionship often find it in communing with animals, plants, books or small machines like clocks or cars or, of course, dolls.

Such a lonely state of affairs is inevitable for some parents and children, if they live on isolated farms for instance. But many parents living close to other children keep their own isolated either through shyness or snobbery. When a child is young this often piles trouble upon the mother as well as the child. When the child is unused to sharing, an antipathy forms with other children when they do come into contact. This makes other families reluctant to have anything to do with them, so that the mother is left with the burden of a miserable child.

Later, when the child goes to school, he finds other children getting on easily together, he himself is left out and often turns to the teacher for protection. The others who may have only just learnt to stand on their own feet are then contemptuous of him, and a chain of unmerciful teasing and bullying may begin. Thus the lonely child thinks that the world of his contemporaries is cruel and hateful. This feeling of chronic shyness may carry on for many years and cloud the individual's sense of well-being even in his adult life. For instance:

One only child was pampered by his mother even during school playtime. She would come in the middle of the morning to hand biscuits to him through the school railings. The other children jeered and called him 'the chimpanzee'. Nearly twenty years later, when he was met in the street by one of these schoolfellows, an expression of discomfort immediately came over his face. He said only, 'I must collect my mother,' and swung round to open his car door when his mother appeared out of a shop.

More unpleasant perhaps than these solitary children are those who superficially learn to play with others, but use them simply as vehicles for their own phantasy. Other children are not treated with concern, but used like dolls to satisfy the whim of the child. Needless to say, all children are prone to do this to some extent. They may bully, steal, tease, torment and act despotically. Such egocentric despotism often continues into adulthood.

4. Siblings[1]

The preceding discussion will perhaps have helped to make it plain why children are usually glad to have siblings. They are people of more or less the same age who naturally share so many of a child's own anxieties. They also see things from a similar point of view. If there is not too great an age gap they usually become firm if quarrelsome playmates as they grow older. Probably troubles between siblings become chronic when parents do not recognize the particular personal feelings of one or more of their children. The child is then left alone and hurt, sulking at not being noticed and, as often as not, begins to take it out on a brother or sister. We cannot enumerate all the eventualities here, but let us just look at one or two salient problems.

The eldest child often has a problem that the younger ones hardly notice. This is that for the first year or so of life he has been the centre of his parent's attention. Then with the birth of the second child this is shattered. It is remarkable how often parents say nothing about a new baby coming, so that the experience comes as a shock to the child. Later the eldest child usually finds a solace by being the 'cleverest' one. He swanks about his knowledge which is inevitably greater than the baby's. Sometimes he remains solitary and bitter, tormenting his siblings in subtle ways. More often perhaps, a mother will encourage her eldest child to identify with her and use his knowledge to become a benign substitute mother and unofficial teacher. Whatever the particular outcome might be, one often finds that eldest children, particularly elder daughters, have a deep sense

[1] Fraiberg, 1959.

of slightly sad, even solemn responsibility which the other children lack.

Younger children probably suffer from feeling helpless and incompetent compared with the older ones. One often sees a younger child going into paroxysms of rage because his senior has sneered at his ineptitude. But the younger child has often the compensatory comfort of protection from his elder siblings.

It is frequently said that a middle child gets the worst of both worlds. Sometimes this may be true, but it is an over-simplification. The middle child is by no means always the maladjusted one. It would only be true where the middle child's anxieties and problems were neglected by his parents in comparison with the other children. Perhaps in general we could say that where recognition of one child is neglected in comparison with others, then we can expect trouble between siblings.

5. A child and his mother[1]

This relationship has been discussed at length in previous chapters and we need only summarize here. Mother is the child's first object. Through her feeding, care and enjoyment of him she becomes the centre of his world. She performs innumerable functions which are impossible for him to do himself, and is his first interpreter of the world about him. He is very dependent upon her, and his feelings of love and hate towards her have an all-consuming importance. In the second year the problem of discipline and social control is played out in the arena of his feelings about his mother. This articulates and complicates his ideas and feelings about her; it does not make her less important. However, as he grows older his father will usually become a more meaningful person in his own right. Let us look more closely at this relationship.

6. The child and his father

We have already discussed in chapters 2 and 3 how a father usually functions primarily as a support and background to a mother with her baby. This means that the child in a nuclear family has a second person to turn to if one fails. It also means that he has two objects for his hostility and not just one. This is a subtle but important point. If a child has only one parent, the main focus of both his love and hostility, his *ambivalence*, is directed at one person. We mentioned before that this mixing of contradictory feelings is

[1] Winnicott, 1964, 1965 a. Fraiberg, 1959.

very hard to bear. With two parents he can feel loving towards the one while he is hating the other, and vice versa. We see this when a child rushes instinctively to his mother when angry with father or, equally frequently, the other way about. Such splitting of feelings towards the two parents can become malignant and stultifying, but it is a transitional way of helping a child to tolerate the internal pain of mixtures of love and hate.

Being a different person from mother means that a father provides different experiences for the child. The child has a broader basis of activity to imitate and identify with, and he can also test himself out in a wider context. The games a child plays with father will often be different from those with mother, so he can find enjoyment and self-assurance in things he might miss with his mother. In particular a father, who goes out to work, often takes on the quality of being a representative of the more distant world outside the home, while at the same time being close and intimate. It is often he who leads the more distant expeditions with the children. Thus both boys and girls equally learn from and identify with their fathers.

There is also a more subtle and less understood way in which fathers make a unique contribution to their children. We have already mentioned how males and females have differing physical and hence underlying psychological shapes. A male's phantasy seems more directed outwards, whereas a female's is directed towards inner space. Hence mothers and fathers have underlying differences in orientation towards themselves and the world. This means that boys and girls, being also of differing genders, tend to have differently shaped relationships with their fathers and mothers. A little boy soon knows that he is of the same gender as his father, and becomes involved in trying to emulate him as well as feeling jealous. This occurs whenever two people are alike in a characteristic but one is in advance of the other. For a little girl such rivalry is usually most markedly reserved for her mother. For her father, on the other hand, she often nurtures a yearning for intimacy which manifests itself in flirtation. Family patterns however are never simple, and a parent's relationship with children is always many-sided and can become very complex indeed.

The actual patterning of feelings a child experiences will depend not only upon his father or his mother, but also upon how his parents get on with each other and how they together relate to him. Until now we have only considered the *dyadic* or two-person relationship between child and parent. We must now consider the triangular or *tryadic* relationship between a child and his two parents together.

7. The child and his two parents

Parents are *big* in the eyes of a child. Not only are they physically big but psychologically also, because of his helplessness. In comparison with his own incompetence they are idealized in his mind. Their bigness is matched only by the strength of the child's own feelings. These, as we have seen, can be overwhelming. If the reader recalls some of his earliest memories of his parents he will probably become aware of this childhood experience for himself.

Generally speaking, the child is faced with problems from two directions. On the one hand, he has to comprehend the world outside himself. Particularly he must bring coherence to what his big parents are doing. On the other hand, he has his own passionate feelings to control and bring into an acceptable relationship with the outside world. We have discussed how the child attempts to make sense of the physical world. He has to do this about his parents as well. This is often very difficult. The physical world is on the whole consistent but parents are not. Parents' moods change for no apparent reason, they say crazy things, and become violent or silent in the most inexplicable ways to a child. Yet his parents mean so much to him that these actions easily throw him into states of confusion, helplessness and anxiety. It is likely that confusion about a parent evokes as much long-lasting anxiety as, for instance, does a parent's severity, or discipline (Lidz, 1963, 1968). Here are a few examples of people's complaints about their parents. They illustrate this sense of helplessness when they did not understand what was happening 'inside' their parents.

(i) My mother used to say, 'Oh, you are a clever boy,' with a twist to the word clever which was a sort of admiration but also somehow hatred. It terrified me, and even now the word 'clever' makes me shiver.

(ii) My father was never angry with me openly. He used to storm at my mother and other people but never at me. He just got somehow listless and 'clicked' with his mouth – it terrified me.

(iii) My mother always spoke as if I agreed with her in everything. I could never argue with her in all the forty years she was alive. As I grew older I was sure she was wrong, but then I would feel she must be right, so I was never sure what I thought at all. I feel this still long after she has died.

These tales have probably been distorted by self-justification in the years since childhood, but they also have the ring of truth in them.

It is difficult enough for a child to cope with the incomprehensibility of each of his parents separately, but he also needs to integrate his ideas about the relationship of his two parents to each other. This can be impossible for a child, especially if they rarely show open affection or mutual recognition of each other in front of the child. For instance:

(i) A boy was quite strictly yet warmly brought up by his mother. His father also did a lot of things with him. But whenever his father and mother were together, mother would tend to lapse into passive subservience, forget things and be called a fool by her husband, so that all confidence went out of her. From this, the boy got little idea of how a man and woman could enhance each other.

(ii) A girl and boy were closely united to their mother; father was more distant yet interesting and admired. But with mother he seemed to give up all sense of responsibility, so that there were continuous quarrels. Eventually husband and wife would not share the same bed, but as there were only two beds, father and son slept together, and mother and daughter. As with the previous illustration, both children became very confused about the relationship between man and woman.

(iii) A girl's parents quarrelled violently, usually about money. After a hostile exchange of words they would both lapse into silence and not speak to each other often for months. However, every evening they still played cards together, silently passing the cards to each other. The confusing effect of this need not be elaborated.

Incidentally, none of these children had themselves married by their mid-thirties. We need not be concerned with later consequences here. These anecdotes serve only to illustrate the problem faced by a child attempting to integrate his feelings about his parents together.

Integration of ideas about parents is particularly important because they are of different gender, and sexual feelings become directly involved. As we have seen, sexuality inevitably comes under spoken or unspoken taboos. This means that the subject is not only very exciting, but also mysterious and evocative of vivid, often uncontrolled phantasy.

8. The child's sexuality and his parents[1]

The importance of sensuous body feelings to the little child has already been described. He loves and needs to be stroked, cuddled and kissed. When he is anxious or hurt he runs to his mother or father to be comforted with caresses. Thus his parents necessarily become the objects of sensuous love. This is obvious when we see the cuddliness of most pre-school children. By the second or third year the child has usually found his genitals, so that this becomes an area of sensuous gratification like the other surfaces of his body. And the child, not yet knowing the rules of politeness, usually seeks sensuous gratification from his parents in these parts as he does with the rest of his body. This wish, however, meets with a taboo or prohibition. His parents do not usually caress his genitals like the rest of his body.

Parents' attitudes about their own and their children's genitals naturally vary from outright shock, disgust or punitiveness to playful admiring comments. It has been suggested that, with modern liberal attitudes towards sex, difficulties about it are a thing of the past. This would seem to be unrealistically optimistic. The problem is a complex one for each individual child and parent. For instance, if on the one hand fondling is tabooed by parents, the child's unfulfilled urges give rise to very powerful phantasies. Sometimes we hear these being more or less openly expressed with a sadistic flavour to them. 'I'm going to spike you, I'm going to spike everything.' Or – 'I'll lay you on the floor and stamp and stamp till you are flat.' Where such violent impulses are directed at his all-important parents, a child's phantasies can become frightening (Klein, 1947, 1953. Freud, 1917. Cameron, 1963. Lidz, 1968). On the other hand, if no taboos are imposed the child can become over-excited by his impulses, and these in themselves can be felt as overwhelming and frightening. Simple permissiveness provides no more of a solution to a child's sexual anxieties than does simple suppression. It seems that every parent has to fumble an unsteady course between the two to the best of his ability without any simple rules of thumb.

[1] Freud, 1905, 1917. Cameron, 1963.

Because of the taboo involved, the genitals become a focus of frustrated impulses for the child towards his parents. Furthermore, it seems that a host of other ideas and feelings, particularly hostile ones about parents, get elaborated by genital phantasies. For instance:

(i) A boy used to get driven frantic by his mother's general teasing of him. Later in childhood, he indulged in torturing his penis, tying it up and pricking it with a knitting needle.

(ii) Another boy's father was a doctor, and operated to remove his son's adenoids and tonsils. The boy was terrified that his father would detect his sexual excitement and operate upon his penis too.

The reader will probably recognize similar wishes and fears in himself.

We have alluded to the sadism which frequently enters into sexual phantasies. Since the child is small and his genital excitation is strong, yet cannot be fulfilled until he is an adult, sexual phantasy is likely to take on *paranoid or persecutory* meaning just as his general anxiety did when he was much younger. This means that sexual ideas become dichotomized or split in the primitive ways which we described earlier in chapter 4. Ideas then take on an all-or-nothing quality where tenderness and concern have little place. Rivalry, envy, jealousy and cruelty tend to rule these sexual phantasies (Klein, 1947, 1953). Perhaps because of this emphasis upon rivalry, dominance and submission, these phantasies have been called *phallic* (Freud, 1917).

We have already said that the shape of sexual excitation and hence of phantasy, is different for a boy from a girl (chapter 6). A boy's concern is with external size, thrust and stab. Girls on the other hand tend to be preoccupied with internal *contents*. Hence a girl's sexual sadistic phantasies are often elaborations of destroying the insides of things, or biting off and then taking inside (Klein, 1947, 1953. Deutsch, 1944). However, both boys and girls undoubtably entertain ideas of many mixed varieties.

We are usually well acquainted with phantasies like this in us as adults, but often forget that children have them as well. Most parents, wisely, do not probe into the phantasy life and sexual ideas of a child. To do so only confuses, over-excites and frightens him.

They leave him to get on with the business of sorting things out himself.

The reader may complain that this is an exaggerated and horrific portrayal of children's sexuality. Here it is important to recognize not only that sexual phantasy exists, but also that it is only a part of a child's life, and little spoken about, so that other, happy and less sensitive activities take up his communications with adults. Furthermore, it must be remembered that sexual excitations, for all their troublesomeness, are not only the origins of later reproductivity but also the probable source of much creative imagination.

9. The oedipus complex[1]

The propensity of children to feel rivalry with parents of the same sex is of particular importance. Let us first consider the little boy. From about the second year of life he seems to recognize his physical similarity with his father, and often wants to emulate him in the things he does. Thus in the ordinary course of events he loves his father for loving and attending to him. He also admires him, feels small in comparison, idealizes and wants to copy him.

These positive feelings will, as we have seen, be juxtaposed with negative and painful emotions derived from frustrating and confusing experiences with his father. So a boy's impulses towards him are naturally ambivalent. Over and above this a third factor comes into play. The little boy loves his mother. This in itself does not worry the little boy. He can love both his parents at the same time. But where he experiences his genital excitement he is in trouble. First of all, it has the forbidden quality we have mentioned. Furthermore, it has no satisfactory direct outlet, so that as with any frustration, lurid and vivid phantasies are provoked. In particular he wants to overcome his father. One often hears this quite explicitly stated by a boy. 'When I am grown up I will have the biggest willy (penis) in the world, bigger than daddy or anyone.' Since he entertains such grandiose feelings towards his father, in his phantasy he expects revenge in return. This, needless to say, is often confirmed to some extent by his father, who may well feel really jealous of his son, especially if he is spoilt by his mother.

The *internal* (usually unspoken) sexual phantasy systems within a little boy are termed the *oedipus complex*. You will note that this refers to what is going on inside the child, not to the family situation. This is often referred to more loosely as the *oedipal situation*.

[1] Freud, 1913. Cameron, 1963. Lidz, 1968.

H

The oedipus complex of a girl naturally takes a different form. Her gender identity and hence her rivalry lies with her mother. Thus the girl's feelings tend to be the reverse of the boy's. There is an added complexity, however; for both boy and girl, the first and deepest attachment is usually to mother. Hence a girl's first love becomes her sexual rival. With a boy on the other hand his first love becomes his first sexual love.

We need not go into the complexities of this any further. The variations of emphasis seem to be as multitudinous as there are people on this earth. We shall say more about the ways in which children resolve the tensions involved in the oedipus complex in the next chapter.

10. *Theoretical summary*[1]

In this chapter we have described how a child begins to turn his interest from his parents to include other children of his own age. His social capacity to get on with other children must mean that he develops representations inside himself of these children as being like himself, and yet at the same time being different. This we have termed *empathy*. It is evident that such empathy is highly complex, but certainly involves concern for the other person, which in turn involves putting of oneself in the other's shoes while still recognizing one's separateness.

At the same time, we have noted how the child's development brings new problems. From an early age he has been forming representations of his parents within himself, his *parental objects*. When younger he had no great need to reconcile these two either outside or inside himself. He could deny one while relating to the other. Now his awareness is broadening, he *needs to integrate* his feelings about himself to have a self-coherence, particularly when with other children. This means he must reconcile ideas inside himself, particularly the representations of his two parents with whom he has identified and who have become internal objects.

This brings a child face to face with the triangular situation of himself and his external parents (the oedipal situation). His sexual feelings make an internal reconciliation of his two parents together a complex and anxious experience for him (the oedipus complex). The next chapter discusses the resolution of this.

[1] See also Lidz, 1968. Cameron, 1963.

8

FOUR TO FIVE YEARS OLD

This chapter will perhaps be one of the most difficult in the book. This is partly because the developments described are subtle and internal to the individual, so that they are not readily noticeable upon cursory acquaintance. It is necessary to know a child well before the changes become evident. We shall also be drawing a number of threads together in an attempt to form an integrated idea of underlying psychological happenings, and this means that we shall be abstract and theoretical in our formulations. Until now we have confined our theory to a summary at the end of each chapter. Here, however, we shall try to embed theory into the main body of our thinking. The reader may well find himself particularly puzzled and dissatisfied, in which case he may prefer to return to it later after a brief first reading. Even so he will probably still be doubtful. This is perhaps inevitable because some fundamental issues are raised and we cannot afford to present much evidence about them. If, however, the reader has been stimulated to further thought, the time will have been well spent.

1. Unintegration in the pre-school child

In the preceding chapters we have observed the pre-school child as fundamentally sensuous, eager and passionate. With fullhearted-ness he *invests* the attention of his whole body and mind in the experiences of the moment. This readiness for passionate involvement is perhaps one of the key factors in the child's enormous capacity to *learn* which has been stressed. From our adult experience we can recognize how much more quickly we learn things when we are deeply involved or 'lost' in an interest. The same seems to apply to a greater extent with the small child. The child's state of relative *unintegration* facilitates learning. This state of unintegration was observed in an earlier chapter when describing the child's quick changes of mood. One minute he will be immersed in one concern, the next he will be involved in something quite different. There is little integration from one experience to the next.

We have also noted, however, that he is also trying to make experiences meaningful. This is a process of *mental integration* which is intrinsic to the development of an intelligent human being. Integration of ideas about the outside world has already been noted. For instance, you will recall the boy who was puzzled by people having bonfires on the roof. When it was explained that it was smoke from their fires going up the chimneys and coming out of the chimney pots, he was delighted. He had made a new conceptual integration. The world was less puzzling as a consequence.

Such integration occurs also with *inner* experiences and impulses. We can hear this going on when children reflect about themselves in the following sort of way.

(i) I like you most of the time Mum, except when you get cross with me, then I want to bash you.

(ii) I don't like it at Granny's because there is no one to play with, it's boring, but I like it at Susan's because we play together there.

Such integration, both in understanding the outside world and in recognizing inner experiences in relation to them, allows the child to become more independent. Knowing his own likes, dislikes and propensities he can anticipate events, and control himself during them.

This mental integration is often referred to as *insight*. It will be noted that it is possible to have insight about either external or internal events. It is also possible to gain insight about the relation between the two, internal and external. Independence of thought and action goes hand in hand with insight.

2. Spurs to integration and inhibition

The natural urge to integrate various experiences and impulses is given added stimulus by two aspects of the child's social situation. First of all he is venturing more and more alone into the world outside his family. He is playing with other children in the street and other houses. He may be going to a nursery school. This means he is less able to run back to his mother to be cuddled and comforted. Other people act differently from his parents and also have their eyes attending to things other than him. In such circumstances a child is usually frightened, shy and lonely to begin with. It is yet another experience of separation anxiety. But unlike the younger child he has usually developed enough integrated sense of himself alone to cope at least for short periods. His memory for instance is organized sufficiently to know that his mother will return. His sense of space will also have become organized so that he knows roughly where home is.

Being separated from home makes the child feel anxious. But, since he is more integrated in his ideas, this anxiety can be minimal so that, instead of his feeling overwhelmed, it acts as a spur to further integration. He can now envisage the advantages of self-contained independence. It offers new experiences in the physical world and intimacy with other children. The discovery of this capacity to be separate from his family is usually felt as a triumph and a new-found freedom. Many children cannot wait to get out of the house to play with others. Mothers often then sigh with relief. The easy achievement of this freedom seems to depend very much upon parents' attitudes, as we discussed in the previous chapter.

A second stimulus to integration arises out of a child's sensuality and sexuality. We have already recognized how in the earliest years he needs a full and satisfying play of his sensuous impulses with his parents. But this cannot go on if he is to find a way of independent self-possession. For instance, he cannot be cuddled quite in the old way if he is distressed in somebody else's house. His yearnings for sensuous comfort become a nuisance to his independence. From being a pleasure, sensuousness begins to be also a source of shame and anxiety. He deals with this by various modes of *self-inhibition* which we shall discuss in a few moments.

Genital excitation has to be specifically contended with, as mentioned in the last chapter, so he needs to inhibit both his general sensuous wish to be cuddled and, more specifically, his genital excitement also. If he fails to inhibit either of these yearnings, he remains fixated upon the continuing presence of members of his own family. We can recognize that this task of inhibition is a fateful one for the child's future. His independence is at stake. We all partially succeed and fail, at least at this stage of childhood.

This is not a problem or task that the child is aware of in the focus of his consciousness. He will not explicitly talk about it as a whole problem. He may however mention aspects of it, such as when he expresses revulsion at being cuddled, or pride in enjoying himself away from home.

We can see the immediate results of this slow process of inhibition in the five-year-old child ready to go to school. He tends to be a different person from the cuddly, sexy, passionate three-year-old. He has a self-possession and *dignity* which is missing in the younger child. If all has gone well he is still enthusiastic and eager, but he does not usually want to be cuddled so much, he is not so sexy, flirtatious or passionate. He is reflective and, as we shall see, often very moral.

This new phase of life is often referred to as *latency* (Freud, 1916. Cameron, 1963). This literally means the period 'of lying hidden' and refers to the fact that the child's passion and sensuality now lies hidden (to emerge later in adolescence). This latency is of course only partial, but it is a characteristic which is none the less observable to those who know children well.

The child's inhibition evokes thought rather than action, and substitutes phantasy and imagination for impulsiveness. Imagination allows him to reflect and think independently if it is directed towards the world around him. He is becoming ready for school and later to go into the world by himself.

3. Mental processes involved in inhibition: formation of an organized super-ego

What processes go on in the child's mind to produce the inhibition we have spoken about? As with many aspects of the human mind we are largely ignorant. The individual's general underlying urge to integrate experiences has already been mentioned. This involves the formation of wider and wider representations of the world. A gain in breadth like this must require a partial inhibition of the passionate involvements in specific activities which are typical of the younger child. The very young child is, as it were, fascinated with each piece of a jigsaw puzzle. When he is older he wants to make up the picture as a whole. As he does this he becomes less interested in the parts.

This may give an idea of what happens, but it does not tell us how. We know little of the answer to this. But it seems that one fundamental function plays a large part. This is identification with adults.

Previous chapters have noted how the baby and then the toddler imitated other people's actions (Millar, 1968. Sluckin, 1970). Through this imitation and other processes as well, the child forms representations of the people in his world, particularly of his parents and siblings. These representations or internal objects become part of his inner world and hence part of his sense of himself. The process of imitation, and then internalization to form internal object representations is termed *identification* (Cameron, 1963).

One function of this copying of adults is that of providing a short cut in learning. A child does not have to go through the complex process of discovering how to do everything on his own. He can copy an action ready-made as it were.

A parental activity that is particularly noticeable to a child is their *scrutiny* and *criticism*. In chapter 4 on the second six months of life, we described the child's experience of his mother's positive and negative responses to him. We noted particularly how distressed he became at her negative or critical reactions. Later in chapter 5, it was noted how the child controlled or inhibited his behaviour, on his potty for instance, in response to his mother's positive and negative critical reactions. He internalized these critical functions of his parents, so that *self-critical* agencies began to be observable in the *guilt* of the young child. It was noted that these self-critical functions were not yet organized and were often contradictory. They were referred to as precursors of *super-ego functioning*.

It will be evident that self-critical scrutiny plays a part in mental integration and inhibition. Take for instance the potty-training situation. A child feels he wants to wet. His self-critical scrutiny comes into play and he thinks to himself something like this. 'If I wet my pants, Mummy will be irritated and I'll be miserable. I'll hold on and do it in the potty. Mummy will be pleased and I shall feel good.' So he holds on, does it in the potty and everyone is pleased. Here self-scrutiny has been instrumental in inhibition and the formation of newly-integrated activities. The reader will be able to think of many other instances of the value of self-scrutiny in the development of new activities.

When a child is young self-scrutiny is often largely dependent upon the actual presence of his parents. For instance, he will pick up a stone, then remembering what his parents said, look round to see if anyone is watching. Then, if he sees no adult, he may throw it.

Later, in his pre-school years, he will be feeling more competent and hence more able to imagine himself to be like his parents. His identification will become more solid as it were. As this happens he is more able to identify the image of *himself* with the scrutinizing aspects of his parents. An organized *voice* of conscience begins to be

apparent. For instance, our stone-throwing child will pick up the
stone, hesitate for a minute, then put it down, perhaps muttering,
'It's bad to throw stones, I don't throw stones.' This identification
of the self with his conscience can be heard in all sorts of conversations by the three and four-year-old. 'Don't do that, it's nasty.' 'I
didn't cry when I fell over, did I?' 'I didn't start fighting with
Johnny, did I?' 'I didn't do it, it wasn't my fault,' – and so on.

These examples show how the child's self-scrutiny is becoming
integrated into the whole conception of himself as a person. The
four and five-year-old, for instance, takes pleasure in moralizing,
even forming vague general rules of conduct so that he tends to
become meticulous, pernickety and conformist. At this age,
conscience is not very humanistic, it is on the whole rather smug.
The self-scrutinizing voice of conscience, derived in the first place
from parents and siblings, is now beginning to have a coherent
organization of its own within the child. It is termed the *super-ego*
(Freud, 1923).

4. Id-impulses, ego-functions and super-ego[1]

We can now draw the various aspects of our discussions together
and develop a rough theoretical framework. This may be useful to
have in the back of the mind when thinking generally about people
and not only about children.

We can see the child being faced by data from various directions
all at once at any moment in time. There are first of all the demands
of the *outside world*, the need to fit into it, make sense of it and gain
satisfaction from it. Secondly, the child experiences his own inner
impulses to do things, his *id*. Thirdly, there are the demands of his
inner scrutinizing conscience, his *super-ego*. At any moment in time
the child has to find a satisfactory compromise between the demands
and prohibitions of all three agencies. The functions he develops
in more or less satisfactory attempts to find enjoyable compromises
between these three have been referred to already as *ego activities*.

The demands from the three sources (the external world, impulse
life and conscience or *super-ego*) very often give rise to *internal
conflict*. Here are a few very simple examples.

A properly brought-up little girl of four is out alone with her
father. She needs to go to the lavatory. Her father begins to take
her to the gents. She sees that she is not going to the ladies where

[1] Freud, 1923. Cameron, 1963, Lidz, 1968.

she has been taught to go, and becomes frantic. She dare not go alone, she needs to go to the lavatory, but she ought not to go to the gents with her father.

We see here the conflict between:

(a) her impulse life – her need to go to the lavatory,

(b) her conscience or super-ego – her sense that it is right and proper for girls to go to the ladies,

(c) external reality – her father's taking her to the gents.

Faced by a conflict between these three, her ego is unable to find a compromise – so that she breaks down into a bout of anxiety. We might note that a few years ago this child would not have had the same problem. She would not have discriminated 'ladies' from 'gents' and would have gone happily with her father. Incidentally, this is an example of how new developments create new problems all the time for the growing individual. Another example:

A little boy of four, who has proudly learnt how to be brave, cuts his knee. He runs towards his mother, who is ready to comfort him. But he stops still in his tracks, his face crumples and he breaks into distraught tears and will not be comforted.

Here again we see a conflict between:

(a) his impulse life – running to be kissed better,

(b) his conscience – he hesitates, his voice inside him, 'be brave', has spoken,

(c) external reality – his mother is ready to comfort him.

He breaks into tears but refuses to be comforted. He tries to compromise between the dictates of his impulses and his conscience.

At any moment in time each individual, be he child or adult, finds his own compromise or adaptation between conflicting demands. Most often of course the conflict is not intolerable and life goes smoothly on, but at some time for all of us conflicts arise which engender anxiety until we have found a new mode of adaptation.

The nature of conflicts that may arise will be different for each individual child. Each will have his own particular pattern of impulses to satisfy. He will also have received his own particular quality of upbringing from his parents. Hence he will have his own idiosyncratic conscience with its own quality of approval and condemnation. He will also have developed his own particular capacities to cope with himself and the world (ego-functions). Hence an identical external situation is experienced in different ways by different individuals. For instance, the various readers of this book will be reacting differently to its contents even though the copies in front of them will be identical.

5. Defence mechanisms against anxiety

We have just investigated how an individual child or adult experiences internal mental conflicts and feels anxiety when they seem unresolvable. Fortunately perhaps for an individual's immediate peace of mind, the human being seems to have a capacity to divest attention from anxiety even though the conflict is still present and unresolved. The modes by which an individual automatically *turns away* from *conscious* awareness of internal conflict or anxiety are termed *defence mechanisms*.

The study of these mental mechanisms is of fundamental importance, particularly for those working with disturbed people. It is a subject which is not easy to grasp and the reader is certain to feel puzzled by reading this brief exposition given here. At the least he will need also to discuss and clarify his preconceptions with other people at some length.

We have already mentioned some defence mechanisms, although not given them that name before. For instance, we noted how a young child cannot tolerate both loving and hating his mother at the same time. He tends to *split* both his feelings and ideas of her so that he sees her as either all good or all bad. This prevents anxiety, which occurs when loving and hating become mixed in consciousness.

Another primitive mechanism has also been alluded to. This is *projection*. The reader will remember how the very young infant has not yet differentiated the sense of himself as distinct from the outside world. From such beginnings it can easily happen that feelings or ideas which really belong to the self are attributed to the outside world. Long after infancy and after the child has consciously discriminated self from others, he can continue *unconsciously* to attribute ideas to the outside world which really originate in himself. If consciously felt as about himself they would cause him to feel bad or anxious. This is projection.

A similar but opposite process is very common and probably also originates from early infancy when self and the outside world are still undifferentiated. This is termed *introjection* and occurs when attributes of the outside world are automatically ascribed to the self. Here are a couple of examples which illustrate these two processes. In an earlier chapter we mentioned a little boy who had been spanked by his mother. He spent the rest of the morning scolding his playmates, telling them how naughty they were. Here he projected his anxious sense of guilt and shame on to the other children. An example of introjection would be that of a child, say, who is deserted by his mother. His ideas that she is bad for doing this may be intolerable. So he feels instead that he himself must have been bad to provoke her desertion.

Projection of representations of unpleasant parts of the self is most common in everyday life, both in children and adults. It occurs markedly in paranoid illnesses. It functions also in everyday prejudiced thinking and behaviour. To scapegoat a minority group, for example, by feeling that they are dirty, evil or uncontrolled helps one to forget one's own failures. Likewise introjection plays a common part in everyday life. The person who blames himself for everything is very common. Acute self-blame – which uses intro-jection to a marked degree – is also very noticeable in *depressive* illnesses and their extreme form *melancholia*.

These are just two defensive processes which are of a primitive nature, yet profoundly affect us all. As a child gets older his internal life becomes more complex and rather different defences can be employed. We will not elaborate upon these. More detailed ex-positions are given for instance by A. Freud (1937) and Cameron (1963); Storr (1960) has a very lucid introduction for the general reader, so also has Rycroft (1968 *a* and *b*).

Our description of defences may have given the impression that, since they operate to alleviate the experience of anxiety, they must act under conscious wilful control. This may sometimes be the case but it must be stressed that usually defensive processes occur quite *automatically* and unconsciously. Being automatic, a person cannot justly be blamed for them. Much pain is caused by thoughtless busy-bodies who accuse others of avoiding anxiety defensively, as if they could have controlled things differently.

Another misconception may have arisen from our description, this is that defences are always bad or pathological. This is not so; they perform a necessary function in ordinary comfortable living. They can only rightly be considered as pathological if their operation debilitates the life of a person or disturbs other people.

Even though defences act automatically and unconsciously their function is to rid the self of awareness of anxious or unpleasant ideas. The term *repression* refers specifically to this mental act of obliterating anxious ideas from consciousness. It usually acts in conjunction with other defences. This implies that an individual may be experiencing many ideas of which he is *unconscious*. We have evidence from many quarters about unconscious processes continuing after repression. The reader should acquaint himself with some of this evidence. The most lucid discussion of this is still by Freud himself (1916), but see also Cameron (1963) and Storr (1960).

The reader may recall some instance of this repression in himself when he has felt tense and ill at ease about something but does not know what. Then, perhaps in a flash, he realizes what he has been worrying about. He may feel a flood of anxiety at the lifting of the repression, but is usually also relieved because the object of this worry is now known.

This is probably a rare occurrence for most of us and will be unconvincing to many readers who have not had such experiences. The idea of unconscious mental processes is always baffling because by their very nature we cannot be directly aware of them. At best we can know of their content by hindsight, as in our example, when we know we were unconscious of something in the past, but are now aware of it. In most circumstances we can only know that something is pressing from within us, but we know not what.

Recognition of the operation of defences is of the utmost importance to us all. It makes us realize that we have a propensity to make things mentally comfortable for ourselves even at the expense of recognizing the truth. For caseworkers it is especially important to recognize that both oneself and the client or patient are prone to distort or obliterate the truth if it is unpleasant.

A caseworker, doctor or nurse for instance will sometimes find themselves in a mess if they blindly accept that a client or patient is mentioning the whole undistorted truth about a matter. A doctor for instance may be very grateful for an honest report of symptoms by a patient. But if he does not use his own eyes, ears and knowledge as well, he will be failing the patient as well as himself in making a diagnosis. Evidence from his own knowledge may well contradict the patient's report and he has to be aware, at least intuitively, that the patient could be distorting the truth to assuage anxiety about the complaint.

The same situation arises with caseworkers, and here the problem is often even more difficult, for there may be no concrete definable symptoms displayed by a client for the caseworker to recognize. By slow trial and error, experience of people and self-criticism of his own perceptions he has to learn to trust his own judgement. This is the purpose of casework training and practice and is of course outside the scope of this book.

Professional practice is not the only place for the recognition of unconscious activities. It is often thought that this is the sole prerogative of specialists like psychoanalysts, therapists and caseworkers. This is not so. We have already mentioned doctors making physical diagnoses. The recognition of emotionally-toned experiences, which may or may not be recognized consciously is also used by every sensitive parent with his children and also by any responsible person living with other people. Here is an example:

A six-year-old boy in a country village was very fond of his grandmother, whom he visited every day down the road. After a brief illness his grandmother died. He was told about it and his only response was, 'Oh bother, everything is wrong today, I couldn't do my sums at school.' No more reference was made. He said nothing about his grandmother and neither did his parents. However, some weeks later he brought his newsbook home from school. In it was a drawing of a church, a gravestone and under the ground a coffin with a Union Jack on it. His parents got the message, and decided to be more open in talking about their feelings about the death.

Here you will see that they did not make any direct comments about their son's feelings but simply decided to be more open in general. They did not make interpretations about anxiety to their son (which is the particular skill of professionals), but they used recognition of unspoken, probably unconscious processes none the less.

6. The significance of childhood defences and adaptations for later life
By the time a child is ready to go to school, he will probably have

formed his own quite strongly entrenched modes of defence and adaptations with regard to anxiety. His style of inhibition and satisfaction will be organized more or less sufficiently for him to be of a piece to be at school all day alone. The way in which he has organized himself will have depended upon many influences. It will be an outcome of the interplay between his impulses, the ways of doing things which he has discovered for himself and those copied from others.

The child's immature mental organization has, perhaps, a fateful quality about it. It will probably mark him for many years to come, in some measure for the rest of his life. No cut and dried proof of this can be given here, but a few illustrations may make the contention clearer.

(i) I myself as a boy was rather overawed by the intellect of my father and older sister. I found great satisfaction in playing soldiers. This game satisfied my rivalry with my father, who unlike nearly every other man of his generation, had never fought in the war and was ashamed of it. Soldiers also satisfied my conscience, they were brave, and fought for the right, they were 'Christian soldiers'. From the age of five or six I determined to become a soldier when I was grown up. Schoolwork was of no great interest. It overawed me as my family had done earlier. So I became even more determined to be a soldier. Later I went into the Forces but, faced with the reality rather than phantasy, was appalled by its waste of life and uselessness.

(ii) The eldest of three brothers was the son of a kind but rigidly conforming mother and a father who was a footballer. The boy himself was rather sickly as an infant, and his inexperienced mother was prone to react with horror because of her ideals of good health. Later, when his brothers were born, their mother became more confident and easy-going than she had been with him. He felt he was the sickly horror in the family and was frantic about it. But he found his compromise. From the age of five or six he quite consistently chose the path of being the 'oddity' in the family. Everything that shocked his mother, and she was easily shocked, he found a pleasure in doing. Later, in his mid-school years he loved to investigate everything that was 'different'. By ten or twelve he was absorbing himself in Oriental mysticism. In his teens he naturally espoused any activity, philosophy or cause that was different from Western conforming standards. He was erudite upon Buddhism, Taoism, Zen, Shinto, acupuncture and macrobiotics. Athletically he could not be a beefy footballer like his father and brothers, but he found athleticism with a vengeance in ju-jitsu.

(iii) In her first years a little girl adored and was thrilled by her father. At work he was a carpenter, at home he was artistic and imaginative. However, he was irresponsible and tended to let the house go to ruin. The little girl's mother began to grumble about her husband and a chronic rift and bitterness grew up between them. By the age of six or so, the little girl had become convinced from her mother's arguments that men in general were no good and her father in particular was a useless mess. Later in adolescence she entrenched her sense of contempt for him. In the early years of her adulthood she consorted only with women who likewise held men in contempt. Later, when forced to work with men, she tried very hard to hold to these beliefs. It was only with great pain that she allowed her good feelings about them, which she had had as a very small girl, to find a place in her conception of them, herself and the world.

These illustrations suggest that the actual patterning of a person's character depends upon many influences. There is also much formal evidence that different cultures tend to enhance differing characteristics in individuals (Mead, 1928, 1963. Erikson, 1950). This chapter has noted the importance of the particular patterns of influence within the family. There is much evidence concerning this (Lidz, 1963, 1968. Laing, 1964. Goldberg, 1958). We have, however, also stressed the importance of the physical make-up and internal impulse life within the individual as being as crucial as social influences.

9

FIVE TO ELEVEN: EARLY SCHOOL DAYS

1. Family and the outside world[1]

The law in Britain requires that a child must go to school at the age of five. This means that for six hours a day someone outside the family, a teacher, takes responsibility for him. This is a fateful transition which impinges upon the skill and conscience of many people, not only parents and teachers, but also politicians and administrators. Policies and techniques of education are of vital importance to every individual child, as well as a community at large, but we cannot hope to do justice to such questions here. Rather we will focus upon events as they affect a child and also upon some of the emotional changes that take place within him.

Up until now much of a child's awareness of the outside world will have been filtered by his parents. Not only will they have informed him about the world according to their beliefs, but they will also have acted for him in most transactions with outsiders. This will probably have protected him from overmuch anxiety in dealing with strangers. The child will also have attuned himself to the habits and moralities of his family. He will have taken these into himself and, since he knows no other standards, they will seem the only ones possible to him.

On going to school the child finds himself alone with new people. He is placed in the charge of a strange teacher who will in many ways be different in her habits and morality from his parents. He also finds himself with unfamiliar children, who will have carried their own habits and beliefs from their families. They, like the child himself, will probably assume these habits to be absolute and common to everyone, but will soon discover that there are many divergences and contradictions. Lastly, the child finds himself in the classroom which is first and foremost a setting where he is expected to learn formal intellectual skills.

[1] See Winnicott, 1964, 1965 *a*.

Here are a few memories of early days at school which distil some of the worries of this new situation.

(i) We were Welsh-speaking, but had to sing hymns in English. I know what they mean now, but can still remember the incomprehensible jumble of words from those school assemblies.

(ii) I remember going to the medical room with a cut knee to have what I thought was 'flints' (lint) put on it.

(iii) I saw a teacher fall off her bike, hurt herself badly and cry. I remember being amazed that teachers could cry just like us children.

(iv) I got stuck on a page of reading and felt awful. The next day, the teacher made a mistake and thought I had mastered it. I didn't say anything, but felt very guilty, because it was really a lie.

(v) I jumped on a see-saw to show off to the Mother Superior, who was standing near. The other end shot up and knocked her over. I was frantic because I thought I had killed a saint.

(vi) I recall going to a strange school and standing petrified as the other children bullied a boy with no hair. I can still see his reddish wig being thrown around and the boy crying with his hands covering his face.

(vii) I was a tall girl and used to be laughed at for it with names like, 'lofty', 'skyscraper', or 'what's the weather like up there?'

(viii) I can remember my first day. I was all right but another child screamed when his mother left him. He must have been uncontrollable because he was put inside the wire guard around the fire, like a cage, and he screamed all the morning. I remember thinking, 'Is this what it is going to be like?'

These memories have no doubt been distorted by time, but they re-create the underlying trepidation in the midst of strangeness which will be remembered by most of us from our early school days. This anxiety is many-sided. There is shame at incompetence and fear of being scorned or bullied by the cruelty of other children. We also

I

see anxiety aroused by the child's own inner sense of guilt. Being assailed by fears, a child is often tempted to lie or cheat in defensive attempts to avoid awareness of them, but he may then be castigated by his own inner conscience, or by the teacher if she catches him out. This is illustrated in our list by the boy who pretended he had mastered a page of reading.

A child has not yet learnt to control his actions to conform to the requirements of the new situation. He is likely to act impulsively and then feel ashamed or thunderstruck with guilt at the consequences. This was epitomized by the girl who knocked over the Mother Superior with a see-saw. The reader himself will be able to remember other aspects of anxiety in the new situation of school.

Our sample of memories is culturally limited to the British Isles. The transition from home to school may be very different in other societies. Here is a memory from Nigeria which highlights this:

> There were few cars in our town and everyone wandered around and played in the streets. Most people knew each other. Yorubas are rather proud of being friendly, so you might spend the whole day out even if you were very tiny. Going to school was eagerly looked forward to because it was very important to be educated. There weren't any birth certificates so you had an entrance exam. All those wanting to go to school were lined up and told to put their right hand over the tops of their heads. If you could touch the lobe of your left ear you could go to school, and jumped up and down with joy.

(You will find that this method of selection works. Children can do it between the age of five and six.) In Britain where the gulf between home and school is wider, a child may be glad to go to school, but is usually also openly worried.

We have so far stressed the multiple demands, from himself, his family, the new teacher, and from other children, which play upon a child. Such a multiplicity of new experiences must occur for every child, whatever his home background and culture. They evoke anxiety until integrated within the ego. Most children have by the age of five developed sufficient inner self-control to make it a relatively easy business to assimilate the new demands. This readiness for school is usually detectable in a child's general demeanour when he relates to children and adults outside his family.

If he disposes himself with a certain self-contained dignity then one can feel fairly confident that things will go well.

Yet however well-prepared a child may be in his internal organization, he inevitably meets conflict when he gets to school. A child is often susceptible to being torn apart, as it were, in efforts to conform to and placate the multiplicity of people and their expectations. Let us examine the three main groups in this – the family, the teacher, and other children – in a little more detail.

2. Early home development and school[1]

The child carries the way of home with him to school. These may have been happy enough in themselves, but can nevertheless conflict with school. For example:

(i) An only child was much loved but most of his time was spent alone. He felt happy in this for, from a very early age, he populated his imagination with people and things that he loved dearly. He was reading at three and this increased the scope of his imaginative loves immeasurably. He normally never played with other children. By the time he went to school he was very well equipped to deal with his lessons, but the presence of other children was quite outside his experience. They shook him out of his rich solitary inner world of imagination. Because of his cleverness, he became a teacher's pet, and hated by his schoolfellows who unmercifully bullied him. He never made a friend all through his primary school years.

(ii) An Indian girl spent her early years in India. She naturally attuned herself to living in the open air and to an easy-going 'timelessness'. When she came to England, the way that school life ran seemed strange, cold and machine-like. Precision and timing seemed almost to attack her. She made many friends at school and was well liked. But her school days and class-work were strained and unhappy. She appeared a dull, slow learner.

Such examples could be multiplied many times over. Most parents try to ease these discrepancies by explaining the differences and by adapting family ways so that they do not clash with school. If they

[1] See Green, 1968.

do not, a child often becomes distressed and then resentful. Here are two examples:

(i) A family, happy enough in themselves, were extremely erratic timekeepers. The daughter was thus very often late for school. She was reprimanded at assembly and became terrified of being late. She began to refuse to go to school and became 'ill' with a multitude of minor complaints. Her mother let her stay at home, which only made matters worse. In time her mother, with the help of neighbours, got her off to school regularly on time and the tendency towards school refusal ceased.

(ii) A mother was very worried about her son's health, and insisted he wear long black stockings throughout the winter when the other boys all wore shorts. He was teased about this by the other boys, but dare not go against his mother. Later he found acceptance of a sort by becoming the clown of the class, but says he never forgave his mother.

Both these are examples of parental failure to recognize the importance of differences in habit between home and school. Such failures of recognition are often noticeable with parents who have been brought up in one culture and come to a new one. Never having been children in the new culture, they naturally find it difficult to make the imaginative leap towards what it is like for their own children, who are growing up in a setting different from their own.

The alien quality of school is also a problem for many other parents as well as immigrants. It has been suggested that schooling is essentially a middle-class institution with its emphasis on verbal and abstract thinking (Bernstein, 1970). Such abstract thought is only of peripheral use to many manual workers, and may play but little part in their family conversation, so that their children are not attuned to it. Teachers on the other hand must have valued abstract thought in order to become teachers. When they meet the children of manual workers at school they find them poorly exercised in such thought, and may grade them as of low intelligence. The children for their part then grow up feeling inferior, since teachers who are their first representatives of the world outside the family have made them appear so. Their parents, having suffered the same fate years before, are in no position to disabuse them.

It is of note that going to school, for most people, is the first transition from one situation to another. Similar experiences are usually felt later in life whenever the individual becomes vitally involved in a new and strange institution or environment.

3. Teachers and formal learning[1]

It is perhaps useful to discriminate two functions of a teacher. One is to introduce the ways of people outside the family to a baffled and anxious child, and the second is to preside over formal learning. The first task has been given much thought by infant school teachers in recent years, so that it is now often common for a child's introduction to formal learning to be slow and playful, with much intimate conversation between teacher and child. But just as we noted earlier that parents often fail to recognize the anxiety a child may feel about the difference between home and school, so often do teachers fail also. Children themselves are not sufficiently developed to resolve contradictions by themselves. Both parents and teachers are called upon to help them with the transition. Teachers and other professionals are often prone to attribute all blame for distress in a child to home circumstances, as it absolves them of feelings of shame and guilt. Our approach to the question will perhaps have made it plain that a child's anxiety is likely to be a product of what he brings from home meeting a new environment, which in its way may be just as inadequate for his needs as home. Such personal considerations can only be peripheral for many teachers. They are faced with a class of up to forty children, and their main responsibility is usually seen as fostering formal learning. Let us briefly turn to this.

In his early years at home a child will no doubt have been disciplined to conform to his parents in behaviour, but his imaginative mental processes will normally have been his alone. He will usually have been left to play with toys and ideas to suit himself and his phantasies. The situation of school learning is different from this. Whatever means are used to achieve it, the aim of school is for the child to become disciplined in thought, so that some of his ideas at least conform to rules. It is then expected that he will be able to manipulate these disciplined ideas in his imagination in abstract conceptual thought.

This being so, a teacher must inevitably be a disciplinarian of thought. She must expect to raise the antipathy of children that any

[1] Morrison and McIntyre, 1969.

disciplinarian or inhibitor of self-willed phantasy evokes. There have been many innovations in recent years concerning the methods of achieving this intellectual discipline (see, for instance, Isaacs, 1930). Old-fashioned teachers perhaps saw themselves as the enemies of self-willed imagination, and set out to destroy it early by the imposition of iron discipline and repetitive learning. More recently some teachers have come to see that self-willed imagination lies at the core of every person's being and, if recognized, can act as a spur for the child towards a wish to discipline his own thoughts. The teacher thus becomes an aid to the part of the child which wishes to master a subject rather than an enemy to the whole of himself. However, as we discussed in the earlier chapters on parental discipline, there is inevitably a part in all of us which loathes any form of constriction. To this part of a child the teacher, however kind, must be felt as harsh and antipathetic.

Old-fashioned discipline perhaps shattered a child's natural wish to learn and discover for himself at his own pace. Modern methods do not commit this crime, but when mental discipline is too slack and the teacher unwilling to face antipathy, then a child is left with inflated and unrealistic ideas unchecked. The new free methods of teaching are often very rewarding to teachers, because their children's spontaneous ideas are new and interesting. However, they also produce strains, for now a teacher must steer a difficult path between enjoying the pupils' ideas and at the same time checking wild phantasy.

4. The child's changing conception of himself

Through his activity in class and achievements in learning, a child now develops a quality of relationship with his teacher which has previously only been experienced within his family. As at home, he is watched over and protected. The teacher also introduces criteria both of general behaviour and of scholastic achievement towards which the child can strive. Previously a child's parents and siblings have been his primary regulators of self-esteem. Now the teacher joins them as a centrally important person. In so far as the child does things which the teacher enjoys, his self-esteem and sense of worth are enhanced, but if he falls away from her implicit criteria of valued behaviour or achievement, he feels unwanted and useless. Thus the child makes contributions to the teacher, and is now just as dependent upon her idiosyncrasies and values as he is upon his parents.

5. *The society of other children*

The wish to be enjoyed by his teacher means inevitably that a child *competes* with the others in class. Comparison with other children is likely to be continuous, and poor performance relative to others usually leads to silent despair and listlessness in a beginner, unless a teacher can spare time to give special attention. Doing better than others can be equally unpleasant, since he is in danger of being envied and ostracized by the less successful. 'Swot', 'bookworm', 'teacher's pet' are epithets designed to distress the clever child. Here are a couple of comments by clever children which make this plain:

(i) Nobody likes me much at school because I win all the time.
(aged seven)

(ii) I sit at the front because I am top and never dare look round, because I am sure they are hating me. (aged twelve)

Around these core experiences of competition in the classroom, however, a child has the opportunity to find himself in the special society of other children. This is often a crucial turning-point for his later enjoyment of other people. Previously his companionship with others will have been mainly under the eye of a mother, but in the school playground and afterwards in the street or fields, he will be alone with others of his age.

Other children can be frightening because they may be strange, hostile and are less controlled and responsible than adults. It has been stressed that children are fundamentally rather anxious and in fear of shame when they go to school. They will do all sorts of things to alleviate this sense of inferiority. On the positive side, they will be spurred to learn new skills, both in class and with other children. They will also bring less creative defensive manoeuvres into play in order to feel at ease.

Some of the most common are bullying, teasing and scorn. Here is a simple example of this mechanism. A child who is upset because he cannot read a passage in a book will feel better if he sees someone else in greater difficulty. His self-esteem is enhanced by the comparison. This itself does not amount to bullying. For example, the private inner thought or even public comment, 'I can read better than Ann,' might have scorn in it, but it is not teasing or bullying. But when a child actively repeats and repeats, 'Ann can't read, Ann can't read,' until the little girl is in a paroxysm of humiliation, this is teasing, which is a verbal form of bullying. This probably uses a projective form of defence. In emphasizing someone else's weakness or badness, an individual can avoid the painfulness of some similar feeling about himself.

Togetherness in groups lends itself to such projective modes of defence. Teasing and bullying is then transformed into scapegoating. In this children (or adults) gang up together and feel mutual enhancement while they obliterate their own anxieties in the discomfiture of another. Needless to say this can become institutionalized, teachers can subtly encourage it and young children can eagerly side with an adult leader against a scapegoat.

For all the dangers of being physically or mentally hurt, the company of other children usually enhances the reciprocity of feelings and ideas which is hardly possible with an adult. We have already mentioned the child's pleasure in being with another fellow-sufferer. He can identify himself with his companion, and feel him sympathizing back on equal terms. Such reciprocity also gives a unique opportunity to develop that aspect of conscience which is based upon sympathy for another human being, who is as precious as oneself.

It is useful to emphasize again here two aspects of conscience or super-ego functioning; they could be termed *sympathetic* and *punitive*. The sympathetic aspect of conscience is aware, however vaguely, of others as being like oneself. It scrutinizes the self with regard to the real or imagined pleasure or suffering given to others. The punitive aspect, on the other hand, is not directly concerned with the sense of another's well-being, but scrutinizes and measures the self against the strictures of real or phantasied rules. These rules may have been originally imposed upon the individual by threats of punishment or loss of love of various kinds, but now form an organization of internal strictures within the individual. Here sympathy for others plays little part, the voice of this aspect of conscience speaks only when rules are contravened and when the conduct is likely to evoke imagined or real punishment.

We noted earlier in chapter 5 that the voice of sympathetic conscience is likely to arouse depressive anxiety, whereas the punitive conscience arouses more primitive persecutory feelings. Both forms of conscience are interwoven and play their part in the child's becoming a social being. The company of other children is an exercising ground for both aspects of conscience, but particularly the sympathetic one.

6. The development of industriousness

Perhaps of even more importance than inter-personal developments, a child gains skill and knowledge in the company of other children. A moment's reflection upon the variety of boys' and girls' games, conversations and hobbies makes us realize this (see, for instance, Opie, 1969). It is hard to judge, but children probably glean as much information about the world from informal conversations with friends and family as they do in the classroom.

Through the classroom, games, hobbies and conversation a child slowly integrates his understanding and skill in dealing with real objects and situations about him. Our earlier chapters noted how the little child resorted to make-believe to alleviate his sense of trepidation, surrounded as he was by a big and incomprehensible world. Through the medium of such phantasies, he was enabled to develop knowledge and skill in dealing with things around him.

As he grows through the school years his skills develop, and with them his awareness of *self-efficacy*. As this becomes more solid, the need for make-believe gives way to sheer pleasure in *industry* (Erikson, 1950, 1968). Here is a memory which illustrates this transition; it recalls a boy in his early teens and represents a culmination of the activities of earlier school years.

> I used to do a lot of tinkering and carpentry. When I was young I can remember pretending to be a carpenter or engineer when I was mucking about. It was fun doing it, but of course nothing ever really worked after I had finished. One day the handle of my mother's iron broke and in examining it, I realized I could shape a new one if I selected the right wood from the pile in the garage. I did this, screwed it on, and my mother could use the iron again. I didn't have to pretend any more.

The reader will recall similar experiences.

The practice of explicit make-believe play perhaps falls away earlier in girls than with boys. It is common for boys in their early teens and later to be absorbed in make-believe games and hobbies, such as model aircraft, cars and so on. Girls of this age may have as many make-believe daydreams as boys, but on the whole their skills are limited to reality. This may in part be due to the fact that a girl is of the same sex as her mother and most of her teachers, whom she has seen at their tasks every day. It is thus easy for the girl to imitate and identify with them, and to develop her skill and sense of efficacy. A boy, on the other hand, is of a different sex from his mother and probably his early teachers also. He tends to become antipathetic to identifying with them at quite an early age, yet usually has only a transient acquaintance with the tasks of men like his father. With less opportunity to learn he may be less sure of himself and hence more prone to make-believe.

7. The school child and his parents

As a child gains more confidence to be alone he usually seeks out the company of like-minded children and turns away from his parents' conversation. It is often stressed that children no longer want their parents' company during adolescence, but this progress towards separation starts much earlier. Certainly by the age of nine or so most children quickly tire of being with their parents alone. They itch for the society of other children, which has a life of its own, with many secrets hidden from adults. Older children also like ganging up together to scorn and giggle at the real or imagined silliness of their parents or adults. This doubtless uses similar mechanisms to the scapegoating of other children mentioned earlier. During these years it is usually transient, so that a child can be laughing at his parents one minute and crying to them for help the next. It is probably not until adolescence that the perception of faults in adults plays a central part in development.

The child's tendency towards separateness is only partial. A general consideration of these years makes us realize that parents' behaviour is still of overwhelming importance to him. The conscious focus of a child's mind may be directed away from his family, but fundamental decisions are mediated through it: he lives where they live, is fed and clothed according to their notions, and goes where they go at week-ends and holidays. Both economically and psychologically he is incapable of independence. Children, by and large, are quite aware of this and accept the ways of their parents without open question or rebellion. This does not mean that the child acquiesces in all his thoughts and feelings. These will be kept in his inner world and may even be quite unconscious. At most, negative feelings will manifest themselves in nervousness or 'difficult behaviour'. His ego-functioning has not yet developed sufficiently for him to come out in open self-determined rebellion. This must wait until adolescence.

8. *Theoretical summary*

We will add no new theoretical concepts here to our list. This does not mean that the child remains static in his internal developments We have stressed how the child tends to turn his interest and emotional investment from his family towards friends and teachers in the outside world. With this comes an enhancement of his self-sufficiency, and hence a strengthening and articulation of his ego-functioning (Erikson, 1968).

A predominant process in this ego development is that of identification; contact with teachers and schoolfellows means that the child is sensitive to imitation of their behaviour. He then tends to take these patterns into himself and consolidate them so that they become part of his functioning personality; as we mentioned in chapter 5, the whole sequence is referred to as identification. The importance of these identifications with teachers and other children hardly needs stressing. They are evident in numerous habits which a child picks up at school. Through such identifications he becomes more like his school-friends and perhaps less like his parents.

Since an individual's identifications with those around him outside the family seem to be so important, we are drawn to ask what differences there are between these and those with his parents. Here the answer seems to be that the child's identifications with his parents, coming earlier, are more primitive. They involve stronger physiological reactions and hence have more violent feelings attached to them. The very young child also has no choice over the parents he finds himself with. This means that his parents become objects of ambivalence (as stressed in chapter 5). Hence his parental representations within himself, his identifications with them, also become the seat of internal conflict. Later identifications with people in the outside world may be strong and used a great deal by the child, but they are not likely to be the source of such primitive internal conflicts. As the child is now older and more developed, he has a greater freedom of choice to pick up or cast aside identifications with others to suit himself.

PUBERTY

1. Adolescence

The next four chapters, on puberty, mid-adolescence, going to work and being in love, are concerned with the gradual transition from child to adult. We have seen that by the age of ten or eleven a child may have considerable freedom in his choice of play, but major decisions of life are still vested in his parents and teachers. By the mid-twenties, at the latest, our social expectations are that the individual will be able to support himself and take responsibility for his own choices. The development of *self-responsibility* involves transformations within the individual which match these changes in social expectation. This is a process which goes on throughout adult life and is not exclusively tied to one period. We should perhaps speak of the process of 'adolescing' rather than adolescence. But the attainment of self-responsibility is paramount during the teens and we focus upon it now.

2. The social background of adolescence[1]

The law in our society reflects the transition of responsibility from parents to the individual himself. By the age of eighteen or so he has reached his majority. After this, parents have no legal hold over or responsibility towards a young person. This legal position is matched by our general expectation that a person is free to choose a spouse, rear children, and decide upon his own place of living and leisure. To do this he is expected to support himself.

Our society is epitomized by the ideal of independent responsibility in love, work and leisure. We must recognize, however, that this is not universal, nor has it always been the case in our own history. In many cultures it is common, for example, that the younger generation, however mature, obeys its elders, in all major

[1] Erikson, 1950, 1968. Fleming, 1967.

decisions. This obedience throughout life perhaps epitomizes static or traditional societies.

In many parts of the world techniques of production and social practice have remained virtually unchanged for centuries. Here practical knowledge and wisdom is vested in those who have lived longest, in other words the older generation. Their children reap the benefit of this knowledge, but may not assume power of direction until the death of their elders. They then take over the elders' image and expect obedience in turn from the next generation. Such societies often have great stability, but are not conducive to the development of new techniques of production or variety in personal relationships.

Western cultures, on the other hand, have a long history of turbulence and instability. Encroachment and conquest have never been far from any European. Quiet solidification into traditional societies has never been left in peace for long. These cultures have been noted for their technological innovations and also the variety of their social and family relationships.

The young person in a traditional society will usually be expected to assume the adult functions of full-time work and marriage soon after puberty. But he may remain obedient to his elders until old age or death. Thus the process of throwing off parental obedience, or adolescence as we know it, is either very prolonged or never completed. In our culture, on the other hand, the assumption of independent responsibility is expected to take place within a span of a few years.

Such considerations as these make it evident that the experience of adolescence must vary from culture to culture, family to family and between individuals. However, physical puberty remains more or less constant throughout the human race. This is the keystone of adolescence everywhere. Let us consider it within the limitations of our culture.

3. Bodily changes at puberty[1]
These are so well known that there is no need to detail them. The maturation of the genitals in both boys and girls makes reproduction possible. These, together with the development of the secondary sexual characteristics (hair and body growth), give the appearance and stature of an adult by the age of about sixteen.

[1] Stone and Church, 1957. Fleming, 1967.

4. The experience of puberty in boys[1]

The increased excitability of a boy's penis has notable consequences for his self-awareness and behaviour. He becomes physically fully sexual, but often does not know what to do with his urges. Even if he knows about sexual intercourse, such activity has no place in acceptable social behaviour. He tends to become fidgety and unsure.

Privately, most boys find themselves having waves of excitement about the idea of a girl they know or imagine. They may also find themselves disturbingly interested in their mother or sisters. But these passions usually remain secret and dreamy. Overtly, boys often retire to the company of their friends and display a loutish contempt for women. This is obviously not from lack of interest, it is probably largely defensive manoeuvring against unsureness about what to do with ideas and feelings.

In recent years pubescent romance and petting with girls have become more common, so that it is not unusual to see two twelve-year-olds kissing or holding hands (Blos, 1963. Schofield, 1968). This is usually a playful exploration, largely copying adults, to see what the bodily sensations are like. The two petters often care only about parts of each other's bodies and are indifferent to each other's characters as a whole. A boy will fluctuate between such transient affairs and the more secure company of his male friends. From these he usually learns most about sexual practices.

5. Masturbation[2]

The self-stimulating or *auto-erotic* behaviour of infants and young children has been mentioned in earlier chapters. By stimulating parts of his own body the child can obtain relief when distressed. This auto-eroticism has a wish-fulfilling function and acts as a flight from a painful reality. It is thus conducive to the creation of *illusions* or phantasies of satisfaction.

At the same time it seems that auto-erotic activity helps in discriminating the boundaries of the self. For instance, if we touch an external object which is not-self we receive sensations from only one organ – the one that is touching the object. But if we touch ourselves we receive a different signal, sensations from two organs, the toucher and touched. An infant probably learns about himself in this way, so that auto-eroticism plays a part in differentiating the sense of self. Yet it is also conducive to the denial of reality and to

[1] Blos, 1962. Fleming, 1967.
[2] Blos, 1963. Cameron, 1963.

illusion. This is a paradox with which each individual is faced, of whatever sex or age.

With puberty, a boy can give himself a full genital orgasm by masturbation. By creating attendant phantasies of love-making, he uses this as a substitute for the real thing. He usually feels both proud and guilty about this. Many boys wank and vie with each other about their masturbatory activities. But it has also been openly condemned by adults throughout history. The medieval Church, for instance, often considered it a greater sin than adultery. This condemnation is reflected in the tales of physical and mental damage resulting from 'self-abuse' that permeate the ideas of both adults and adolescents.

We need not debate this here but simply note that there is no physical evidence to suggest that damage is caused by masturbation. However, we have just noted that, psychologically, auto-eroticism involves a paradox in that it seems to be instrumental in self-differentiation but is also a lapse into illusion.

The young person has found something that is privately and uniquely his own in genital stimulation. But this is subject to taboo, so that he feels guilty and embarrassed by it. Such conflicts as this act as a spur towards alienation from the older generation, a subject to which we shall return later.

6. The boy's changing body-image[1]

Dramatic growth in body size takes place at this time. A boy may grow a foot taller within two or three years. His physical self-representation or *body-image* must change rapidly to keep up with this growth. This, together with his genital development, presents difficulties in integrating his idea of himself, so that a person in his early teens is often ungainly and shy. For instance, a fourteen-year-old boy, when asked to speak about himself, began as follows: 'It is difficult to know all my motions. Normally I stand upright, occasionally with my weight on one leg. When sitting I rest my head on one hand and cross my legs.' An older person talking like this would sound distinctly odd, but not a boy in his early teens.

Boys, anxious about their body-images, are often preoccupied with comparing themselves when in each other's company. They vie over the length of their penises, their height, strength or whether they have started shaving. This is often manifest in horseplay which

[1] Blos, 1963.

can seem oafish to girls or older people. To the boys themselves it is fun about their bodies, which are crucially important.

7. The experience of body changes in girls[1]

The coming of menstruation and the development of the breasts are if anything more dramatic for a girl than their male equivalent. Here are a few memories of puberty which emphasize the girl's unsureness about her new body-image.

(i) I was eleven when I started menstruating, and remember looking after two six-year-old boys. One day I overheard them saying, 'Is she a girl or a lady?' 'She's a girl because she plays with us.' 'No, she's a lady because she's got titties.'

(ii) I developed young and was the only one in the class to have breasts. The others laughed at me and punched them. I did all sorts of things to flatten them, wearing big loose sweaters and so on.

(iii) I remember being excused gym when I started, and having to just sit there feeling foolish while no one else said a word.

These are memories of people who started puberty young. For those who start later the embarrassment may not be so acute, but most women will recall their clumsiness and self-consciousness.

In recent years the exercise of explicit sexual attractiveness has been 'allowed' at a progressively younger age. Thus, twenty years ago a girl often had to wait for seven or eight years before she could make up, dress or use her body attractively. Now girls in their early teens dress to show off not only to boys but also to their girl friends and to themselves. This often leaves older people aghast. For instance:

We were all very interested in being as grown-up as possible and I was determined to have a bra. I asked my mother but she said 'Oh, no.' So I bought one for sixpence from a friend who had pinched it out of her sister's drawer.

It seems that a girl's interest in puberty is predominantly directed towards her body-image and menstruation rather than upon the

[1] Blos, 1963. Deutsch, 1944. Benedek, 1952.

excitement of the genitals as it is in boys. Girls feel swept by sexual urges, but they are perhaps more diffuse and internal than with a boy. Genital masturbation perhaps plays but a small part in development at puberty as compared with a boy. Even if a girl discovers how to achieve an orgasm for herself (and they seem to experience similar feelings of pleasure and guilt as was described with boys), menstruation is still the most important experience of puberty. It may be experienced with embarrassment or pride, but unlike masturbation its onset is inevitable and not subject to choice. Although it differs from masturbation in that it cannot be self-induced, they both contribute to self-realization and an awareness of physical maturity. For the boy this may simply be interpreted as an interest in girls as sexual objects, whereas the girl's thoughts may turn to dreams and talk of marriage long before boys think about it. They will ponder upon the characteristics of possible lovers in quiet intimacy with their best friends, scorning boys of their own age who are still horsing around with cronies.

8. The sexual climate in different schools[1]

We have just suggested that girls' attitudes mature earlier than boys'. This may be due to different rates of physical maturation as well as to the differing impacts of menstruation and masturbation, the former being conducive to seriousness, the latter to phantasy. However, psychological maturation may also be affected by cultural climate. Sexual attitudes certainly seem to vary with the school a child goes to (as well as with his family background).

Different schools, even in the same area, have different climates of attitude. Here are a few examples.

(i) Ours was a co-educational school with boys and girls in the same class, but we didn't have much to do with each other. We girls had our best friends, while the boys seemed to go about in gangs with their own interests.

(ii) We girls never had best friends at school because everyone from thirteen onwards had to be seen going to the bus stop with her boy friend.

(iii) We lived in mortal fear of sex at our boys' boarding-school. Masturbation was never discussed except by priests in sermons. I had a photo of a film star in a bikini which I lost. It

---

[1] Fleming, 1967. Schofield, 1968.

K

was found, and there was a witch-hunt by the masters for the owner. Fortunately I was never caught.

(iv) We all paired off at various times with girl friends from the local girls' school. Dances between the schools were held every term.

(v) I rather think that you were a bit of an oddity at our school if you didn't have some sort of love affair with another boy.

(vi) There weren't any homosexual liaisons between the girls at our school. But crushes on teachers or older girls were 'the thing'. And we would spend hours talking to our best friends about them.

Whether these differences in climate have a lasting effect upon children remains an open question. This is of interest because it is often suggested that later homosexuality is bred at school. This has been mentioned in these reminiscences, but we will wait until the next chapter to discuss it further.

9. Sexual curiosity

The young child is usually very curious about how babies come, and this interest continues through latency. There is naturally renewed excitement at puberty. The reader will recall his own memories of this. However well informed by teachers and parents, children seem to distort and elaborate the facts into weird and wonderful stories.

An earlier chapter mentioned how sexual excitation seems to play a powerful part in the functioning of imagination generally. Nowhere does imagination weave itself with such intensity as upon the actual subject of sex itself. The market for stories of divorce, perversity, rape, broken love-lives and violence indicates the millions of adults and children needing to satisfy fevered sexual imaginations.

The following quotations show how in curiosity a need for factual knowledge is interwoven with pleasure in distorted phantasy.

(i) The actual birth of a baby was shown on television, and some children were allowed to stay up and watch. It was the only subject of conversation in the playground next day. The general consensus of opinion was that everyone now knew how babies were born, through the chest and out between the breasts.

(ii) I remember drinking in knowledge of a twelve-year-old boy who 'knew'. I produced a secret drawing-book of his teachings, which were of babies being born through the anus. Later, by reading our *Home Doctor* while my mother was out shopping, I discovered my error.

(iii) I learnt most of what I knew at a Saturday afternoon market stall. There was a book about reproduction which I read chapter by chapter Saturday after Saturday. I used to go down after lunch praying that it had not been sold.

(iv) I remember hearing my mother talking about someone who had to be cut when her baby was born, so I assumed that all babies had to be cut out of their mothers. I duly spread the word at school.

(v) We had a theory that a woman's genitals did something like biting the man's penis and swallowing it to make a baby.

These practices may be rejected as the silly consequences of adult prudery. But they are also great fun, and exercise initiative and curiosity in a way that no serious formal instruction can entirely replace.

As a contrast to these ways of gleaning sexual knowledge, here is a description from Zambia.

The practice in our villages used to be like this. When a girl first menstruated, she went to stay for a month by herself in a house. No one visited her except her mother and certain other knowledgeable married women and mothers. They would look after her but also give her instruction about the facts of life, how to make love and also about the duties of a wife. At the end of a month the isolation would end in a grand party. This was to indicate that the girl was now ready for marriage, and that her family was willing to consider offers.

This is not only unlike the British modes of sexual instruction, but also shows a fundamentally different attitude by both adults and children to the transition of adolescence.

10. Children at puberty and adults[1]

In British cultures at least, *alienation* between young people and their parents tends to begin at puberty. A much younger child may be out of sympathy with his parents, but this will not have been explicit. He will have had to conform overtly to their ways.

We have discussed how a child is flooded with excitation at puberty and does not know what to do with it. He is embarrassed, and when in company with others of his age he can share this with them. With adults it is different, for they went through the phase years before and seem to be distant from it. However, the child now feels the sexual urges of an adult and is also probably just as tall. He compares himself more directly with adults than before, but tends to feel unsure and incompetent in the comparison.

In compensation his body size, aided by masturbation phantasies, provides the seeds of a subtle grandiosity of mood which helps him forget embarrassment and clumsiness. Being elated and yet having an underlying sense of doubt about himself, the young person can quickly spot the elements of foolishness in adults. This heightened sense of criticism is shared by friends, so that they can club together in mutual admiration and giggle at adults. This is a form of defensive scapegoating against the anxiety of inferiority. The mood of slightly arrogant grandiosity also provides the assurance needed to formulate realistic criticism of adults, and the refusal to take things for granted. Without it, we would perhaps remain like sheep.

From the parents' point of view, their child's sexuality usually brings their own private practices into question so that they feel embarrassed. This can soon be spotted by the children, who become adept at exposing their parents' weaknesses. Parents then react in their own ways to defend their self-esteem. The overt split between the generations of adolescence has begun. Some adults fall over themselves to cure this split by pretending that there is no difference between them and the child at puberty. They will give details of their own love-making as if they were brother or sister rather than parent and child. Young people usually loathe this because it implicitly allows no privacy on either side. In sexuality above all things the individual needs to be able to be *private*. This is not simply a matter of social convention. We have seen that when sexual ideas are allowed free rein, an individual is given to 'crazy' flights of imagination. Privacy allows this imagination to be contained. Public sexuality breaks the psychological boundaries between

[1] Blos, 1962. Fleming, 1967.

inner phantasy and reality. This can be fun on occasions, but is very confusing if unchecked. For example:

A young man discussed everything with his mother, often when they were both naked in the bathroom. With other people he was frozen, because his imagination was full of sexual ideas which raced through his mind in an uncontrolled fashion.

We shall conclude by suggesting that there must inevitably be a difference of attitude between young people and their parents, because the life problems they face are different. Only where one generation succumbs to the ways of the other will the split seem to disappear. When the individuality of both is asserted, clashes may well occur.

II

MID-ADOLESCENCE

1. Social background
In a traditional society, puberty and the transition to adulthood
would be a major life event which had been publicly organized into
the social pattern. This is not so with us. Social expectations facing
any one individual are vague, various and contradictory. He is given
a generalized freedom of choice and thrown back upon his own
resources. This chapter is about the second phase of assuming adult
choice and self-responsibility. It is particularly concerned with the
overt rejection of parental authority. This can predominantly be
seen happening in the teens, but it must again be stressed that
'adolescing' is a process that varies from individual to individual
and has no definable time limits.

2. The situation facing the individual
By the mid-teens a person finds himself vaguely looking forward.
He will soon be expected to be an adult, but he is neither sure what
he wants to do nor what he can do. He is at a threshold, but in a
limbo of uncertainty. This could be epitomized by the words, 'What
shall I do – to work, to marry, to enjoy myself?' Because this is a
time of uncertainty it is often called a *crisis*. This is not meant to
imply that great danger is involved, but simply that a turning-point
has been reached where the individual cannot remain as he was.
Change must take place, but the new direction may be for better or
worse (Caplan, 1964. Erikson, 1968). Naturally few adolescents will
formulate their predicament quite so decisively as this, but most
would agree that these questions often permeate their thoughts.

3. The disruption of the individual's mental organization[1]
The child has his own private phantasy life. His *public image* of
himself was confined to his school and friends. Apart from this he

[1] Blos, 1963. Erikson, 1950, 1968. Deutsch, 1944.

simply assumed he was his parents' child. He may have hated and loved them, but being immature, he had little opportunity to do anything but accept their ways and beliefs as part of his natural order. In large measure he was *identified* with his parents. For example, a child brought up by religious parents may have no deep personal conviction, but he will assume religious truth, say 'I believe in God', and feel there is something strange about atheists. Similarly, a child brought up in an influential family will grow up assuming that influence is an automatic part of his life. If he grows up with humble parents who assume that 'the good things are not for the likes of us', he will imbibe these expectations as applying to him also. The reader will recall similar assumptions taken in from his own parents. I myself remember my private phantasy that I would be a martial leader. At the same time I knew I was middle class and lived in a small house. I envied the rich and pitied the poor just as my parents seemed to.

With adolescence, these assumptions begin to be called into question. The influences which bring this about must be various. Educationally the young person may have developed so far that he is moving into scholastic areas which are beyond his parents' comprehension. The climate of his school and friends will be encouraging him to argue. He will also have the body and sexual impulses of an adult, so he is ready to confront his parents face to face, as it were.

The overt manifestations of his new development will probably be to disobey, argue and be irritable with his parents and other adults. The internal counterpart of this argumentation is subtle but important. Part of the young person begins to *attack parts of himself which are identified with his parents*. He begins to dislike thinking like them and being subservient to them. As mentioned in the previous chapter, the adolescent's slight grandiosity of mood enhances his sensitivity to the absurdities of his parents. The reader will probably remember being disgusted by certain things his parents did and rejecting them from the idea of what he would like to be.

Here are some other instances:

(i) My parents were always waffling about morality in a vague abstract way which made me sick. I was rather a prude, but at sixteen then decided to devote my life to science concerned with hard facts untrammelled by boring morality.

(ii) My mother was very shy, so that at holiday times we hardly had the company of any other families. I was shy, too, but determined to be sociable when I grew up and married.

(iii) My father was religious and I wanted to be as grown-up as possible, so got confirmed quite young. The next Sunday I decided that religion bored me. I refused to go to communion, my father and I fought physically on the way to church, and I haven't been interested since.

Just as the young person attacks ideas of himself which are like those of his parents, so also counter-attacks take place and he tends to doubt every motive of his own. His psychological organization is unstable and in flux. This is manifest in bouts of self-absorption, irritability and restlessness (Blos, 1963. Deutsch, 1944).

It is sometimes assumed that everybody must have some acute and noisy crisis in order to have a proper adolescence. There is no evidence to support this. Many people throw off blind acceptance of their parents quite quietly over a long period, so that it does not seem to have been a crisis at all. However, questioning parental attitudes is central to the process of adolescence.

There are various immediate consequences of this relative dissolution of the individual's old mental organization. We shall now discuss some of them.

4. The adolescent's conception of himself [1]

We have already mentioned the young person's unsureness of himself. He is prone to discard his likeness to parents, but does not know what he wants or is competent to be instead. He often has an underlying fear of being nothing to other people. This seems to be confirmed by the fact that he has not yet been recognized as an adult. Spurred by such anxieties he makes intentions for the future. But nothing is settled in himself, so he may plan several different careers within a week. Failing to find any solution to his insignificance, he often becomes noisy and exhibitionistic. This gives a transient sense of impact upon other people.

The young person is often fired by espousing great causes in his mind. We have already mentioned his proneness to *disgust* at parents and himself. This can quickly be turned towards ideas about the world at large, so that the institutions of mankind are seen in all

[1] Blos, 1963. Fleming, 1967. Erikson, 1968.

their vileness. Causes are then espoused which seem to offer future salvation.

Unsure of himself and held back by being a minor in the estimation of others, he usually confines himself to feeling the power of words and ideologies. The educated adolescent is renowned for his interminable talking and idealism. This bores or infuriates tired adults, but through it the young person is usually sorting out his own beliefs and testing them. Furthermore, being so sensitive to disgust, he can be a particularly acute diagnostician of personal and social ills. Hence young people are often in the vanguard of social changes.

If a person in adolescence is inarticulate, he may find a sense of power at one remove by belonging to a gang. Being unable to intellectualize, such groups often violently *act* the inner predicaments that are assailing their ideas rather than talk about them in ideological terms. This is the well-documented province of sociologists and social psychologists. It would serve no purpose to extend ourselves here (see Fleming, 1967).

Apart from these gang activities, the intimate company of friends provides sympathy and a means of testing out new integrations of ideas and behaviour without being scorned catastrophically. He may be fiercely criticized, but will not be regarded as a silly child.

A young man may walk along the street wearing the boots of a Cossack, jeans of a cowboy, jerkin of a Red Indian, smock of a paratrooper, necklace of a Tibetan, hair style of a maiden and beard of a prophet. This is an enjoyable way of experimenting with appearance to others. The freedom for such *experimentation* is a natural consequence of the rejection of parental models.

Exploration is akin to experiment. Physical adventure and feats of endurance have long been accepted as rewarding by both young and old. This seems old-fashioned to some, who then turn to exploring inside themselves instead with the aid of drugs.

Drug trips combine the thrills of exploration, risk and strangeness, together with a pleasure in assaulting parental and adult conventionality. My personal impression is that self-discoveries under drugs are usually short-lived. They are rarely integrated into the individual's everyday functioning. Without reality testing, such insights retain an illusory quality. There is also the risk of addiction. This of course often adds further excitement.

5. Sexuality[1]

After our discussion of puberty, there is little need to consider heterosexual feelings again at present. This will be taken up in the chapter on being in love. Homosexuality has, however, so far not been discussed.

With the coming of puberty and then the dissolution of old mental structures, the individual may find himself assailed with a welter of discordant impulses and ideas which have hitherto been held in check. In particular, infantile urges come to the fore. These are often perverse and many-sided. They involve both active wishes to stimulate and passive yearnings to be stimulated in both sexes. Active wishes are usually equated with masculinity and passive ones with femininity.

Urges to be both active and passive occur in everyone whether male or female. Homosexuality is more specific than this. It puts into practice the wish to be active or passive genitally with someone of the same sex. This often involves a *fascination* with *parts* of the body. It is thus close to fetishism. A frequent occurrence is that an individual, feeling extremely inferior himself, *idealizes* (see Segal, 1964) or worships a body part either of his own or in someone like him of the same sex. This becomes sexually exciting, and satisfaction is sought in loving, or being loved, about the body part while mutually masturbating or performing some other form of intercourse. For instance:

> A boy was very shy and bullied. He was also self-conscious about an undescended testicle and the smallness of his penis. When eleven years old he was enthralled at the penis of a boy whom he saw masturbating. From then on he became a penis worshipper.

Worship of body parts is often associated with compulsive role-playing, either by pretending to be an ideal specimen of one's own sex or an adoring member of the opposite. Either way, self-illusion is prominent.

Young people, especially boys in their teens, being unsure of themselves are prone to idealize body parts and experiment with homosexuality. As confidence is gained, this often falls away. The processes which fixate homosexuality into adult life cannot be discussed here (see Cameron, 1963. West, 1960).

[1] Schofield, 1968. Blos, 1963. Deutsch, 1944.

6. *The adolescent and his parents*[1]

We have suggested that the internal rejection of identifications with parents is a core event of adolescence. The actual home situation makes this either more or less easy. Where parents give their children *room* to carry on their transformations in relative privacy, where they give them freedom to work out their ideas in their own time, adolescence is usually worrying but pleasant for both generations. It is inevitably worrying to parents because they are giving up responsibility for decisions, and neither they nor their child are sure that he is ready to take over. For instance, a mother said, 'My husband and I want to have a holiday. Jack, sixteen, doesn't want to come. But we're not sure about his looking after the house for a fortnight. Last time he left an electric fire on all the week-end.'

We have been stressing an adolescent's wish to be rid of parental influence. At the same time the opposite is true. Parts of him wish to remain dependent. Not only is he habituated to reliance upon adults, but also life is easier when others look after the necessities. So parents are expected to allow freedom of action while still burdened by the responsibilities of home, food and money. This is infuriating, and a most common cause of rows between parents and children.

This reluctance to leave off being a child must not be overlooked. Many parents and teachers report how they need to push young people into self-reliance, only to be met with hot resentment and grumpiness.

The passing of dependence is usually experienced with some *sadness* on both sides. Parents are losing a function in which they have been deeply involved for many years. They are getting older and perhaps envy their children's vivacity. From the adolescent's point of view, he is giving up the gratifications of childhood and its dependence. This entails a form of *mourning* as well as freedom. Grief in adolescence is little mentioned, but many people report moments of conscious sadness about home when tears well up in their eyes (Blos, 1963).

Some parents find it hard or impossible to give up their old ways of nurturing their children. In doing this they are not giving room for independence. Young people frequently complain that their parents cannot see them as they really are but only as little children. They are *infantilized*. For instance:

[1] Blos, 1963. Fleming, 1967.

   (i) My mother still watches everything I do. Her eyes seem to be everywhere. She can't even stand my being in the bathroom alone.

  (ii) I went for an interview for a job, and it was the devil's own job to stop my mother coming.

 (iii) My father still corrects my table manners. He's done it for years and it never changes.

These are examples of behaviour which might have been appropriate in childhood but are now intrusions upon the adolescent's autonomy. When a young person retains some independent determination, violent quarrels often arise in such families. Other children succumb and remain docile but subservient into adulthood. It is possible that such children only find independence from their parents through the passage of violent mental breakdowns.

Because adolescents seem to ignore the older generation, it is often said that they are careless of their parents. In behaviour this is no doubt true, but their inner feelings are often otherwise. The young person is struggling between rejecting his parent's ways and then feeling remorse for hurting them. They may not act with responsibility but nevertheless feel it. For instance:

   (i) My parents are my only responsibility (girl aged sixteen).

  (ii) I must find a job which I want, but which does not hurt my parents too much (man aged twenty).

This second example perhaps epitomizes the young person's situation. He has a responsibility to himself. It will also be expected of him by others in the outside world. He usually wants, at the heart of himself, to feel that his parents are happy about him as well. His predicament is to find ways of life which satisfy all three.

7. Theoretical summary

Adolescence entails transformation in all aspects of mental organization (Blos, 1963. Cameron, 1963. A. Freud, 1937. Lidz, 1968). The coming of puberty means that new patterns of bodily urge appear. Putting it theoretically, there is a resurgence of *id* demands. At the same time changes in body image also tend to make the child's habitual *ego organization* out of date. Furthermore, the young person's attacks upon parental identifications means that his previous *super-ego*, or organization of conscience tends to be broken up.

All these transformations act as something of a threat to the individual ego which attempts to reorganize the new incoming data into coherence. The individual's struggle with his id is perhaps most manifest in his general fidgetiness. Tribulations with his super-ego are seen in preoccupation with moral issues and the desire to develop ethical opinions of his own. The overall attempt to reorganize ego-functioning is seen in trial and error behaviour, both by action and thought.

Such an ordeal of ego-function is often referred to as the adolescent *identity crisis* (Caplan, 1964. Erikson, 1950, 1959, 1968). This requires a little explanation. The ordinary healthy person has an underlying *sense of himself as being continuous in time and separate from all other beings*. This contains the idea of *identity* (see also Rycroft, 1968 a). Such a sense of 'being' involves not only awareness of feelings and ideas within the individual himself, but also that other people have them as well. In particular it entails the recognition that other people are affected by the individual and have *opinions about him*.

The concept of identity emphasizes the *public* as well as the private experience of an individual. A child's public experience is confined to a small circle of family, friends and school. Since adults are responsible for his well-being, the child needs to worry but little about his public impact. He is thus free to play and enjoy his own private explorations and phantasy life.

With adolescence, this is coming to an end. He will soon be expected to look after himself and contribute to an adult world in ways that are satisfactory to a wide variety of strange people. Public appearance and usefulness take on importance. The young person worries acutely about how he appears to others, and what he can do in adult life to satisfy both himself and others. This is the adolescent's identity crisis. It is only slowly resolved in the teens and young adulthood by the discovery of satisfactory work, leisure and love. We shall discuss the first two of these in the next chapter, the third in the one following it.

12

LATE ADOLESCENCE AND ADULTHOOD

1. The concept of adult identity

From this point onwards we shall dispense with theoretical summaries at the end of each chapter. It is hoped that the reader will have grasped some of the essentials of our theoretical concepts by this stage. They will thus be brought more directly into the main body of our discussions. New concepts will also be introduced within this context. This chapter draws threads from many sources and condenses them into an abstract form. It is thus perhaps the most difficult in the book.

We have now come to the time of life when an individual tests out his activities in an attempt to find an integration which is satisfactory to his inner self and to people around him. A *specific* activity in relation to others is referred to as a *role*. At any time in life a person may function in a wide multiplicity of these. But when he has found a personal patterning of roles together with inner satisfactions, the individual usually experiences a sense of wholeness and well-being. This integration is often referred to as *adult identity*; it is essentially idiosyncratic and private to each individual (Erikson, 1950, 1959, 1968. See also Lynd, 1958).

Coherence like this is not easy to find. It probably takes a good many years of trial and error even for the most fortunate. Many people seem never to find it. What is more, as the individual goes through life, new situations arise, which demand new roles and hence the development of new integrations within the self. So, although a person may have found an overall direction and style for himself by perhaps his late twenties, the details of his identity will be changing until death. Psychological development does not cease with physical maturity. Since transformations are called for throughout adult life, some of the enthusiasm and romance of childhood and adolescence must be kept alive by the adult. Failing in this, he is likely to become stultified, so that he experiences the world passing by while he remains an onlooker.

This chapter, being about adult functioning in general, cannot hope to be comprehensive. Even a multiplicity of books about the subject could not do it justice. We shall discuss a few aspects which have at least a fairly wide applicability.

2. *Work and adult identity*

Perhaps our ancestors made one of our greatest provisions for personal freedom in the invention of currency. By the use of money to stand for a wide variety of goods and services, an individual's choice of satisfaction was greatly enhanced. In our society adult freedom is largely dependent upon a capacity and willingness to earn money.

We need not dwell upon the iniquities and injustices of distribution that occur in our economy but simply note that, by and large, the individual earns money and hence choice by making *work contributions* to others. This is one of the key characteristics of an adult as opposed to a child.

It could be said that an individual has not *come out of adolescence until he has discovered the contributions he can make to others and been recognized for them.* This recognition needs to be both in money and in personal appreciation. Contributions are found first in work, but also in leisure and love. These necessitate some sacrifice of egocentric wishes. The particular pattern of *compromise* between egocentric wishes and contribution to others delimits an individual's life style and adult identity. Here are some examples of people reflecting about this in the course of ordinary conversation.

(i) I am a cowman of course, and it's good enough work. But politics is what stirs me. I wouldn't like it as a job, but it and and the job go well enough together.

(ii) In doing social work, I at last found I was happy. It was me. I felt pleased with myself for what I was doing and people liked me. I couldn't imagine doing anything else. I relaxed, I suppose, in the evenings, but the middle of me was being a social worker.

(iii) In those days football and motors were my life. I wanted to become a professional, but my dad said I must really help in the shop. Being in a village with no one else to do it I could see his point, so I said, right I'll do it, but Saturdays must be mine for football, and it was agreed. Later, I ran a taxi from the shop and everyone hereabouts came to me if their cars wouldn't go.

Here we see different people organizing their lives to satisfy both themselves and the circumstances in which they are placed. We shall return to the subject of compromise at the end of this chapter.

3. Choice of work

In a traditional society, the nature of a person's work would probably be pre-ordained by his father's occupation. There would be negligible choice. There is perhaps little of this in its pure form in our society, but the work people take up is still delimited by what is available as well as by individual wishes. We also see a great variation in the personal investment put into their money-earning work by different people. Many individuals, particularly those in repetitive jobs, aim for little satisfaction of their inner phantasy, but seek it in leisure time instead. There are two such instances in the examples just given. Others invest a great deal of themselves in money-earning work, and expect to get a great deal of inner satisfaction in return. This is epitomized by the social worker in the examples just given. The demand for inner satisfaction is particularly noticeable with professional people.

It has been suggested that an individual's choice of work can be categorized as to whether it is tradition-directed, outer-directed, or inner-directed (Reisman, 1950). The reader will note that our brief discussion has been along these lines. However, it is likely that every choice of work involves an interweaving of all three influences in varying degrees.

4. The first job[1]

Perhaps the most common memory of first going to work is of feeling a nobody in a vast machine. The contrast with school is impressive. At school, the whole organization was, ostensibly at least, for the sake of the pupils. The primary purpose of an office or factory on the other hand, is not for its personnel. They come second to the work objectives, be it production or care of other people.

A young person going to an industrial organization is prone to be a nameless item in the machinery. Even if the actual work situation itself is congenial and intimate, he can nevertheless feel a lonely sense of being next to nothing in the context of the wide adult world in general.

[1] See Carter, 1966.

Awareness of being a nameless item often throws a young person back into a paranoid mood where 'the machine' or people in it become acutely persecuting. A young working person is often fraught with worries about what other people are saying about him or whether he is being done down. But being unsure of himself, he usually dare not voice these discontents or even let himself think about them clearly. Often such ideas about the impersonality and even malignancy of work conditions have a great deal of truth in them. Many people find such ideas alarming and prefer not to dwell upon them, but rather try to find a way of doing the job in as pleasant a manner as possible. It is a situation which bears comparison with going to school for the first time.

Each type of job has its own skills which must be developed and mastered. It also has its own particular anxieties which have to be held in check, so that new defence organizations are called into play. Thus, for instance, medical students and nurses have to organize themselves against the fear of causing death, and against the impulse to vomit. A steel erector must find ways of absorbing any anxiety he may have about heights. The lorry driver must hold his imagination about accidents in check, while still maintaining enough anxiety to be safe on the road. The reader can easily add to this list (for accounts of different forms of work see Frazer, 1967).

5. Repetition, creativity and responsibility[1]

When a person settles into any job he will find varying degrees of *repetition*, together with opportunity for *creativity* and *responsibility*. Let us consider some of the personal strains and satisfactions involved in these.

All jobs entail physical or mental repetition, some more than others. The epitome of such tasks is in conveyor-belt assembly and packaging. They are not the sole prerogative of manual workers. Perhaps the most taxing are in offices, copy typing, costing or filing. Industry and commerce have an omnivorous need for the mechanical capacity of the human body allied to the minimum of creative intellect.

The essence of repetitive work lies in speed of movements carried out time and again without variation. From the personal point of view *choice of action* is excluded once the skill has been mastered. This seems to constitute the drudgery of repetitive work more than gross physical toil. Just as a child does, the adult mind seems to need

[1] Jaques, 1970. Carter, 1966. Brown, 1954.

exploration and variety for its satisfaction. When a task cannot be invested with imagination, intolerable boredom is likely to set in.

The means by which repetitive workers find variety often have to be ingenious. Some people slightly alter their mode of carrying out a task from time to time. Music is another way. In listening, one can play in imagination while the body carries on with something else. Daydreaming is, of course, the most common outlet. For instance, a widowed packer recounts that she carried out intricate accountancy as she worked. She dreamt of a trip to Australia to see her family, and calculated with each packet how much nearer she was to saving the money required. Without this, she says, she would have gone mad. Romantic and erotic daydreams are common. Secret masturbation is quite frequent in some jobs. Talking to while away the time is only possible where the noise level is low. Women's talk is usually personal. For instance, one typing pool is reported as being interested in nothing except romance. Marriage was of no interest, the conversation seemed to be a continuous race game about engagements and breaking them off. Older women will, of course, gossip about family and local affairs. Men's talk is less personal – about sport, pools, horses, grumbles about the management, politics and so on.

Using such means of relief as these, many people find it easy to submit themselves to being mechanical. Perhaps this is because anxiety about the task is reduced to a minimum with repetition. Other people, probably when they have a high estimation of themselves, find repetition insulting and intolerable.

Many jobs require a greater degree of individual *choice*. Thus a fitter has more choice as to how to go about a task than does a conveyor-belt worker. The greater the freedom for invention, the more skilled does the individual have to be. With freedom of choice comes opportunity to act *creatively*. In creative activity a person uses his imagination to construct some ordering of objects or ideas that was not present before. It is one of the most deeply enjoyable activities of the human spirit. At the same time, choice entails uncertainty and gives room for anxiety about performing the task. This was spared the repetitive worker.

The purest form of creativity is art and invention, but it is not confined to these. For instance, an electrician rewiring a house is exercising his creative functions when deciding where best to lay his leads and fit his switchgear. A shopkeeper organizing his sales will do likewise when he estimates his customers' needs, decides what articles to stock and arranges them in the shop for display. So also is a housewife furnishing a house and organizing her family's day. It seems that all planning has elements of creative functioning in it. A person denied this at work will often seek to fulfil himself in his leisure, in gardening, needlework, social organizing, handiwork and so on.

It will be remembered that both repetition and creativity were exercised in school, so they will not be new to the working adult. But full *responsibility* for a task upon which other people depend will be relatively new to the young adult.

Responsibility for a task means being *entrusted* with its successful completion. The reader will remember how the infant first needed to trust his environment and then began to trust himself. With this he began to be self-responsible for his own functioning. By adulthood this has come full circle. Other people expect to put their trust in him. They become infants, as it were, in his hands during the period of the task. Thus passengers need to trust their driver, housewives their plumber or patients their nurse.

The individual's sense of responsibility involves knowledge of the task to be carried out. It also requires other functions. His *conscience* must be operating so that he recognizes the existence of others and feels *concern* for their well-being. This operates to inhibit impulsiveness or withdrawal from the reality of the task. Lastly, and of fundamental importance, it involves *anticipation* of possible trouble and disasters. The responsible person must be able to tolerate anxiety about possible *faults*, both in himself and in the situation in hand. Only then can he realistically watch over it and look forward. The exercise of responsibility has great satisfactions. The individual is master of the situation and is also being *parental*. But it involves burdens of personal anxiety and guilt. To be responsible, a person must use these feelings without being overwhelmed or being carried away by egocentric phantasy.

Each task provokes its own particular anxieties, so that some people can bear its responsibility while others could not. For instance, an individual may find that anxiety about heights is too much to contain, so he would not make a good airline pilot. On the other hand his anxiety about vomiting, death and damaging others may be under control, so that being a doctor would be quite tolerable.

Many tasks involve no direct responsibility for other people's well-being. But all jobs do this at least indirectly. Thus a man making spare parts for washing-machines is not directly responsible for other people's lives. But if he fails in his job, a housewife may be affected months later and miles away.

Our emphasis upon responsibility may give a solemn and pedantic impression of adulthood. Certainly awareness of responsibility tends to be antithetical to the urge towards romantic exploration and creativity. The former aims towards conservation while the latter searches for newness. The individual who identifies himself exclusively with responsibility is prone to become conservative and even reactionary. He shrinks into being a 'square'. On the other hand, if he identifies himself completely with romanticism he shrinks into immaturity. It seems inevitable that an adult is faced by inner conflicts between responsibility and the search for newness. Identification of the self with either one side or the other is a form of splitting which avoids experience of this conflict.

Turning now from responsibilities at work to more general considerations. An individual's *maturity* is allied to his capacity to feel and be responsible in an underlying way. When a person's mental organization of skill, concern, guilt and foresight has developed to the point where he is aware of responsibility in a variety of situations, we say he is mature.

There are many adults who are able to act responsibly in specific tasks, but who seem still to have an underlying wish to hand over to others. This may not be spoken about openly, but is manifest in subtle ways such as when he relates to others with a naïve begging, placatory manner. We usually say then that he is emotionally immature. His unconscious impulses rather than conscious attitudes are being noticed here.

Responsibility as we have defined it should be distinguished from power. The idea of power refers to an individual's effect upon and control over other people. Responsibility on the other hand refers to his recognition of power and concern for those affected. It describes a person's psychological functioning, and is not here a sociological, legal or political concept.

6. Irresponsible role play

People may have power but little responsibility if they are interested primarily in *satisfying their own* phantasies while obliterating their sympathetic conscience and concern. This often occurs in social and political relationships.

When an individual takes up a role to indulge his phantasy of power without responsibility towards others, it is often said that he is practising one form of 'gamesmanship' or playing games (Berne, 1964).

The reader will recall the function of games in childhood. The impulse to play often arose out of anxiety in a situation which had not yet been mastered. The capacity for make-believe was then called into action, so that the child could pretend to be a grown-up character who represented mastery of the anxiety. Such games were entered into quite consciously with the recognition of all concerned that it was make-believe.

Such consciously contrived games are also played by adults in leisure time, but the time for open indulgence in them is limited. However, *compulsive covert role play* often interweaves itself within other activities. Here, an individual fraught with anxiety finds relief in a phantasy system; other people may then be drawn into his system so that they become pawns in his 'game'. Thus for example, a person still fraught with anxieties about his helplessness may repeatedly search out situations where he can pretend to himself to be in command. Yet another person might on the other hand find the experience of guilt and shame intolerable, so that he is driven to finding situations where he can feel a martyr and is thus freed, at least temporarily, from guilt. Other individuals may readily enter into such compulsive role play. Thus a person driven to playing the master, for instance, may find accomplices who find relief in being martyred servants and so on. The essence of these compulsive roles is that recognition of the real feelings of other people is obliterated for the sake of satisfying an inner phantasy system. The function of responsibility falls asleep, as it were, when such games are being enacted.

It is perhaps important for any individual working closely with people to be aware of this human propensity to play roles. The reader will be able to add to our brief description from his own memory. He is also recommended to read Berne (1964). This is a popular and witty book, somewhat slick, so that the reader may feel that the writer himself is playing a game of know-all. But its descriptions make plain the misery caused by compulsive role play. In it not only is responsible concern lost, but the role-player is impoverished, so that the essence of being a feeling human being seems to disappear.

We have repeatedly noted that phantasy is present within every individual and can act as a spur to creativity as well as being the root of passion. Thus, no doubt, elements of games are being played out in the recesses of every person's mind. We have been stressing here that such phantasies take on a neurotic or compulsive quality when the functioning of responsibility is lost.

7. Residues of childhood[1]

The recognition of responsibility as opposed to being childlike is central to adult identity formation. We have noted that among other things this involves seeing the self in part as *being parental.* This would seem to mean identifying with one's parents again, and raises a paradox, for it was only in the last chapter on adolescence that we said a vital part of growing up was the rejection of parental identifications.

Such a paradox arises out of a loose usage of the idea of identification. The adolescent was rejecting submission to automatic identification with his parents. The assumption of adult responsibility involves feeling the self being like a parent, and is not the same as submitting to the pattern of one's childhood parents.

With the loosening of ties to childhood parents, the individual has a freer choice of parental models upon which to base his adult responsible ideas of himself. We see this happening, for instance, when young people work out how they are going to bring up their own young children. They will accept some of their own parents' ways and reject others.

As a person assumes the responsibilities of being an adult, we see his childhood-dependent attitudes slipping into the background. But this does not mean that they have died within him. The childish parts of himself may remain very active, often unconsciously. Introspection will probably make it plain to the reader that there are parts of himself which continue, either in thought or behaviour, from his own childhood. Here are a few brief illustrations from other people.

(i) A young girl's father was a clergyman who became quite well known locally as a social reformer and efficient organizer of protest movements. Her mother was intelligent and warm, but quiet. When the little girl was five or so, her mother began to suffer from epileptic attacks. Her condition deteriorated and she became generally confused. The young girl's later childhood was clouded by worry and shame about her helpless disordered mother who died when she was twelve.

[1] M. Klein, 1960.

The girl became a lively and intelligent adult. When happy she was often fired by social reforming zeal. But these moods alternated with crippling depressions when she felt she could not put any coherent thoughts together, and sat for hours on end unable to move, just as her mother had been years before. There were no signs of brain disease, but during these periods she was quite incapacitated.

(ii) A young boy was brought up in the country. His father ran a progressive boarding-school which was regarded with some suspicion by the local people. The boy's mother cared little about this, and ran her family with a 'back to nature' philosophy. Her pigs, goats, hand-loom weaving and home-made pots were unusual and were laughed about in the neighbourhood. The young boy grew up isolated from the local children, though he went to school with them. He was baffled by them and envied their conventional toys and games, so that he rarely felt at ease to join them.

When he grew up he became a schoolmaster like his parents. His resemblance to them seemed to end there, for he went to work in a city and was more conventional in his ways. He was respected and very well liked, so that he quickly came to head a department. However, as soon as he cast off his professional mantle he was crippled with shyness. He could not bring himself to be at all intimate with others in the neighbourhood. When not at work, people outside his family seemed like a race apart, who would look askance at him just as they had done years before.

(iii) A girl was an only child, but brought up in close contact with a large extended family of uncles, aunts and cousins. Each member of this network was intimately interested in what the other was doing, and life was full of family dramas. There were numerous quarrels where each person blamed someone else for trouble caused. 'It's your fault.' 'No, it's your fault,' would echo backwards and forwards as blame was tossed to and fro by both adults and children. Sometimes the blame would settle on the little girl herself. The others then turned on her like moralistic wolves, and she would suffer torments of remorse interspersed with fury at the unfairness of it all.

When she grew up, she was lively and witty so that she had

many good friends. She was very sensitive to injustice, and when difficulties arose at work she would spend hours obsessively working out who was to blame. Her childhood experiences had given her a swift tongue, so she was regarded by her friends as someone who liked a good row and argument. However, if these arguments centred upon personalities rather than abstract principles she would feel distraught, tearful, and exhausted for days after.

(iv) A boy, many years ago, was one of the elder of many children. He was very fond of his mother, but each year brought another birth, so that he had but little of her company. He took this stoically, and in fact became particularly admired by his family for his bravery both at home and in childhood exploits. His mother died when he was ten and his father struggled on alone to bring up the family. Two years later the young boy said he wanted to relieve his father of one mouth to feed and was determined to join the Navy. His father gratefully accepted this further demonstration of bravery.

When he was eighteen, after six years at sea he fell ill and was invalided home from the East. In the ship on the way back he seems to have gone through an acute adolescent crisis. He became aware that he had no future in the Navy, and could see no way of life that would fulfil him. He wondered whether to throw himself overboard and finish it all. Then 'a radiant orb was suspended in his mind's eye'. He exclaimed 'I will be a hero and confiding in providence will brave every danger.'

Later in adult life this is just what he did. As Lord Nelson he became the brave hero not only to his family, but to England at large and succeeding generations of schoolboys.

These are just a few examples, and can do no more than suggest further thought for the reader. Some childhood residues become an enhancing part of adult life. This is often the case when propensities are loved by parents; this occurred with Nelson, whose bravery was admired in childhood.

Other residues, however, are not so enhancing. When experiences become full of anxiety they cannot be usefully integrated into the individual's style of life. They continue with a life of their own inside the individual, but are largely out of his control. Elements of such fixations can be seen in the first three examples just given. No doubt they occurred in the case of Nelson also, but we have not described them.

It might be said that every adult has an outer layer, as it were, with which he relates to the world, but the child is still active within him. These childish parts give zest and richness to his life, they can also intrude as useless and disturbing repetitions both for the individual and people around him. Compulsive role play is one manifestation of this.

8. The compromises of adult identity[1]

We now come to the last point in this discussion of adulthood, and turn away from childhood residues to more general matters. Throughout adult life, demands to *conform* to other people's standards and requirements are continually impressing themselves upon the individual. At the same time, he has his own inner wishes, so that a conflict between interests becomes inevitable. For an individual to maintain the *integrity* of his personality (Storr, 1960) so that he senses an integration of his wishes, his conscience and the demands of the outside world, he must repeatedly make *compromises*. Integrity is lost when splitting of awareness occurs, so that one set of interests obliterates others for any length of time. Fanaticism is one instance of this, and a person preoccupied only with himself is another. So, too, would be one who surrenders himself totally to other's demands. For example, compare these two men, both bank managers.

(i) Mr A. was highly esteemed by his superiors and customers. However, his whole life was consumed by his bank life. He had no hobbies. People were invited to supper on the basis of their business connections. His family life was invaded by ideas and strictures about the bank. He would say to his wife, 'You mustn't wear trousers in the front garden because customers pass.' Or, 'You should order your groceries from Jones's because they bank with us' and so on. In submitting to the bank he was unable to enjoy either his own bodily functioning or the inner lives of his wife and family. He repeatedly fell sick and his wife, failing to make an impression on him by ordinary means, soon found herself turning into a

[1] Storr, 1960. Erikson, 1968

chronically hysterical individual. Although esteemed by many, he had failed to go through the agony of making a compromise between the various demands of his situation.

(ii) Mr B. was actively interested in athletics, music and literature when young, but went into the bank to earn a living. When quite an old man he said, 'I often thought I would leave the bank and do something that directly interested me more, but I fell in love and decided that getting married was the more worth while. And to do this I had to stay in the bank.' However, he did not forget the expression of his inner life. He continued to be a reader, talker and musician in his leisure time. 'The bank was satisfactory in a way. It was secure, and looking after people's affairs was interesting. But everyone knew my heart was in other places as well, and because I wasn't married to the bank I didn't get far up the ladder.' Here we see evidence of making compromises, but not of losing self-integrity.

We see in Mr A. a form of fanaticism. He was obsessed by ambition and conformity to banking. Mr B. on the other hand tried to evaluate the various aspects of his life and sought to compromise between them. Because of this he may have suffered the fate of being thought ordinary, but no one would say he was a nonentity, and many were glad to have known him.

The examples illustrate how social pressures, particularly those in large impersonal institutions, can be deleterious of a person's integrity unless resisted on occasion. Mr A.'s superiors at the bank, for instance, no doubt valued his unswerving loyalty and commitment to its own interests. They cannot be blamed for this, but it is noticeable that no help or encouragement was offered to him to balance his interests.

Perhaps most people are faced with situations rather similar to those of these two men. The course through adult life seems to be a continuous process of compromise between conflicting issues. As new situations arise, so the individual is called upon to develop new patterns of thought, to find new compromises which will maintain his own and others' integrity.

13

COURTSHIP AND BEING IN LOVE

We have so far described the formation of adult identity without reference to falling in love or to sexuality. This chapter will discuss being in love, particularly as one of the steps towards *marriage choice* and the formation of a new family (see Westermarck, 1926. Harris, 1969. Bell and Vogel, 1968).

1. The social background of courtship

Although pairing of males and females for reproduction and companionship is universal, the method of choice of partners and forms that the partnership may take vary enormously. Perhaps the only universal rule is the *taboo on incest* (Freud, 1913. Flugel, 1945), the forbidding of sexual relationships with offspring or siblings.

Among lower animals there is no incest taboo as such. The behaviour of domesticated animals, for instance, shows that they have no scruples about this. In the wild, choice of sexual partner is determined by animals of one sex giving signs of their preference, or by those of the other sex asserting dominance over their possessions by force or threatening modes of display (Storr, 1968).

By these means among social animals a group leader emerges while the others of both sexes remain submissive to him. Thus the leader delimits the sexual activity of other members of his herd. Among humans this kind of limitation tends to be imposed from within each individual by means of taboos and guilt, which have in turn been imposed upon the young by their elders. This process was described in chapters 7 and 8 (Freud, 1913, 1916). Throughout the world these taboos crystallize into rules about sexual intercourse and about marriage choice, although they are not identical in different cultures.

Not only do cultures differ as to these rules, but also as to who is responsible for the marriage choice. *Arranged marriages*, for instance, where the families rather than the individuals court each other and conclude a deal between them, have been and still are very common (Bell and Vogel, 1968. Harris, 1969. Mead, 1956). This form of marriage choice probably predominates where a society depends upon extended family networks for its stability. Here it would be natural for families, or their senior representatives, to do the choosing for the sake of family continuity. Individual choice would disrupt this.

In our society the childhood taboo on sexuality and sensuality tends to be lifted in adolescence, so that by adulthood an individual is, in law, free to make his own marital choice. By the standards prevalent today both male and female partners are expected to be responsible for their own courtship and ultimate choice. What is more, it is assumed that the decision to marry will be based upon *mutual romantic love interwoven with sexual passion for each other* (Gorer, 1955. Harris, 1969).

Seen in the context of history, these criteria for marriage are unusual and of fairly recent origin even in Western society (Westermarck, 1926). Although acceptance of them as a social norm has only recently become widespread, the origins of the concept of romantic love lie further back in history. What is recent is that it should now be expected to form the basis of marriage choice. Let us consider this briefly, as it will provide a context for our discussion of the individual experience of love.

The concept of romantic love owes something to Plato's notion that each person was born incomplete in himself and searched for the 'other half' which would make him whole. This bears a resemblance to our idea of romantic love, but for the ancient Greeks such love was frequently homosexual and irrelevant to marriage. In a patriarchal society where men are politically dominant, it is the men who make the choice of marriage partner, whether it is done by the senior members of a tribe or family on behalf of their youngers, or whether the choice is made by the young men themselves.

In the early twelfth century there occurred a remarkable movement in Western Europe which reflected a new preoccupation with thought and feeling, and ultimately changed man's attitude to himself profoundly. In religion a new emphasis on Christ's humanity led to a new awareness, a recognition of his human sufferings and affections, and from this to a new adoration of his mother the Virgin Mary. If Christ was human enough to have been a baby and dependent upon his mother, she could therefore intercede with him now and his affection for her could be counted upon. Until this time she had played only a small part in Christian doctrine. This *Mariolatry* was paralleled by a secular movement in the cult of the *troubadours*. The knightly ideal which the troubadours celebrated showed a man who would now devote his life to his lady, content merely to carry out her commands and earn her favours. It was *for the lady* to decide whether he was worthy of her.

Two things to note here. The love relationship celebrated by the troubadours was still irrelevant to marriage, and indeed often cut across its bonds, so that the love of Tristan and Isolde or Lancelot and Guinevere is adulterous. Secondly, these romances clearly formed an escape from the harsh realities of the marital customs of feudal Europe, still very much a patriarchal society. However, the idea that the woman is no longer a chattel, that she has the power to say no to the man's advances, and that she is worthy of a lifelong devotion is seen here for the first time, and became enshrined in medieval literature. This can be seen as a step away from male dominance, and certainly the whole courtly ideal contributes towards our present-day aspirations concerning the relationship between men and women. What was originally an ideal, standing in time and space outside the ties of marriage and family, has been grafted on to the main stem of marriage and child-rearing. How far this can work is another question. (It is just this which in the fourteenth century formed one of the main themes of Chaucer's *Canterbury Tales*, the marriage debate, illustrated by stories ribald or idealistic depending on the teller.)

We have a fairly clear picture of family life in England, at least among the literate, towards the close of the Middle Ages from sources such as the Paston Letters (Davis, 1963). Marriage was still a matter of family convenience. Men were expected to consult their seniors, and women to submit to their parents' or elder brothers' choice. After marriage women were expected to identify themselves with the interests of the family they had entered, and often did so with great drive, thus wielding influence and authority. This is not to say that isolated instances of mutual romantic love did not occur. The Paston Letters contain mention of at least one such romance where the lovers succeeded in marrying in the end, although family pressures were maintained against it for years.

In Elizabethan and Jacobean writing, the idea of mutual love is widely expressed. The devotion of the troubadours can be combined with the sensual passion so ribaldly expressed in some medieval literature. Here is John Donne mocking the devotional love approach:

> Who ever loves, if he do not propose
> The right true end of love, he's one that goes
> To sea for nothing but to make him sick:
> <div align="right">(<i>Elegie</i> XVIII. Love's Progress)</div>

But he can express genuine devotion and a mutual affection which speaks straight to the twentieth century. Here he is talking *with* his love in reciprocal conversation as equals.

> I wonder by my troth what thou and I
> Did till we loved? Were we not weaned till then?
> But suck'd on country pleasures, childishly?
> (The Good-morrow)

John Donne's ideas of reciprocal appreciation between lovers may seem very near to our own, but several centuries were to pass before this became solidly confirmed and socially accepted as the main basis for marriage. One of the factors which we have perhaps to thank for this change is the Industrial Revolution.

With industrialization people became mobile in their search for work. With this mobility the extended family is replaced by the nuclear family as the primary social unit. When this occurs individual men and women have to make their own choice of a partner with whom to start their new family, often many miles from relatives. In the nuclear family, intimate reciprocal appreciation of husband and wife is vital for stability. Thus romantic love which taps and enhances this mutuality comes into its own as a main criterion for marriage.

What is more, industrialization has meant that women have come to be employed in large numbers outside their family networks. The opportunity for employment has made it possible for them to say no to a suitor without fear of family repercussions or destitution. They can earn a living until they meet another more acceptable mate. Up to a point, women's freedom now makes a social reality of the troubadour's fiction. Women can really pick and choose and leave the men to pine.

This summary sets the stage for our understanding of the modern man or woman 'in love'. Such a historical context enables us to see how residues from the past, such as the power of family influence, still have great strength in the habits of love and courtship.

2. Individual development of being in love

We cannot hope to do justice to the complexity and importance of the capacity to love. Our summary will have the quality of dispassionate dullness inevitable to an over-view. Perhaps only lovers when speaking to each other or poets in the written word can come close to representing the real inner experiences of love and hate. But an over-view may illuminate connections between aspects of the individual which might otherwise be omitted.

A glance back to the chapters upon infancy will find the first mentions of love. We saw the infant as seeking objects, particularly his mother, to satisfy needs. In general, it could be said that an individual feels love for external objects or people when they *enhance his functioning*. The first enhancements an infant receives are largely concerned with the mouth and gastro-intestinal tract. He is fed, kept warm and soothed.

Soon he begins to recognize the person behind these satisfactions, and seek little ecstasies of mutual 'conversation' with his mother. He chortles with wide smiles on seeing her, relaxes in her arms, eagerly snuggles up against her and laughs with her. When she goes he is grumpy. The parallels between these expressions and the passions of a lover twenty years later are perhaps sufficient for us to assume that there are direct repetitions within us between love feelings as a baby and as an adult.

A child may enjoy his mother intensely but will usually also turn outwards to love other people as well when they enhance him. As a child grows older, the enhancement he experiences will become more and more of a psychological nature. For instance, he will adore adults and other children for the games they play, or the stories they tell. A child will also love others for enjoying him, for he is enriched and affirmed by this.

The reader will recall the particular sensitivity of the young child's genitals and the phantasies that arise from this. A special note was made of the oedipus complex. At the same time as these excitations a generalized inhibition is also growing which culminates in the self-possession necessary to go to school.

During the latency school years, inhibited love flourishes in friendships. Here the individual has the opportunity to experience

both the comfort and enhancement which come from the togetherness and reciprocity of friends. Passionate crushes are rare.

The coming of puberty brings a surge of genital excitation. This
is hardly directed towards any specific object at the beginning;
rather it provides grounds for phantasy and self-absorption.
However, sexual phantasies are soon felt consciously to be about
external objects, even if imagined ones. Boys tend to dream about
girls they are making love to, girls dream of their heroes. Then the
boy or girl will perceive some aspects of their dream person in real
people they see. But they are usually content to worship from afar.
Film stars and pop idols provide the public with ready-made speci-
mens for this level of love. They are essentially transitional, that is,
they are used to attach what was originally an inner phantasy to
something real in the outside world. They are a first feeler of love,
as it were, from phantasy out into reality.

Some time in the early or middle teens most people start upon
a sequence which begins perhaps with casual and tentative dating
and may end with commitment to a life-long partnership. Here it
must be stressed that each person has his own sequence. Its order
varies from individual to individual and from culture to culture.
What is more, it would be presumptuous to think that any particular
sequence was more 'normal' in the healthy sense than any other.
Some people may be in love many times before marriage, while
others commit themselves for life to their first love. Each person
finds his own particular ways of being in love. It is perhaps one of
our essential freedoms (see Schofield, 1958. Gorer, 1955).

First love affairs mean a lot to each person, but they are undoubtedly a testing-out both of what someone of the opposite sex thinks
of oneself, and also of one's feelings and performance. There is often
a 'don't care' mood about these relationships. Girls treat their boy
friends with a certain indifference. 'He's nice but I'm not in love
with him.' Likewise boys are offhand. 'She's soft on me but she's
not going to catch me.' Many young people are far more wary of
falling in love than of losing their virginity. We shall see later that
they have good reason to fear the experience.

At some stage, perhaps, a person finds himself being in love. The
earlier phantasy, crushes and idealization are now attached to a real
person whom one knows. This is usually quite out of conscious
control, it just happens. Characteristics of the loved one are seen as
gleaming with a certain beauty, while for his part the adoring lover
is likely to feel small and humble yet surging with ideas and life.

It must still remain largely a mystery as to what happens when we fall in love. A welter of feelings well up which, in a large measure, have probably been denied expression since infancy, when we naturally and explosively emoted about our parents and siblings. Added to this are unbridled sexual feelings which even as infants were not gratified by our parents. With this surge the individual is thrown off balance (Lidz, 1968. M. Klein, 1960). Emotions which have been held in check for years are loosened. A person falling in love goes somewhat crazy or mad. He appears rather daft. We get some idea of the painfulness of *unrequited love* in realizing that the individual is boiling over with ideas and feelings which are out of his control. The loved one is felt to be the most important person in the world, just as were parents in infancy; but these passionate feelings are rebuffed. The loved one does not love back; the individual has nobody to whom he can safely attach his adoration. Feelings are met by an empty space as it were. This is humiliating and frightening. The vicissitudes of unrequited love need no further elaboration. The reader will be acquainted enough with literature to recognize that this is a deep source of drama for all of us. We can also recognize why many people are afraid of falling in love.

When feelings are reciprocated, the lover is usually very humble It amazes him to find the other person is in love also. He often mutters something like this, 'It's marvellous, it's happened to me, I can't believe it. I am not worth it. It's fantastic.'

Reciprocal love might happen at first sight. But it is more often a slow tentative business on both sides. One person may love first and the other not until later. Both may have known each other well as friends before being in love. Probably many married people have never felt it much at all. Let us dwell for a moment on the experience. When two people are in love a widespread *reciprocal appreciation* of each other occurs. This is an enhanced awareness not only of each other's ideas, but also of psychological characteristics and of each other's bodies. Each individual idealizes the other. We have mentioned the earlier manifestations of idealization in the crushes that young people have on a phantasy person, film star or pop idol. In this the individual perceives characteristics in the idol that he *misses in himself yet would dearly like* to possess. Thus, for instance, a shy young person with limited impact upon others will dote upon a star who impresses millions, or a rather frightened conformist might idolize a gay buccaneer. Such idealization is a counterpart to projection. In projective mechanisms the individual perceives

M

characteristics in others which he does *not want* to possess himself. He then takes up a stance of scorn or disgust towards them. In idealization he adores features in others which he *does want* for himself, and slips into a position of adoration towards the idol.

When idealization remains in this primitive form, it can often lead to a corrosive envy of the loved one. The individual is repeatedly being made aware that another person, the idol, possesses characteristics that he would like to have himself. This often occurs when love affairs turn sour. Another outcome is also possible. The lover may still idealize and want the characteristics of his loved one, but then sense that if he had them they would be antipathetic to himself as a whole person. When this occurs, the individual is glad of a partner with these ideal attributes, so that he can possess them at one remove.

Here is a simple example. The characteristic used is a part of the body, but it could apply to any part of bodily or mental functioning. A man may particularly idealize and dote upon his girl friend's delicate expressive hands. In one case it might be that he simply wants expressive hands like hers for himself. He may yearn to be a beautiful musician, but feels he could never be one because of lack of dexterity. In this case he will simply feel his own lack, and his loving idealization may turn to corrosive envy. In another case the young man might equally feel moved by his girl's delicate expressive hands. It might equally be that in *part of himself* he would like to have such delicate hands for himself. But the same time he is proud of his own heavy muscular hands, and delicate and heavy muscular hands just cannot go together in the same person. So as a *whole person* he does not want delicate hands. But he is very glad that he can 'possess' them at one remove in his loved one.

Likewise his girl might want, in part of herself, to have strong hands and yet be proud of her own delicate ones. She reciprocally will thus dote upon his strong hands, while being pleased by her lover's appreciation of hers. Both partners are happy. This is a trivial example, but the notion can be applied to many more complex characteristics.

The most fundamental attributes that are reciprocally appreciated by lovers are of course masculinity and femininity. Here we see men wanting to possess feminine characteristics, but feeling they are antipathetic to themselves as whole people, so are glad to enjoy them in a partner. Likewise with women. This is an everyday instance of the ancient Greek notion, mentioned earlier in the chapter, of each person seeking 'his other half'.

Reciprocal appreciation has enhancing functions. When an individual feels appreciated in what he does, he gains new courage and assurance. Likewise when he actively appreciates, his partner is enhanced. A benign process begins to form. Each partner is valued and enhanced, but because the other is doing the same in return, there is little question of a weight of debt or of corrosive envy.

Such intimate loving has probably not been felt since childhood with parents. We have already drawn attention to the repetition of the mother–child and father–child emotions in lovers. Feelings which have lain dormant for years emerge again. It would, however, be a gross over-simplification to say that reciprocal love is only just a repetition of early childhood experiences.

The situation in early infancy is one-sided. The child might contribute greatly to his parents, but is not sufficiently developed to recognize this fully. He is essentially small and dependent. He has to use his parents' capacity to know the world in order to survive. Lovers are more equal in their reciprocity. Like a child, a lover feels the enormous importance of his loved one, but unlike a child he is aware of the contribution he himself is making to the other. There thus grows that sense of 'I–thou', of 'we together', 'us' which although experienced by all good friends and colleagues, is felt at its most poignant and meaningful between lovers.

It is plain that there is a fundamental difference in *intimacy* (Erikson, 1953) between friendship and being in love. Lovers are essentially private, and reveal to each other not only their bodies but also their most privately held dreams and feelings, which in the ordinary course of life have to be kept safely hidden. Ordinary everyday relationships have a transience and superficiality which make it too painful or overwhelming to reveal the most intimate dreams and ideas. We can see from these considerations that a lover puts himself at considerable risk when he falls in love. Exposure of his 'crazy' loving emotions throws his old modes of guarded adaptation out of balance. If appreciation is not reciprocated he is left with a distressing inner chaos.

It is not only idealizing appreciation that the lover needs to support him in his revelations of himself. He demands also *sympathetic* appreciation. He yearns for his loved one to feel along with him, see things from his point of view. Lovers need to identify with each other. This can be heard when they say to each other such things as: 'Oh, you poor darling, how beastly of them.' 'That's wonderful for you, I am so glad,' or 'Now look after yourself.' In this way each person feels he is supported and encouraged by the concern of the other in his path through the cold, hard world. This is a togetherness, which, silly as it may seem to the cynical outsider, is what most of us yearn for in our hearts.

3. Being in love and adult identity

It has just been mentioned that in the state of being in love, characteristics are idealized when the individual misses them in himself. We noted that this could lead to corrosive envy except in so far as the individual is aware that the characteristics are anti-pathetic to the sense of himself as a whole. In this case he can enjoy them at one remove in his partner. The sense of self as a whole person was referred to in the last chapter as adult identity.

When an individual has formed a relatively stable organization within himself with a realistic awareness of his overall capacities, then he is in a position to admire his partner's characteristics, because he will know he does not want them for himself. But if an individual has not developed this *integrated* awareness of himself, he may fall idealistically in love, but then later become prey to overwhelming envy and humiliation. Lacking contentment in his own identity, he will be prone to idealize qualities which contrast with his incapacities, but then may realize that he wants them for himself. He may also find himself bitterly disappointed by his lover. Lacking an integrated and coherent sense of himself, he will have fallen in love with parts only of the other person. As time goes by, other parts are likely to emerge which are less adorable. And being immature and unintegrated in himself, he is unlikely to find these tolerable.

These considerations suggest that it is important for an individual to have developed a coherent sense of adult identity before committing himself to a life-long relationship based on being in love. It is, for instance, an argument against marriage in mid-adolescence. But we have also noted how variable people are in the phasing of their developments, so that it would be rash to be dogmatic on this question.

4. Courtship[1]

Falling in love is a far cry from two people knowing each other for what they really are and yet still loving. Courtship is the process

[1] For descriptions of courtship see Gorer, 1955.

whereby two people, who have found certain lovable characteristics in common test each other out and discover the realistic basis for affinity. It is a process which may have started before falling in love, and certainly continues long after marriage. The frequency of divorce and emotionally sterile marriages tells us that courtship is often incomplete.

Young couples in the privacy of tables in cafés, country lanes, back alleys, the backs of cars and bed-sitters do a lot of talking as well as love-making. In this each discovers the other's interests, likes, dislikes, and ways of doing and thinking. Most people want to feel that the other's general outlook on life is similar to their own. Without this underlying agreement about philosophy of life there can be little sense of togetherness through the later years of marriage. What is important in a person's underlying philosophy will depend upon the inner make-up of each person. For instance, for some couples differences in religion or political opinion will matter little, while for others the differences are irreconcilable. The philosophies that usually seem most important are those which deeply involve an individual's own sense of identity. Thus a person whose conception of himself rests upon a certain religious or political orientation is likely to need a lover who is broadly of the same mind. These are only two examples of underlying philosophy. Just as important for others may be such attitudes as the wish to have children, views on their upbringing, attachment to or independence from relatives, country living versus town living, or ambitions for intellectual activity, money, status and sociability.

It is around the discovery of divergences of attitude that lovers' quarrels may arise. Let us look at such quarrels in a little more detail. We have described the process of reciprocal love and indicated how one falls in love with characteristics that are internally important to the self. We have also suggested that these characteristics can only be parts of a whole personality. When a lover discovers attributes that are antipathetic to himself he often gets angry, demanding that the other should change to fit in with what he wants. The other feels this as a threat and a quarrel may ensue. For instance:

(i) Two lovers got on fine until the man realized that his girl friend had never invited him to her flat to cook him a meal. He was terrified that she did not like cooking, as this meant a great deal to him. He burst out with this one evening. She, being very unsure of her cooking ability, defended herself and remained adamant that such a thing didn't matter these days. After this all sorts of differences of philosophy arose, and within a few weeks they had parted.

(ii) With another couple, the beginning of the story was rather similar, but the ending was different. The girl confessed to being unable to cook, the man then rose to the challenge and said he would teach her all he knew. Soon she had outstripped him. Incidentally, they married, moved out into the country and opened a restaurant where husband was manager and father to their children, while wife was chef and mother!

This example gives us an indication of the function of lovers' quarrels. They are the grist of *reality-testing* about each other. When a part of the other person is discordant with an ideal, then anger ensues and there is a demand for the other to change. The value of the quarrel lies in its outcome. Some quarrels do initiate a change in the individual, as in the case of our second girl who couldn't cook. Quarrels may thus be creative.

Other quarrels do not initiate a change so much as acceptance of each other's characteristics. For instance, two lovers were very different in ideas about punctuality. A quarrel ensued where a lot of things were thrown about and smashed. It was appalling at the time, and no dramatic changes in behaviour came about in either partner. But they may have changed somewhat inside themselves. The man thought, 'Well, I am pretty punctilious and she isn't, but so what, it doesn't really matter.' Likewise, she thought something like this, 'He is insufferable about time, but I am pretty sloppy, and anyway it doesn't matter as much as I thought.' Other quarrels, of course, do not have these creative outcomes. Many couples get locked in sterile and repetitive attacks upon each other, neither side changing nor accepting the other.

Having an underlying sense of individual history and development helps us to understand, if only roughly, the particular vehemence of lovers' quarrels. The individual falls in love with attributes that have a deep inner significance to himself. Throughout his earlier years they remain inside him and emerge only as phantasy. Then, when he falls in love, these are realized in an actual relationship.

The characteristics which have such significance are often connected with childhood parents. For instance, a man loved his mother's vivacious feeling for people, but as he grew older he lost touch with her. He fell in love first with his girl friend's expressive face and then with her vivacious feelings about people, which quite consciously reminded him of his mother. Their lovers' quarrels often arose when he felt she was not being as thoughtful as his idealized mother.

Individuals may also be attracted to characteristics which are essentially unlike themselves or their parents. Thus a woman loathed her father's irascibility and fell in love with a man who seemed comfortable and easy-going. Here quarrels arose when the man was too soft. As well as this, we have already mentioned that people fall in love with characteristics which have no direct relation to their parents, but are rather concerned with attributes that they lack themselves. Thus a shy woman fell in love with a man who was, by and large, an easy-going extrovert. Quarrels arose then when he wanted to be sociable while she wanted him to herself.

It is perhaps an over-simplification to suggest that the shattering of phantasy is the only cause of lovers' or marital discord. We shall discuss this at greater length in the next chapter. We confine ourselves to it here because it epitomizes one of the fundamental functions of courtship, which is testing of reality. Each individual discovers what the other is really like and finds out whether he is still in love. In this testing, one discovers new things about the self and one's lover which are real and delightful, just as much as those which are painful. Courtship may be an exploration fully as exciting and frightening as any voyage of discovery. John Donne said this of his lover when he wrote of her, 'Oh, my America, my new found land.'

5. Lovers and their families

So far we have described lovers in privacy. This very private and personal finding of each other is the keystone of marriage today, with its emphasis on the intimate nuclear family. But both partners also come from families and usually look to them for support. Most people want to be allowed to be free to marry with their parents' good wishes behind them. They thus want their parents to like and accept their lover. People who marry against their parents' wishes often find it works well, but it is a strain, not only because of the conflict of loyalties but also because they cannot easily look to parents for help in later years.

Falling in love means a fundamental turning away from parents, and many people for their own or family reasons are unable to do this. The boy who is very comfortable with his mother is an old joke, but it happens often enough. So too is the girl who will not go out 'because mother wouldn't like it'. Others actually do fall in love but with someone who wants to join a family and is easily incorporated into the old structure. This comes very close to an extended family system.

Probably most couples see themselves as creating a new family with its own autonomy, related but not subservient to the parental family. In this case lovers have to go through a process of turning away from their parents, which psychologically involves at least a partial rejection of them, with anxiety arising as a consequence. This has to be lived through and accepted by both parents and children for easy separation to take place. It is a process which hardly has to be faced in an extended family social system (Harris, 1969. Bell and Vogel, 1968).

6. Engagement

When a couple feel they want to commit themselves to marriage for life, they usually get engaged. This custom is sometimes scorned as an archaic triviality. Such a view omits notice of some social and psychological functions in engagement. By being engaged, two people *make public* that they are a pair who are united. This is epitomized by the engagement ring, which is a useful badge. With it a woman indicates 'I am no longer on the market,' without going through the palaver of saying so. Any observer at parties will see how young men look at women's fingers as they talk to them.

By being publicly engaged, the young couple test out the new identity of themselves as a couple. Each one is no longer a single individual person to their friends. They are part of a new entity, a couple. This inevitably means they will be treated differently. They will lose some friends and gain others.

7. Weddings

Like engagement, the marriage ceremony is essentially a public act. It focuses in a short space of time upon a pattern of processes in the development of a married couple. These have probably been going on informally throughout courtship and engagement.

First of all, in the privacy of courtship the couple have been deciding whether to commit themselves to each other for life. Secondly, in engagement they have disengaged themselves from their parents and shown themselves as a couple to their friends. Their families have probably been attuning themselves at the same time. Thus a great many people are involved in a wedding. In the ceremony these people join together and put into the words of marriage vows what has been, and will be, going on psychologically within the individuals. This ceremony, whether in church or registry office, is not meaningless. It makes public in one place and at one time things which have been going on privately. It is, of course, a meaningless ritual if those inner private processes of commitment and acceptance have not been taking place.

14

BEING MARRIED

1. Some background considerations[1]
You will recall from the last chapter that the process of mutual
testing and discovery, called courtship, continues if all goes well
right through the marriage. Much of what was discussed then
applies to this chapter also.

We shall, of course, be thinking primarily of people who form
themselves into a nuclear family. To put this into perspective, let us
contrast it briefly with marriage into a hypothetical extended
family. When this occurs, the individual joins a new group of
people who have their own long-established ways. He knows
roughly what is expected. He must fit into the family's code of
behaviour if he is to be accepted. Thus his problem of social
adaptation is already defined. This may be a difficult task, but the
fact that it is present must give him a sense of security. The partner
who remains in the extended family can keep most of his or her old
habits grown from childhood. The individual forming a nuclear
family has little of this security from habits of established codes of
behaviour.

The extended family may be a situation which is claustrophobic
for the adventurousness at the core of individuals, and is fraught
with tension for one who finds it difficult to conform. It is also not
conducive to the development of new ways of living or techniques.
But it very rigidly provides a simplicity for those living in it. A
sense of security comes also from the knowledge that there is always
a network of relatives to rely upon. Responsibilities in work,
housing, caring for children, the old and ill are spread so that no one
individual need necessarily be overloaded.

The delight of a modern young couple setting out to start up a
new nuclear family lies in being free to mould their own fate un-

[1] For more discussion see the work of sociologists, e.g. Young and Willmott, 1957.
Gorer, 1955. J. Klein, 1965. Harris, 1969.

trammelled by the restrictions and codes of older generations. They are pioneers. But the couple must test out what to do in each new circumstance without any sure knowledge that it will turn out well. They are unlikely to have well-known family members around them to turn towards for help. Thus responsibilities of work, housing, caring for children and illness crowd in upon them. This becomes only too obvious when one gets to know parents with young children in Britain today. They may be proud of their achievements and fundamentally happy, but they are usually very tired, worried and overworked for years on end.

For the young married person, life is a long series of problems to solve. These are partly intellectual, like organizing housing, finances and the material things of a marriage. They are also emotional, for with each new situation the person has to develop new ways of relating to his partner, children and people around him. It is a tale of continuous development, and of reorganizing inner functions to respond to new situations. Thus the individual is burdened with responsibility and the guilt and anxiety that go with it. But, as we observed about the exploration and play of young children, human beings seem to take delight in seeking out problems to solve for themselves. It is this freedom to discover, develop and master problems which is the essence of being human.

When a partner's physical or mental functions break down, or if he fails to develop adequate new functions, then there are few people well known to the family to take over or help. In these circumstances, the State and its social and medical services are intended to be at hand to provide the assistance which in other places is largely given by members of the extended family.

While the State can provide services which an extended family cannot, particularly in medicine and education, it is inevitably impersonal and ponderous. When help is sought from a family member it is from someone who is known and hence largely trusted. But when help is sought from a State agency, the first communications are with people who are strangers, who have no knowledge of oneself as a person, and are hence mistrusted. The agency also has a dual responsibility, to the State and the individual, and these often conflict. Similarly, conflicts naturally arise in an extended family also. But such considerations make it plain at least that State aid is not necessarily simple.

2. *The married couple as a team*[1]

The integrity of a nuclear family rests upon the co-operative activity of husband and wife together. Its whole functioning is organized by the husband and wife solving problems together. In so far as they work together as a *team*, the various aspects of the family, work, housing, children remain integrated. The word team may have a sporting connotation, but it is very generally used to describe a group of individuals, men or women, who join together to solve a set of problems by their communal efforts rather than individually, to win a game, design a building, fight a battle, or restore a sick person to health. Husbands and wives solve problems and carry out tasks which have a very similar general form.

People who join together as a team form a unit which is recognized by others as a separate social entity. Team members relate to each other, at least as far as the task is concerned, in ways which are different from those of outsiders. They develop private languages, quick and intimate ways of communicating which both aid problem solving and give a sense of intimacy and togetherness. From the days of engagement onward, a husband and wife will have formed themselves into a team in a similar way. They will have been recognized as a unit together by others and, if all goes well, will both have experienced the pleasure of developing intimate, quick private communications together.

The experience of solving concrete problems together is the deepest delight of being married. The difference between a married team and others lies in the breadth and variety of problems tackled and in its long-lasting continuity. No others can match it in these qualities. We could list the problems tackled by the ordinary couple, and it would stretch a very long way. Here are just a few. Many are external to the couple as it were, like finding and organizing housing, decoration and furniture; working out finances, finding new friends, allocating work, reorganizing their contacts with relatives, bringing up children. Other problems are internal to the married couple, such as finding ways of quick easy communication, finding how to give each other sexual satisfaction, or how to change towards each other as they grow more experienced and older.

Since the integrity of a nuclear family rests upon the husband–wife team, then if this team gets split, the family breaks up as an autonomous unit. Clearly, married couples vary greatly in the things each member does alone or as a team with his partner. Each partner,

[1] Harris, 1969. Blanck and Blanck, 1968.

however happily married wants time to be alone. But when co-operation is required but does not occur, then there is trouble. A partner must turn to outside agencies for help. It is necessary here to make a differentiation. There are many problems which married couples cannot solve together, but for which they turn to outsiders for assistance. This happens when a doctor is called in to a sick child, when children are sent to school, or when a husband consults a friend about repairing a house. These are problems tackled by one partner and outsiders with the acceptance and encouragement of the other. The case is different when a pathological split occurs. Here one partner repeats a pattern of his own without the acceptance of the other. When this occurs, family functioning becomes dis-integrated, the individuals begin to live in worlds of their own and problems which require attention remain in the air. It is often in such circumstances of splitting between husband and wife that social agencies are called in. Not all split marriages demand such assistance of course, but it is likely that many so-called 'problem families' originate in this.

In recognizing the team nature of a married couple we can perhaps see why being in love is an important criterion for a nuclear marriage. With the nuclear family, the married couple must, if all is to go well, work together as an intimate team with their own private and rapid means of communication and understanding. They must do this over a wide variety of problems involving both material and personal matters. Furthermore, they must have the commitment to go on together for a very long time. The mutual enhancement arising out of the reciprocal appreciation of being in love provides the background for these team tasks. Obedience to a family's dictates may give sufficient impetus to make a marriage when an extended family forms the team, but not when a couple are out on their own.

If we are correct in this argument about marriage, we might in passing generalize to team situations outside marriage. These teams working together also seem to function best through reciprocal appreciation between their members. The involvement of the individuals is of course not so widespread or sexualized as with a married couple, but appreciation within the limits of the tasks in hand is important. It has been said that the only sane bosses and members of staff are those who can realistically appreciate others. This is perhaps forgotten by those who can think in terms of efficient organization and nothing else.

Our understanding of reciprocal appreciation in institutions outside marriage can perhaps be used in another way as well. The melting away of male dominance, which we have noted historically as occurring within marriage, has not taken place at the same pace in many other work situations. Here men and women still often behave according to stereotyped masculine and feminine role play. Such compulsive games must shrivel the capacities of both sexes. Yet women are taking up careers and working with men at an increasing pace. The individuals in mixed working teams will then have to divest themselves of stereotyped sexual role play and appreciate each other personally in ways that must similarly occur in marriage.

3. Individual gratification in being married [1]

We have so far stressed the value of teamwork in the married couple's solution of problems. This alone is hardly continuous and gratifying enough to keep two people together for the main part of their lives. We are after all fundamentally selfish animals. What deeply gratifying experiences can marriage provide that other more transient relationships do not?

Consideration of being in love answers some of these questions. The individual can feel valued above all others by someone else. This stimulates his functioning, just as a baby is enhanced by being loved. What is more, by reciprocating this he is not overburdened with guilt. There is also being cared for and watched over by the equivalent of a watchful parent who alleviates anxiety.

As a husband and wife get to know each other over the years they can, if all goes well, take things for granted in each other. A set of assumptions and shorthand communications grow up between couples. The individual can come to feel he has someone he can fundamentally *trust* in a world where he is faced with bafflement, anxiety and uncertainty. It seems that many people look for trustworthiness and sympathy as the prime values in a spouse over and above all others (Gorer, 1955). This sense of needing a trustworthy person was described in the infant. As far as these primitive yearnings are concerned, time and age count for little, for the adult still feels them. We still are (if only unconsciously) babies at heart. At the same time as husbands 'mother' their wives, so wives mother their husbands. In being married, there is an underlying integration of these primitive functions which is finely balanced.

[1] See Blanck and Blanck, 1968.

Similar primitive or babyish levels of functioning come to the fore in any team process. When the individual becomes a team member, his sense of separate identity is lost to a certain degree. A person is not just 'I' but 'We'. In a work or sports team this loss is usually transient and easily controlled. It is deeper in marriage. Married couples are recognized as one by others and by themselves in many areas of functioning. This sense of fusion can easily be recalled when a married person is unsure whether he or his spouse said something, or which of them came to a decision or who did this or that part of a task. It is also experienced in illness. One partner falls ill and the other one may then feel ill quite automatically, even though he is not. The bodily feeling of fusion experienced in sexual orgasm is another example. Here again we hark back to some of the experiences which probably occur in the young infant before he has differentiated between himself and his mother.

As primitive emotional patterns come to the fore in marriage, so we would expect disturbances between husband and wife to be also of a primitive kind. Much quarrelling seems to be concerned with the individual's attempt to assert his sense of separate identity from marital fusion. By quarrelling, each individual asserts what he thinks or wants. For instance, phrases like these are common enough: 'You never give me a chance to say what I want.' 'You really think I am just an appendage, don't you?' 'You never bother to think what I might want.' Marital rows occur with such vehemence, the self-assertions are so forceful, even panic-stricken, that one is drawn to the conclusion that the individual is actively struggling against an inner urge of his own against independence of thought. This would be a drive to experience fusion which is common in groups, teams or marriages. Sometimes fusion reaches crazy proportions, where each individual is quite unsure what are his own feelings or ideas and what are his partner's. For some couples this becomes chronic and intolerable in its fruitlessness.

Perhaps in relaxed marriages a flexibility occurs between losing the self in partnership and separating out as an individual. It is probably difficult to do this on all occasions, and quarrels are then likely to take place. Rows can thus have a positive function, they are part of the partners' struggle to experience themselves as separate people (Dicks, 1967).

4. *Making love*[1]

Sexual intercourse is the physical unspoken epitome of marriage. Here can occur in the language of body expression all the functions we have alluded to already, reciprocal appreciation, caring, trusting, fusion, separateness and teamwork. It is also animal. The male uses the female as the vehicle of his lust and vice versa. At its most satisfactory it is selfish, yet in so far as both partners are satisfied no one is the worse for it.

Innate biological mechanisms are involved in sexual intercourse. But learning is required to find optimal patterns of gratification for both partners. Many couples seem to think that sexual pleasure should come without any effort, but as with all other complex functions, learning and exploration seem to be necessary. This learning can have the romance of an exploration. But probably all people find themselves at times in difficulties of shyness, disgust, lethargy or unresponsiveness.

Even though intercourse is biologically primitive and 'animal' it is none the less controlled by a highly complex web of feelings. This will have grown within the individual over the years since infancy, as well as having been aroused by the specific character-istics of a partner. Often such feeling patterns are quite unconscious and beyond active control. These considerations suggest that sexual difficulties can be multi-determined. The partners may be omitting some simple mechanical methods of stimulation. On the other hand they may be in the throes of a web of unconscious feelings beyond personal control. Only an understanding of each individual's predicament can cast light on this.

It would be a mistake to think that intercourse is simply a release of sexual tension. We have just described it as a bodily conversation, and as such it may perform many functions at once. Couples not only express their delight in each other by it, they also make up quarrels, use it as a playful battle, or soothe hurt feelings and stave off boredom.

One such function seems to be the relief of anxiety. Some people want to make love very frequently when they are anxious, and lose interest when not. In a general way this often occurs in wartime, when by rational standards a procreation of children would be greatly reduced. Yet it is not. For instance, many babies were born during the siege of Leningrad in 1942 when the population was starving. Areas prone to famine today also tend to have high birth-

[1] Masters and Johnson, 1966. Brecher, 1966. Blanck and Blanck, 1968.

rates. A similar example is where people are seriously ill but not incapacitated. Tubercular patients often are noted, perhaps unfairly, for their sexual hunger. It may be that in the face of death we reassert our biological urge to reproduce.

We have been stressing that love-making, at its most enjoyable, is a coalescence of physical activity with appreciation of human beings. Recent interest in sexual intercourse seems sometimes to overemphasize the mechanics of stimulation to the detriment of personal loving. For instance, many people obsess themselves about the quality and frequency of their orgasms. In this 'cult of the orgasm' a climax is seen as the only ideal to aim for so that failure brings waves of remorse. Loving tends to become a branch of athletics, which seems to be a limited point of view.

5. Dominance skew[1]

At times in every marriage, one partner is likely to become dominant and the other submissive or obedient. When both are going about a task where one partner has greater skill or knowledge, this is likely to be benign and by mutual consent. It may well be that when another task arises the partners will reverse their roles. In such instances there is a distribution of responsibility.

However, in some marriages it is evident that the wishes of one take precedence over the other repetitively without regard to skill and knowledge. Here, there would be a *skew* in dominance and submission. We allude to this in ordinary speech when we say such things as 'she wears the trousers', 'he is a brute', 'he is henpecked', 'she is a mouse', or 'he is a martinet'. In such instances we usually sympathize with the underdog, feeling that he is being unfairly used. At the same time, however, it is often noticeable that a sort of unconscious collusion may take place between the partners. The underdog may be quite unwilling to change the pattern, for being in this position has advantages. He can be gratified by a sense of virtuous martyrdom, and is absolved by it from guilt. Such patterns have the attributes of role play (Berne, 1964), discussed in chapter 12.

Skew in dominance is often seen as being related to social conventions. For instance, in Western culture the male has been politically dominant throughout known history, and we might expect the same to occur in the intimacy of marriage. But social forms should not be confused with the intimate relations inside a family. For

[1] Mead, 1950. Lidz, 1963.

N

instance, the social form of Judaism has been markedly patriarchal. Yet every Jewish boy or girl will tell you of the underlying power and authority of many Jewish Mamas. Likewise medieval England was politically dominated by men, but our knowledge of family life then shows that husbands were often ruled by their wives, even though the latter were legally mere chattels. My own memories of my grandparents' generation, who were Victorians and paid lip-service to male dominance, are that the males and females were variously dominant according to their individual characters. Certainly today the personal characteristics of the partners seems to determine skew just as much as social conventions.

6. Gender skew[1]

Stress has been laid repeatedly earlier in this book upon the difference between male and female in body shape and pattern of arousal. These patterns of sexual responsiveness tend to be displaced to ideas about other functions as well. Thus the male is sometimes regarded as generally more thrusting and the female more receptive. At primitive levels of body action and feeling, this is likely to be so. However, non-sexual functions are often stereotyped in a sexual way. Dichotomizing between male and female roles takes place where there is no justification for it. For instance, such thinking often occurs about driving cars. Driving is thrustful, and men certainly enjoy playing the fast car game, just as little boys do. This spreads to the idea that women cannot drive properly, which in turn leads some women to pretend to be scatterbrained about driving in order to 'be feminine'. There may be differences between males and females in the phantasies enjoyed when driving. But there is no evidence that men are naturally better drivers than women. If anything, accident records suggest the opposite.

Nursing a baby is sometimes stereotyped as 'women's work', so that some men will not be seen with a pram. Deviations from these social stereotypes arouse anxiety, and so people tend to conform. But if this is cast aside, individuals can be very flexible in everyday functioning. Women are driving cars quite happily by the million, and equally fathers push prams without feeling any the less male.

However, the inner feeling of being male or female is important not only in making love but also to the underlying sense of self generally. The sense of gender can get skewed in marriage. For instance:

[1] Lidz, 1963.

A very tomboyish woman married a soft pliant man. They enjoyed work together, for their professions were the same. Sexually they found satisfaction only when the wife lay on top of her husband. All went well until she had a baby. She felt unable to know what to do. The husband was much better at it. They began to fight over the rearing of the child until one day the wife burst out, 'Oh, for God's sake let me go to work and you stay at home and look after it.'

Here each partner's *phantasy* of being of the opposite sex had solidified and come to dominate their relationship so that undistorted feelings associated with physical arousal could not be fully enjoyed.

Such reversal of roles and gender skew probably become crucial only fairly rarely. But most people, if they are honest, will recall anxiety about it. Being a problem that is fraught with feeling yet hard to put into words, it is a frequent source of distress.

7. Some functions in satisfactory and unsatisfactory marriages[1]

We have already noted how marriage involves a loosening of self-boundaries and that some change of identity is inevitable in the formation of a team. We have also alluded to problems of sexual identity and functioning that may arise. Both these involve primitive, emotionally charged levels of functioning, and hence evoke violent feelings when something is felt to be wrong.

We now come to the question of what are the important functions in married couples who gain harmony together, as compared with marriages which break down. We cannot hope to unravel this question satisfactorily, but will consider one or two points to exercise ourselves upon the subject.

Here are some brief descriptions of married couples. The first four were on the point of breakdown, the second three generally felt to be contented. We can scan these and abstract salient features.

(i) *Mr and Mrs A.* The report says:
   I have never seen any show of love on either side, there was no kiss good-bye or welcome in the evenings. They seemed to have nothing in common, and therefore no subject to discuss jointly. His work and hobbies were his only topic of conversation. These bored his wife, and she spent more and more time with her mother, who came to live with them.

[1] See Blanck and Blanck, 1968. Dicks, 1967.

There were rows over Mrs A.'s mother. He resented her interference but, instead of telling his mother-in-law to mind her own business, told his wife to speak to her. Naturally she didn't or couldn't, and there were more rows. So the family split, he went his way, she went hers. Eventually the grandmother died and the children left home but Mr and Mrs A. stayed the same. They considered living apart, but decided that this would not be possible economically.

(ii) *Mr and Mrs B.*
One day Mr B. outlined his reasons for seeming so depressed. He talked for several hours saying, 'I can't talk to her and she doesn't seem to understand.' On another occasion Mrs B. gave a long account of the hours spent locked in the bathroom crying into a towel. I asked why she need hide her feelings and she said, 'I wouldn't let him see me so upset.'

They never used words of endearment and Mrs B. said they all ended on the wedding day. Her husband is charming to women. In company he would say to his wife, 'Why can't you look like that?' This might have gratified the other woman but hurt his wife terribly. Finally, Mrs B. started an affair with a neighbour, her husband wouldn't believe it even though everyone else knew what was happening. They have separated now.

(iii) *Mr and Mrs C.*
Mr C. was a lecturer at a college and gave a lot of time to the drama society. His wife felt left out and neglected, but being very pretty she soon attracted other men, but he spent more and more time in rehearsals. The climax came when she slapped him on the stage one evening in front of all the students. Her parents encouraged her to leave him and return home to them. She did this and was soon having an affair with another man.

(iv) *Mr and Mrs D.*
Mr and Mrs D. are pleasant to other people. But when you talk to them you are conscious of undercurrents between them. They quarrel openly. Mr D.'s mother is often the cause. She is very rude, but he takes her side in arguments with his wife.

Mr D. says he does not believe it necessary to feel anything for a person to marry them. All he wants, he says, is someone to cook his food. Mrs D. wants to go back to her own mother. She says she could murder her mother-in-law, but still adores her husband.

(v) *Mr and Mrs X.*

Mrs X. is a driving sort of person and her husband much quieter. But if she wears the trousers it is because Mr X. is content to let her do so, and she enjoys it. They have endured considerable hardship together, especially when he was out of work. But this seems to have made them more united. Now in middle age they still show all the outward signs of being in love. They say that they have few major quarrels and most decisions are reached amicably. One suspects that she makes most of these while he acquiesces, but when there is something about which he feels particularly strongly she would not attempt to argue.

The whole family is doted upon by both sets of in-laws. They have helped them out financially in the past, but do not seem to intrude.

(vi) *Mr and Mrs Y.*

In many ways husband and wife are very different. Her liveliness can at times be overwhelming. He is quieter and seems to find her liveliness attractive. His quietness seems to counteract her boisterous nature in a way that is comfortable. They often have different opinions and argue but one senses a tolerance and respect for each other's views.

They say they hardly ever have a row. When they are on the point of one they say they go to each other and swallow their pride until the bad feeling subsides.

He is interested in her clothes and ideas, he likes to talk about his work. Both are rather eccentric and vague, but in different ways, so that between them they get things done efficiently. They are both loyal to each other in every sense of the word.

(vii) *Mr and Mrs Z.*

Mrs Z. is gay, dramatic and untidy. Her husband is critical and can be rude; he is something of a snob. One might not think they would mix well, but they seem to have an inner respect for each other. They appear to me as a couple and not as two individuals trying to keep their own side up.

When he is insulting or flies off the handle, she will stand up for herself and tell him he is wrong if she thinks he is. Rows do not seem to last; perhaps they just have a sense of proportion. Mrs Z. says that he upsets her at times, 'Sometimes I could throw him down the drain, I don't know why he says the things he does, but then there must be things about me he hates. I know I wouldn't really change him.'

If we consider Mr and Mrs A., B., C. and D. we detect an underlying dichotomy or *splitting* of feeling occurring within the individuals concerned. Each tends to see the other in black and white terms. Each openly hates the other. All appreciation has gone, so they are gripped by feeling their partner is just bad to them. They see themselves on the other hand as poor sufferers struggling to keep their end up. Faults are reeled off, resentments of long ago unearthed and chewed over inexorably. Primitive paranoid mechanisms predominate in the partners' feelings about each other. This, however, does not necessarily extend to other people outside the marriage. They do not manifest themselves as generally paranoid characters, but are enmeshed in these feelings only in the intimate partnership.

Regression to primitive modes of functioning occurs. We have noted that this can happen to anyone on all sorts of different occasions. But various factors conspire in marriage to encourage such tendencies. There is its intimacy, its dependence, the loosening of taboos on eroticism and the loss of boundaries in becoming a team. This re-emergence of primitive mechanism has its values as one can be full-blooded, show all of oneself and lapse into that state of disintegration which seems necessary to deep changes in modes of functioning (see chapter 2 on pregnancy). But it also means that violent splitting into loving and hating can occur.

It is also noticeable that the partners' parents were often intrusive with the A., B., C. and D.'s, but not the X., Y. and Z.s. For whatever reasons, the former do not seem to have dissolved their childhood ties to their parents and have been unable to form autonomous adult identities to take to their marriages. Parents often play a part in the splitting processes which occur in marriage. One partner turns back to his parent to be all 'good' while the other is rejected as bad. It is plain that parents often actively connive in this.

Turning now to the X., Y. and Z.s, we see that splitting into good and bad has not solidified into a way of life. This does not mean that hatred is never experienced. To quote Mrs Z. 'Sometimes I could throw him down the drain, but then there must be things about me he hates. I know I wouldn't change him.' Here anger emerges, but close after it comes *depressive concern* ('There must be things about me he hates.'). This is followed by appreciation. The splitting has not taken hold, but rather an integration of feelings and ideas creates perspective and sense of proportion. This has succinctly been described as 'containing hatred in a framework of love' (Dicks, 1967).

It must remain an open question why benign processes such as these occur in some marriages and not in others. Certainly individuals bring propensities from their childhood. But just as important must be each person's choice of partner and their intermingling of feelings as they go through life. Those who strike a note of appreciation and protective sympathy for each other, develop an underlying *respect* which is emphasized in Mr and Mrs X., Y. and Z. When this key is not found, couples tend to retire hurt, bitter and disillusioned, and paranoid splitting becomes entrenched.

15

MOTHERING

We have now come full circle. Our study began with the family in pregnancy, where we now return. Early chapters traced the complexities of infancy and childhood as the individual grew older. We shall now look at a similar period from the mother's point of view. She is still carrying her childhood experiences within her but now, in a different environment, she is faced with the task herself of bringing up the next generation. Since many facets of mothering were discussed in early chapters, we shall only summarize here.

1. Background[1]

Just as in sexual arousal, there must be innate physiological patterns at the heart of reproduction and mothering. Producing young is too universal in the animal kingdom for us to think otherwise. However, prior learnt experiences profoundly affect the capacity to rear both in animals and humans.

Throughout mankind, early learning experiences vary from one culture to another, so that later maternal propensities vary likewise. What is more, variable social expectations about mothering give rise to marked differences in the responsibility and stress placed upon young women.

In societies with a rural economy and little technology, it would be likely that high fertility is balanced by infant mortality. This certainly occurred in Britain until a century or so ago, when illness and death lay everywhere and each child could hardly expect to live until old age. People then tended to be fatalistic, that both birth and death lay not in man's hands but in those of the gods.

Rural living and extended families also meant that the upbringing of children could be spread in space. Children could wander where they wanted and there would be homes of relatives near by. The

[1] See sociological work, e.g. Young and Willmott, 1957. Gorer, 1955. Harris, 1969. J. Klein, 1965. Gavron, 1966.

responsibilities of child care could be spread amongst the family. A mother was prone to be worn out by repeated pregnancies and likely to die, but neither physical conditions nor social expectations were as conducive to the intense personal responsibility which weighs heavily on parents today.

In urban communities mothers and children are hemmed in by lethal motor traffic even if they are not cooped up in high flats. In such conditions children can easily become under-stimulated, bored and restless. Mothers are under continued stress to make provision against these. Being isolated from extended family members means freedom from interference, but throws mothers upon their own resources. Under these circumstances they are often strained by the knowledge that they have only a few hours in which to relax or be ill, for there may be no one else to help (Gavron, 1966).

Medical knowledge, increasing life expectancy, means that mothers can throw themselves into the joy of bringing up their children relatively free from the fear of premature death. But it also means a likelihood of greater guilt than previously if anything goes wrong. Increased understanding of child health and development has probably produced a happier and more vigorous generation of children then ever before. But this greater knowledge implies strict criteria of good care, so that mothers can continuously be under stress of failure, real or imagined. Our greater knowledge has meant enhanced control over the fate of our children, and hence a more intense awareness of parental responsibility.

Perhaps the predicament of parenthood is epitomized by birth-control itself. This gives freedom to choose when and if to have a child. At the same time it means that a parent has to bear the anxiety and guilt of creating another life upon this crowded planet.

2. Phantasy and reality in having a child[1]

If the reader turns back to chapter 2 he will recall the *primary maternal preoccupation* of a mother in pregnancy and infancy. Here the organization of old modes of functioning and defences are loosened so that a woman becomes rather vague and withdrawn. The baby inside the womb tends to become the focus of a play of vivid phantasy and feeling (Winnicott, 1958, 1964, 1965 *a*). For instance, a mother is prone to dream of things for her child that she herself has missed, or to dread that her own bad experiences and unwanted characteristics will re-emerge in the new life. As the baby

[1] Deutsch, 1944. Winnicott, 1964.

is inside and part of her it tends to become part of her own inner world of affect-laden imagery. At the same time the infant is a new creation, an entity of his own who is not just a phantasy in the mind of his mother. These two, phantasy and reality, are in continuous interplay in the mind not only before birth but long into later life also.

The closeness of a baby to his mother's inner world of feeling and phantasy means that her exchange with him is usually warm, deeply emotional and colourful. But it also means that she must be continuously, if subconsciously, testing her phantasy out against the baby as he really presents himself before her eyes. For instance, a mother may at a glance catch a glimmer of resemblance between him and her own father. He may then be endowed with a web of feelings that rise up in her from ideas about her father. But next the baby turns his head and looks like her mother-in-law, and this arouses its own particular imagery. Then the child laughs in his own special way, and with his sensuous wriggling too impresses himself upon his mother as a conscious living person in his own right. The mother's phantasies may well emerge again but now altered slightly by her realistic perceptions, so that coherent representation of her baby slowly integrates itself. This will, as it were, be from a web of real perceptions interwoven with phantasy.

Such a close investment between the inner and outer world means a delicate balance between the two which is readily thrown into disorder. Thus maternal breakdown in infancy is not uncommon (Lomas, 1967. Deutsch, 1945). Sometimes this takes the form of a gross breakdown in differentiating inner phantasy from external reality as in a *puerperal psychosis*. Of more frequent occurrence are puerperal depressions. Here unlike psychosis a mother usually experiences a flatness because she cannot endow her child with enough phantasy from her inner world. Transient states of anxiety and uncertainty assail most mothers, with their first child at least.

Some mothers do not break down in their functioning, but unself-consciously turn their children into the playthings of their phantasy in a chronic way, so that it becomes a life-style. Here are a couple of examples:

(i) A woman, whose own mother had become pregnant two months after she herself was born, produced several children and tried to keep them as babies as long as she could. She seemed, through them, to be trying to have the gratification of a long babyhood which she had herself missed.

(ii) Two parents lost their five children in a fire. They then had five more children, who turned out to be of the same sex as the first. The children were given the same names as those who had died. When the fifth was born the whole family with great rejoicing emigrated to a commonwealth country, just as the parents had planned to do just before the disastrous fire of years previously.

The reader will remember other instances of parental phantasy intruding upon their children's lives given in earlier chapters. The psychiatric literature is full of other instances (e.g. Laing, 1964. Goldberg, 1958. Haley, 1968. Lidz, 1968. Bell and Vogel, 1968). It must be stressed, however, that this is not just a question for psychiatrists. In some measure every child is 'the sport of his mad mother'. It is part of the fate of being the child of one's parents. But, where a mother continues to match her phantasy with an awareness that her child is a real separate person with problems and life of his own, then the experience is rich and colourful for both.

3. Multiple responsibility in mothering[1]
The business of mothering is a continuous *to and fro* between mother and child. Her life is acting and reacting from dawn to dusk, so that both she and her child are enjoying each other yet self-willed, tired and angry. When a mother loses this responsiveness, then the child is *left alone*. Children are glad of this in small doses, but if prolonged it becomes unbearable. We noted in earlier chapters that this loneliness can occur even when a mother is physically present if she is unresponsive to a child's interests or troubles. As a child grows older the areas of activity where this 'to and fro' is required become wide and various.

Perhaps the most common stereotyped idea of a mother is cuddling and nursing a young baby. This may seem too trivial an over-simplification even to mention. But many girls are so enthralled by this idea that they envisage little else. When their children are no longer babies, they may find themselves at a loss and become lethargic, bored and depressed. The children for their part are then left understimulated, drifting about lonely and disillusioned.

[1] Gavron, 1966.

Fathers also tend to limit their ideas to this phantasy of infancy. Being unable to envisage other responsibilities for a mother they irritably dismiss their wives' work as trivial. Years after their infancy, many young people complain bitterly that their mothers could only see them as babies and not as they really were. It seems to be endemic as a source of family friction.

One mother epitomized the essential quality of mothering as *multiplicity*. If we cast our minds back to the ten chapters from infancy to adolescence, we shall recall how complex the patterning of activities was in those years. A mother is called upon to watch over all these and respond to them as her conscience dictates. This is the responsibility of mothering.

4. Changing responsibility with the growth of children[1]
As a child grows up, a mother is called upon to *develop his responsiveness* to match. This entails a continuously new intellectual learning and articulation of patterns of feeling. Let us recapitulate some of the salient features of earlier chapters to clarify this.

The first months of life see a mother preoccupied with attuning her body to the physical presence of a new living being. Later in the first year a child is beginning to recognize his mother, and wants to discover his and her boundaries by playing with her. With the second year he is mobile, and a mother finds her will clashing with his. Personal and social discipline begins to become a crucial issue.

As childhood progresses the young person begins to talk and explore. When a mother has time and inclination, she can spend hours in friendly investigation and explanation which is deeply satisfying to both. If she has neither, they can both lapse into irritated boredom.

By the age of three or so the child will probably be seeking out other children. This means a mother must broaden herself to befriend other mothers and be liked and trusted by their children. For this to happen she has to extend her frame of reference and modes of thought in order to be able to talk to several children at once. The breadth of response must be even wider if a mother has several children of her own of different ages. It is only necessary to be at tea with say half a dozen children of different ages to see how exhausting this can be. All in the space of a few minutes a mother shifts from the conceptual questions of a five-year-old, to understanding a word just invented by a child of two, then to adjudicating

[1] Deutsch, 1947.

in a dispute between a couple of three-year-olds, while at the same time watching for empty plates, cups about to drop to the floor and whether the kettle is boiling.

Coming out of infancy, the child becomes a sexual person. This arouses feelings in response from a mother. These are often dim and little talked about. But most mothers are privately aware of sexual feelings towards their children, and discipline themselves to cope. For instance, mothers often find that they have no trouble over cuddling and kissing their children of both sexes alike until they are three years old or so. They then find themselves being slightly disgusted by too many caresses from their daughters while still enjoying the kisses from their sons. Both sexes want these caresses, and the daughters will get hurt if they are rebuffed while brothers are favoured. One mother, equally fond of all her children, said she finds herself rather guiltily cuddling her son in secrecy when her daughters are in another room.

With school age comes the question of following intellectual progress and finding a working relationship with teachers. Soon after this the child tends to turn towards the private company of his friends. There begins the long process of losing intimacy with a child as he proceeds into puberty. In adolescence all a mother's old ways of doing things are likely to be called into question. It becomes a day of judgement, as it were, for her years of motherhood, so that she is fraught with worries about her failures.

In so far as a mother has kept in touch with her child, recognizing his independent existence however much she may muddle along the way, both of them will probably have found life profoundly worth while. The one-sided parent–child relationship may recede, but the friendship begun years before, in the cuddling and chatter of infancy is likely to remain.

5. Mother and father together[1]

So far we have described a mother's direct relationship with her children. But we have stressed, particularly in chapters 3 and 4 how a child watches and attempts to integrate ideas about his parents together. A child who experiences serious conflicts and splits between two parents can feel very disturbed indeed. Since his external parents are discordant, not only does he fear for his security, but also that his internal parental representations will not 'marry' or function together as an integrated system within him.

[1] Blanck and Blanck, 1968.

Some parents are so sensitive to this that they vow never to disagree in front of the children. This may save acutely embarrassing situations, but children are particularly sensitive to parental moods, and are prone to weave solitary phantasies about them even if nothing is openly said. It is likely that children are always dimly aware of the psychological reality of their parents together, even though they cannot articulate their ideas. For their part, parents must of necessity develop their own personal modes of discussion and interplay that will primarily suit themselves. This was discussed in the last chapter. But these activities are part of the environment a parent presents to children, and are just as much part of being a mother as is breast-feeding or changing a nappy.

6. Mothering and going to work[1]

In times of limited technology and short life expectancy, a young woman could look forward to the rest of her life being consumed by nursing children and domestic economy. Each mother had to exercise a great deal of intelligence and ingenuity to organize food gathering, storage, cooking, long journeys on foot to buy clothing and hours of thought and labour in repairs and dressmaking.

Technology has not only given many women more time to enjoy the company of children, but they can also look forward to many years after their children are no longer a full-time occupation. Thus motherhood is becoming a phase in a woman's life rather than its culmination. This is beginning to be recognized by some education-ists, so that at least a few girls are growing up thinking of future satisfaction in work and careers as well as marriage and mothering.

The present time is transitional with regard to this attitude to work and family. Habits of mind appropriate to pre-technological days coexist and clash with more recent ideals. Thus a woman only in her late thirties said, 'When I got married fifteen years ago I remember thinking that this was it for life. Well here I am now, still married with children grown-up, back sitting in a classroom again starting out on something else.'

When young women have found an identity for themselves through their work life, but also gone on to marry and have children, they often find themselves in two minds over loyalty to their children and the wish to return to work. This is compounded by the dullness of living in a block of flats or new housing estate which is often isolated and lonely, with little opportunity for

[1] Gavron, 1966. J. Klein, 1965.

adventure. Added to this, mothering carries little esteem in many people's eyes. For instance, when asked at a party what she does, a woman may be quite proud to say 'I'm a nurse' or 'I'm a computer programmer', but will feel that 'I'm just a housewife' will sound dull and uninteresting to a listener.

Some women are doubtless engrossed in the satisfactions of their work and will get back to it at the earliest opportunity, farming their children out on *au pair* girls or nurseries. Being successful at work they are usually very articulate, and can rationalize away their guilt about this. They can make their friends who stay at home feel inferior and ashamed of enjoying being a mother. Such splitting of investment is needless to say not necessarily happy either for child or mother.

On the other hand, mothers who throw all of their lives into their families find themselves bored and depressed when their children have gone to school, if they have not begun to search for new satisfactions. They may become prone to cling to their children and infantalize them in consequence.

Each woman will attempt to find the balance of mothering and outside interest that best suits herself. Probably most mothers like to immerse themselves to the full in their children while they are under school age. This is when they are needed most and can stretch the most intelligent of mothers. After this, mothers may have time to turn their zest and creativity to other things.

It is perhaps one of the final responsibilities of mothering, to turn interest away from their children as they grow older. The young are not then burdened with the fruitless task of pretending to be infants for their mother's sake as they grow into adulthood.

16

BEING A FATHER

1. Background[1]

Just as for women, so for men modern technology has begun to transform the social expectations about their function in the family. Whereas industrialization, urban living, education, and greater life-expectancy have extended women's freedom of choice, these have probably conspired together to undermine old illusions of male superiority.

As a consequence of this, there is perhaps an underlying unsureness about male functioning which is particularly reflected in doubt about fathering. There is little documented evidence to support such a contention, but when one mentions this unsureness to fathers there is often a flash of recognition in reply. For instance:

(i) I think we men fall over backwards to avoid being authoritarian like our fathers, but when we try to be democratic and discuss things, our wives complain that we are being soft.

(ii) My grandfather was certain of himself in his narrow confines. But my father had the whole of his world crash about him when he was a young man in the first world war. I don't think he has ever got over it. The only thing he can talk about with pride is the war. I am a bit luckier, but I do wonder where we go from here.

Sometimes one comes across men who seem to have no such doubts, but they often simply reiterate a blind faith in the old patriarchal ways. 'My old man knew how to manage things, and if I do half as well I won't do badly.' A similar question posed to mothers tends to get a different sort of reply. They may grumble that men don't appreciate them or express personal doubts about

[1] See sociological work, e.g. Harris, 1969. J. Klein, 1965. Mead, 1950. Gorer, 1955.

how well they are doing. But they do not seem to feel unsure about the value of mothering in general.

This is perhaps reflected in recent psychological literature. The first decades of this century were full of discussions, particularly by Freud, of childhood ideas about fathers and their importance in the growth and pathology of the individual. In the past forty years the pendulum has swung back to interest on mothering. Very few writers have thought it necessary to consider fatherhood and the problems it poses for the individual, as a central issue. The work that has been done on this often stresses the point made here, that there is uncertainty about fatherly identity (e.g. Erikson, 1950). Incidentally, I know of no recent British work on the subject. This might be because it is not thought an issue worth consideration, or because it has not yet received recognition.

Modern knowledge has perhaps exposed the illusions of male dominance which have pervaded life and thought for centuries. At the same time, the social pattern of patriarchism is hardly viable for the nuclear family in a mobile industrial society. Such a family requires the co-operative use of independent intelligence by both husband and wife. Yet democracy in the family is perhaps not firmly established, so that men are unsure of themselves.

2. The biological circumstances of a family

For a period during her life a mother alone cannot both bear and rear her children and earn enough money to support herself and them. Women can perhaps do this until the last months of pregnancy, and go back to more or less full-time work when children reach school age. But during the intervening years they must be supported. If a mother has, say, three children spaced two years apart, this means that for ten years she must be dependent upon others. Either another individual or an institution must finance her, or she must look to others to care for her children while she works. If a woman is dependent upon an institutional structure, neither she nor her children are likely to reap the benefit of quick and easy communication which, as we mentioned, grows in the intimacy of marriage. So, in general, if mothers want to enjoy being full-time mothers, they need working men to provide for them.

Thus during the early child-rearing years of a nuclear family, the man still 'stands at the door of the cave' just as has been expected of him through the ages. The period during which his breadwinning functions are crucial has been reduced. But the burden of a father's responsibility rests more heavily if anything than in times past, when he could count on more extended family support. Let us glance at the various directions of paternal responsibility.

3. Inner phantasy and responsibility

Like any individual, a father naturally carries his own personal system of active urges and phantasies within him. These will have their primitive roots in childhood and be the heart of his being. They will be expressed in his passions, ambitions and idiosyncrasies. When they are thwarted he will become evil tempered, depressed or anxious. He will find satisfaction for them in his work, hobbies and in the flow of life with his family. The very fact of being a responsible father is deeply satisfying to most men, since it carries a sense of creativeness and fruition together with enjoyment of strength and power that goes with any responsibility. It has been stressed before that without satisfaction of many of these idiosyncratic urges an individual can give little zest or colour to himself or others. Yet at the same time others are dependent upon him, and if he is to care for their well-being he must integrate concern for them with his own satisfactions. Such an integration is a continuing problem-solving process, since a family's needs and wishes are always changing. Just as with a mother, a father's conflicting interests make for anxiety and often tortuous stress.

4. Work

The metaphor of a father standing at the door of the cave highlights how he is required to direct his responsibility and concern. He must, as it were, look outwards from the family to the external world and his work. At the same time he must look inwards to his wife and children. This necessity to face two ways makes a father's orientation rather different from a mother's at the time of child-rearing.

If anything a father's functioning in the world outside the family is primary, even though it seems to have little to do with being a family man. He must work if his wife is to relax in her business of mothering. When a man will not, or cannot work then, as we have said already, the family loses its autonomy. Other agencies must be called in to provide this aspect of fathering. If, on the other hand, a father takes no other interest but provides for his family through work, then at least it can remain an autonomous unit, where its members respect themselves.

Probably because of these circumstances, very much of most

men's zest and self-esteem lies outside the family in their work and relations with other men. We noted in the chapter on childhood how boys grow up with an emphasis upon getting on in a world of other men. They are geared to be both competitive and also to club together for support in ways that often seem strange and absurd to girls and women.

From the point of view of their work, men will develop differently according to its requirements as they progress through life. Thus a mechanic will develop some abilities which will probably remain stunted in a barrister, and vice versa. Naturally we cannot dwell on this here, but it is of note in passing that the skills of work and affairs outside the family are often impersonal and lack intimacy. Most men's working concern is with the non-human world, physical labour, machines, figures, or the soil. If they deal with people it is usually with them in the mass. Boys and men are faced with technology, and usually commit a large part of themselves to it. When they turn in towards their families, quite different capacities are required.

A father will have had no formal education about family matters and, in contrast to a woman, he is unlikely to have learnt very much about them from male conversation or literature. For instance, women's magazines are full of articles about personal problems in a way that is almost unthinkable in magazines for men. Many forces seem to conspire to take a man's interest away from thinking about intimate family questions. Yet these will be his main concern as a father. Let us now consider them.

5. *Family environment*

Turning in towards his family, a father's first worry is likely to be housing. The place where a family settles is usually determined predominantly by the nature of a husband's work. Yet his wife and family will be the first to be affected by where they settle and by the housing that can be afforded from his wages. Thus in this at least, a man will almost inevitably be the leader, and hence either be held or feel responsible for shortcomings.

The predicament of work and housing is seen most poignantly with immigrant families, who move to alien environments because work is available. As often as not, accommodation can only be found which imprisons a wife and stunts the children.

Even amongst those at the other end of the scale who can afford to pick and choose, housing is a very frequent source of a wife's misery and resentment, and hence of her husband's shame and guilt. It is very difficult to assess a house for a family without living in it. The house or flat itself is only one consideration in the long run. The social climate of the neighbourhood and the availability of schools often turn out to be of paramount importance to a mother and her children. Yet these are often difficult to estimate without living in the district first. Thus some families move from one place to another by trial and error, others by force of financial circumstances or lethargy make do with what they have got. Perhaps only a minority of mothers find themselves in an environment where they are deeply contented, and many fathers feel at least some burden of guilt.

6. *Looking after a mother*

When a father turns in from dealing with the environment to intimate interplay with his family, he perhaps finds himself least prepared by his previous learning from men around him.

A father is first of all a husband, so that our earlier consideration about being in love and the married couple apply in this chapter. Perhaps a man's relationship with his wife is of more focal importance than that with his children. For if he neglects his wife, her disturbance is likely to be reflected in the quality of her day-to-day dealing with children. If on the other hand she feels safe and appreciated with him, she is likely to maintain her essential vigour and interest in them.

The reader will recall the discussion of fathering in the chapter on pregnancy. With primary maternal preoccupation a woman tends to loosen her capacity to deal sharply and actively with the world around her. Her husband is called upon to increase his functioning in the areas where his wife has slackened. Most husbands tend to respond by becoming watchful, protective and fussy, particularly at a first pregnancy. Just as she mothers the baby, so his *maternal* feelings arise around his wife. When a father fails to develop this, his wife is left alone. In an extended family she would probably have female relatives to turn to, but in our nuclear family there is likely to be no one to take her husband's place.

A mother's need to be watched over continues throughout child-rearing years. Not only does the environment have to be watched over, but her inner state also needs care. A mother becomes rather loose in her reactivity in order to respond intimately to the ever-

[1] Blanck and Blanck, 1968.

changing requirements of her children. This means that she often tends to feel chaotic, perhaps with wild surges of worry and raw phantasy. On such occasions she may need to be *held* by her husband. Most obviously she wants to be physically held just as an infant or lover is clasped, but *psychological holding* (Winnicott, 1950) is also wanted. What happens in this remains something of a mystery, but it seems that first of all a husband absorbs his wife's anxieties into his ideas. He then responds in his own particular way by checking her phantasies against his views about the reality of a situation, perhaps suggesting solutions to the problems that have instigated his wife's particular worries.

The most frequent instances of this holding will probably not occur in particularly fraught situations, but simply in day-to-day conversation when a mother wants a second opinion for her ideas about the children on routine matters. To a great extent, opinions will be gleaned from other women during the day. But when intimate and crucial questions arise a husband will be turned to, because he is expected to know the nuances of his family situation better than neighbours.

The most usual time for such second-opinion conversations is in the evening after children have gone to bed. Both husband and wife can then relax themselves and off-load their feelings on to each other without hindrance. This is probably the primary reason for the convention of packing children off to bed at the beginning of an evening. Quite a few parents omit to recognize this need for conversation, and fib to the children that they must go to bed simply because they are tired. The children then kick up a fuss saying they are not tired, and feel their parents are being unjust. This is not the only cause of bedtime strife, but is perhaps a common one.

A husband's failure to hold his wife's urges and anxiety is a frequent cause of complaint. For instance, you will often hear such words as 'Oh, him, no sooner is he home than he's out in the garden.' 'When it suits him he'll be as sweet as pie to the children, but help me with them, never.' 'He always lets me do what I want but I never never know what he thinks about it all.' 'He doesn't know what I have to cope with, he just comes in and criticizes.'

Fathers no doubt react to their wives' anxieties according to their own characteristic modes of defence, which have built up over the years. Some husbands, for instance, tend to be scornful by nature. If they care about their wives, they will probably adopt a mode of chiding which can be gentle and helpful, because it absorbs worries while being appreciative. But scorn can frequently be used as a defensive means of ridding the self of emotional involvement, at the same time as shattering a wife's self-esteem. The martinet husband and frightened mouse wife are not uncommon.

This is not the only way a husband may fail to hold his wife. A reverse pattern is quite common in the henpecked husband. Here he may be very attentive to his wife, but frightened and in awe of her. Hence, having no independent strength of his own, he fails to contain his wife's impulsiveness, which can then turn to anxiety. Such a henpecked husband is perhaps epitomized by the man who said with admiration in his voice, 'My wife and I are of one mind, hers.' The reader himself will be able to think of other patterns whereby husbands fail to hold their wives' anxiety.

It is of note that the conception of psychological holding between adults is applicable not only to husbands and wives. For instance, it may be a primary function of working people in managerial or supervisory positions. Although little discussed as yet, it seems also to be of paramount importance between students and their tutors.

Turning back to fathering in return for commitment to his family a man usually expects to leave the responsibility of his day-to-day feeding and comfort to his wife. Most men also call on their wives to hold them in return over worries about work and family. This has been described already when considering reciprocity in love and marriage.

7. A father in direct relation to his children[1]

The last chapter described how a mother is called upon to keep in intimate touch with her children as they go through the phases of their development. We also noted how different systems of her phantasy may be aroused by her children at each stage. These give colour and zest to her as an individual in front of children, but they may also intrude in an uncreative way in her handling of them. Just the same applies to a father. He is unlikely to be as intimately involved in this process as is a mother, because he is out all day. Conversely, since his investment is spread between work and family, his children will invest less passion in him than in their mother. Even so, children find growing up easier if they have two parents to trust. What is more, a father who is blind to his children's affairs misses one of the most profound meanings in life.

Chapter 7 discussed several aspects of the importance of fathers

[1] Erikson, 1950. Aberle and Noegele, 1968.

to their children. Having two parents makes it easier for a child to integrate his ambivalent feelings. Quite early in life a father becomes important as a separate person in his own right. He is of a different gender from his wife, so that boys and girls find their own sexual identity both by watching father and mother together and by the subtle ways in which each parent separately relates to them. A father is also the representative of the outside world, while still being an intimate family person. Parents vary, but it is very often a father particularly who explains and demonstrates the mechanics of the more distant world to children, since he is the one who is repeatedly going out into it and coming back.

Modern urban society presents one particular problem with regard to this learning from fathers. Children rarely see what he actually does at work in the outside world. In days gone by most children could see him and be with him in the fields or in his workshop. Such an opportunity is now rare. Fathers disappear at 8 a.m. to do something incomprehensible until 5 or 6 p.m. A man can say he works in a bank, an office, or factory, but verbal reports are usually meaningless to a child. One has only to see a boy working on a farm with his father to recognize that an experience is lost in urban life. A farmer's son of seven or eight can go with his father, watch him and then do things with him, so that at a very early age he is actually doing useful work himself when on holiday or after school.

Children of a father who works in an office can watch and copy him only in his play, tinkering with the car or in the garden. They cannot experience his primary fathering function of working. It has been suggested that this gap in learning about father's work has contributed towards the devaluation of fathering in Western society.

The last few paragraphs have been discussing the models provided by fathers for children to identify with and grow through. Such models, however estimable in themselves, are likely to be value-less if a child feels personally unrecognized by his father. He will probably be so consumed with hurt anger at being unnoticed for what he is himself that he will be destroying the models his father presents, however useful they might be in principle. Thus a father needs to attune himself to his children and appreciate them just as a mother does.

Some men feel that they can ignore their children in infancy, and postpone entering their children's lives until they explicitly want him as a model later in childhood. Such a policy is probably mistaken. A father who has mingled with his children from babyhood will not only have the pleasure of seeing their growth, but will also know them intimately in all their non-verbal idiosyncrasies. Only when he knows their modes of thought will he be able to be a teacher when the time comes to impart new knowledge. If he has not known them in their early days he will come to them as a relative foreigner, speaking a language which is unfamiliar and imposing disciplines which will seem arbitrary.

Just as mothers have difficulties at different stages of development because of the intrusion of their inner phantasies, so also do fathers. The avoidance of infancy just mentioned is a case in point. Another is reluctance to participate in toilet training. Many fathers are revolted by children's faeces, and hence may never change a nappy. This probably matters little except that a mother can then rarely leave him to look after young children and have time to herself.

Some fathers find discipline easy and provide a useful backstop for a harassed mother. Others find it nerve-racking and impossible to apply consistently. For instance, it is quite common for fathers at times to identify themselves in phantasy with their children against their disciplinary mother, so that they connive in undermining her authority.

We noted previously how mothers often find themselves troubled by sexual phantasies about their children. It need hardly be said that fathers find themselves with the same problem only in reverse. They often enjoy cuddling and kissing their children until they are two or three years old. But after this they may shy off such shows of affection, particularly with their sons. Here a father is usually finding himself worried by homosexual feelings aroused by his son's demands for caresses. Worries about caressing daughters are less common.

These are generalized anxieties, but a father also has his own particular deep-seated phantasies which attach themselves to his children, just as happens with a mother. When these are flexible and allow room for him to recognize his children as they really are, they give vividness to his children's life. However, when a particular system of phantasy remains entrenched, they can stunt the growth of a child or at least embitter him. Here are a few examples:

(i) A father was extremely fond of his only child, a boy. He seemed to be the most precious thing in the world to him. He encouraged him a great deal, but feeling him to be so precious

could show no open anger or hostility. The son in his turn
not only felt disturbed by his father's heavy silences, but also
grew up unable to express his own feelings of anger. He could
be irritable with acquaintances, but he was dumb with anyone
he was fond of. His only way of expressing negative feelings
was to break off a relationship. He had innumerable girl
friends, but walked out on all of them as soon as he began to
feel in the least cross with them.

(ii) A father was brought up in a severe religious faith. After
many rebellions he saw the light and became strictly religious
himself. However, his ambivalent feelings about it seemed to
get attached to his two sons. The eldest was a lively and
rather naughty boy, so that the father became convinced he
had no good in him. The younger son on the other hand was
seen as a shining light of innocent virtue. The two boys then
reacted in character.

The elder espoused unconventional causes and became a
militant atheist, taking every opportunity to torment his
father, whom he loathed. The younger son was obedient and
tied to his parents. He was quite talented as a musician but
could only play in front of them, mostly church music. By
his early twenties he had few friends of his own, and had
never taken a girl out.

(iii) A girl bore a strong resemblance to her mother, who died
when she was quite young. The father doted upon her, but
seemed fixed upon the image of his dead wife. When she had
grown into her teens he would still take her on his knee and
say, 'Your mother will never be dead while you are alive.'
As a woman she was often invaded by feelings of being like
her dead mother, and was overcome with bouts of depression.

(iv) A father felt himself to be a failure just as his own father had
been. He was determined that his son should escape this fate,
so saw to it that he was well educated and encouraged him
to choose a career that he would throw his heart into.

This itself created few difficulties, but the father also felt a
failure with his wife, and encouraged his son to take his place
with her, just as he did over careers. Thus he would ask the
boy to mediate between him and his wife, and also to care for
her in ways where he had failed. The boy felt proud and

triumphant, but also very disturbed. He remained tied to his parents for many years, at least in part because he felt guiltily responsible for both of them, and unable to leave them to their own devices.

These are just a few suggestive examples. Others will no doubt readily spring to the reader's mind.

Because his functions are very diverse and lack the consuming intensity of motherhood, it is rare that a man breaks down complaining that he is unable to father his children. But this does not mean that internal problems are non-existent or that they never rub off on children.

Later in childhood, fathers have problems that are similar to those of mothers about schooling, puberty and the rejection of their ways by adolescents. They are also called upon to let their children go, and not to infantilize them into their adulthood.

8. Mothering functions in being a father

Earlier in this chapter we mentioned that men probably get little information about the intimate personal aspects of family life from other men. We have also noted that these intimacies are called for in the modern nuclear family perhaps more than at any time in the past. The young man will have had his first and most important experiences of intimacy from his own mother in infancy and after. He will have learnt about them literally at his mother's knee. For instance, a young father taking his baby out in a pram and chatting to him as he goes will have done it all before. He will in all likelihood have seen his mother doing it with him, and then copied her himself as a toddler trundling a trolley about with dolls or teddy bears. Boys, when young at least, identify just as strongly with their mothers as do girls. But, for boys, these are identifications with someone of the opposite gender, and we have noted before how children are vehemently conscious of their gender identity.

By the time they get to school age, boys are usually prone to reject the ways of their mother and sisters as 'cissy'. This is often enshrined in our society, at least in later education and in the attitudes of men together.

We could summarize this by saying that there is a tendency to reject or at least feel anxious about *cross-gender identifications*. This seems to be particularly the case with boys and men. But it is also noticeable in women when they are shy of doing things they feel are not in accord with their gender. We noted it earlier in women who refuse to drive cars because it is too masculine.

When a man comes to marriage and then fatherhood, many of the functions he learnt with and from his mother are called upon to be exercised to the full. In many ways it might be an advantage that he has had little education from other men about such matters in his youth. He can be free of indoctrination to make his own discoveries and find his own best modes of caring and intimacy. But it may also mean that he has little support from other men, so that he is lonely, ashamed and unsure when faced with personal or family problems.

17

MID-LIFE

1. Introduction[1]

We now turn away from specific parental functions to more general considerations. In the childhood years it was possible to detect processes of development which were more or less common to all individuals. This is not so easy in adulthood. Here it is more evident that each person develops his own skills and idiosyncrasies according to his work and situation in life. This means that generally applicable ideas about development are largely inappropriate. Perhaps this accounts for the sparsity of literature on development in adult life. There are plenty of works about childhood and a growing number about ageing, but very few about the years between, even though it is the major portion of life. But neither the inapplicability of generalized ideas nor the scarcity of literature should blind us to the highly complex developments that go on within each person's life. Perhaps in future years there will be more studies of the intimate growth of different individuals' functioning.

In discussing parenthood we highlighted certain functions which had some general applicability. On the other hand, people who do not marry probably exemplify the individuality of development. They take many different directions so that it is not easy to summarize their lives. However, some points are worthy of note.

2. Staying single

Much of what has been described in the last three chapters will not have occurred to the single person. He may have fallen in love, but unless he has lived for many years with one person, he will not have experienced a continuity of being able to *regress* in physical and psychological intimacy. What is more, he will not have created children out of his body and been responsible for their rearing.

In our society most single women recognize this loss deeply,

[1] See Lidz, 1968. Wallis, 1962. Neugarten, 1968. Jaques, 1970.

quite consciously, and often talk about it. Sometimes a sequence takes place in the late twenties and thirties when a woman feels anxious that she has been passed over. Then she tends to feel despair at losing her child-bearing function. Lastly, if lucky, she feels sad, recognizing the loss but realizing there are other satisfactions which will do instead.

With men, the story often seems rather different. Probably because they are so much more attuned to work satisfaction and male company, they are less aware of their loss. My impression is, however, that although men do not feel so deeply about failure to have children, they suffer more than women from loneliness and being unable to regress in intimacy with one other person. Probably our social stereotype of a single man is of a gay bachelor. But this is largely a myth. Such men are rare, especially after middle age.

Present-day social attitudes tend to give more room for intimacy to unmarried women than men. It is acceptable and commonplace for women to live together. Men do likewise in the regimented setting of ships, the armed forces or monasteries. Outside such institutions they would be suspected of homosexuality.

There is perhaps an underlying social climate at the present time where invidious comparisons are made between those who are married and those who are not. The single person is seen as one who has failed to be attractive enough to marry and play his part in continuing the species. Married people are conversely seen as narrow in their ways and limited in vision. This view has truth in it, for parents must necessarily withdraw the scope of their interests if they are to concentrate upon their family in a responsible way. However, these comparisons are not usually made for the sake of truth, but rather defensively to enhance self-esteem at the expense of others.

Comparisons of this nature are not new. The Catholic Church, for instance, has often in the past seemed to maintain that the celibate state is higher than that of marriage. On the whole perhaps in our society the opposite view holds sway, so that single people are prone to feel inferior. However, social attitudes are not simple. For instance, considerable valuation is now placed upon individual creativity. And many creative people are absorbed in the products of their minds rather than in families. They have invested themselves in their work; their mental creations are the 'children' they love most. In this they are predominantly non-parental. Such creative people, artists, writers, journalists, academics, are often

the 'stars' of our culture. They initiate ideas and fashions and tend
to carry the charisma of leaders. Such a bias tends to discredit the
functions of real parents. It may be that in this we are not so unlike
medieval times when the celibates of the Church were cultural
leaders. Modern leaders of fashion are perhaps unlikely to be
celibate, but this does not mean that they represent or understand
parenthood.

In more ordinary everyday relationships social splits often occur
between parents and single people. Parents, having so many
interests in common, tend to gravitate towards each other and likewise so do single people. This means that there is often a great deal
of ignorance between the two sides, which gives rise to a traffic in
contempt in both directions. Parents can implicitly be treated like
dirt by some professionals. This seems often to be the case when the
latter are single people out of touch with the problems of family life.
It can happen in education, where some teachers are prone to treat
parents as a fussing nuisance. The same may happen in hospitals. It
has taken many years of campaigning, for instance, to make some
nurses and doctors realize that children may be desperate when left
without their mothers.

An essential difference between the contribution of a parent and
a single person seems to lie in *sublimation* (for definition see Rycroft,
1968 *a*). Parents physically reproduce and rear offspring. Single
people on the other hand do not do this. Rather, their reproductive
urges are *displaced on to other activities*. This sublimation is indicated
in our everyday language when we say that an inventor has given
birth to an idea, a nurse is nursing, a teacher is motherly, a boss is
fatherly, or when a person is given responsibility for a job we say,
'It's his baby now.'

Glancing back at the chapters on parenthood, it becomes clear
that single people may exercise the parental functions portrayed
there very fully but in sublimated forms. Needless to say, the
majority of ordinary parents' activity when bringing up their own
children also involves these sublimations where direct physical
involvement is displaced on to other activities.

We are saying here that the individual uses internal systems of
phantasy and feeling which are concerned with ideas of parental
(and child) functioning when working in areas outside the family.
Such 'family' feelings may either be unconscious or quite consciously recognized. We are not suggesting that parent–child
phantasies are the only forms of thought concerned in work and

play with other people. Rather, such underlying feelings and phantasies play a strong part both in the inner satisfactions a person gets in his job, and in his capacity to empathize with others in social life.

The single person probably has the edge over ordinary parents in the variety of sublimated activities to which he can commit himself simply because he has greater freedom of time. Parents on the other hand have more opportunity for intimate and physical satisfactions. Considerations like this make it plain that it is meaningless to assert that the married state in general is superior to being single or vice versa.

3. The individual's awareness of his life span

From infancy until death, each individual has a sense of his own age relative to others around him. This awareness has far-reaching ramifications. In early chapters we stressed the child's pervasive sense of smallness and incapacity. Later we noted the adolescent's sense of being at a threshold. In the twenties a person establishes himself as a contributor, but is also a learner and servant. In the thirties he usually wishes to be recognized for his contributions, and is less ready to relate to others as a humble learner. He is also usually in the middle of being a parent. Throughout these years he may frequently look back, but is still predominantly looking forward to the future. Then, probably at about the age of forty, he begins to realize that life is half over for him. When the individual looks equally back and forward, he is aware of middle age. We can detect various threads interweaving in his mind to give him his own particular experience of age. None of these are very pleasant in themselves. There is the awareness of a younger generation who are thrusting forward and will be alive when he is dead. We shall say more about this later.

There is also recognition of physical ageing in his body organs. This deterioration is the basis of mid-life as much as growth was in the earlier years. We shall not enter into details of its physiology, but it will be repeatedly mentioned in the next chapters (Bromley, 1966). Physical deterioration takes us to death. This sets the end-point of our existence. Hence ideas about death set a boundary to the conception of oneself, and are central to the individual's sense of identity. Such ideas are critical in mid-life, but have much earlier antecedents. Let us return to childhood for a moment and trace these.

4. Development of the recognition of mortality[1]

The individual has his first ideas about death quite early in child-hood. Certainly children of three and four express concern about dead things. Usually with puzzlement, awe and worry, they will investigate and ask questions about dead animals and birds. They will similarly ask with anxiety about the death of relatives.

The worried emotions children show suggest that they have some dim idea about the implications of death. It cannot be said that they understand what it is like to be dead. No one knows this for certain. Yet a child feels deeply about dead things, and it behoves us to question what it is that moves him to this.

Perhaps among other things, something of the following occurs. The individual (a child particularly) sees a dead thing, and notices that something he expects to be active is not so. It is *non-responsive* in every way to its environment and within itself. Such an external perception echoes *inner experiences* of unresponsiveness, so that death is understood in terms of the individual's own inner feelings. Such inner experiences are frequent, as when one 'feels dead inside', 'cut-off', or ways of relating 'die on us'. We have mentioned the 'death' of relationships at separation on many occasions from infancy onward, and noted that they are usually accompanied by depressive feelings.

The *small deaths* that are continually taking place physically inside the body itself have not been mentioned. These occur acutely in illnesses of every kind which every child experiences. They also occur in the general wastages of the body cells. Thus every child has dim awarenesses of breaks in responsiveness, if not from repressed feelings about broken relationships then from the illnesses of his own body. It is our suggestion that anxieties about all these focus themselves into dread when a dead thing is perceived.

It might be argued that a child's dread is simply a social imitation of adults, and certainly they must reinforce it. But it is so spontan-eous in children and arises so often when adults feel little anxiety themselves, that this seems an insufficient explanation.

Children's conscious personal worries about death are usually expressed in terms of fears about losing their parents or grand-parents. For example (a six-year-old girl talking): 'People die at seventy, you are thirty-five, mummy. So you won't die for seventy take away thirty-five years, what's that? Thirty-five years, oh, I'll be forty-one then. Granny is sixty-five. Well, she won't die yet.'

[1] Anthony, 1940.

Children have inevitably experienced fears of being left by their parents, so the most important idea of a death is the loss of these much-needed people.

The child's own death must usually seem such a long way off that it can easily be disregarded or denied. However, quite young children do think about it. For example (four-year-old boy), 'I don't think I want to be a soldier when I grow up, because I might get killed.' Children who have actually nearly died are often pre-occupied by phantasies about their own mortality when still quite young. For example:

(i) I was six when I fell down under a train just as it was about to move off. I was not badly hurt, but I remember being very frightened and everyone else shocked. From that time onward I thought a lot about my dying and what it would be like. I remember thinking that as I was a child I would naturally become one of the cherubim. I was fascinated by the accident, and returned to the spot years later to go over it again.

(ii) I was seven when I was knocked down by a car and was unconscious for a week. I remember being preoccupied with ideas of my death through my school days. I had a pervasive feeling of living on borrowed time, as if I ought not to be alive. Soon after the accident we left the country where it happened, and it wasn't until I was nineteen that I could return. When I did, one of the first things I urgently needed to do was to return to the crossroads where it had happened.

For children who have not had such close escapes themselves, it may be some years before personal awareness of death comes home to them. Even so, a child of nine or ten will readily be filled with fear that death could happen to him when a neighbourhood child dies or is killed. Such thoughts, though, are usually quickly put aside.

When a young person comes into the teens, his capacity to deny his own mortality usually melts away considerably. This is an intrinsic part of the adolescent's growth of adult identity. The transition is usually gradual. An example of this could be seen in the 1939 war. Children in their early teens or less were often blissfully unafraid of the bombing, at least as far as being killed themselves was concerned. The evidence for death was all around them but was denied. By the late teens young people were quite openly scared.

I myself remember being frightened of being killed in an abstract way during the war when I was seventeen. But when a bomber dived straight towards me, I remember staring at its black shape, and within a few seconds thought, 'This is going to hit us. Somebody is going to get killed. I might get hurt, but I am not going to die.' My capacity for denial was still working. Three years later exactly the same thing happened again, but this time I was very frightened and thought I was going to be killed. I suspect I was a late developer over this, but something of this transition happens to most people at some time or another.

Nowadays, when immediate death is not present, and dying people are usually kept hidden, perhaps this recognition of mortality is more difficult to achieve. However, one can detect that the question is still present, for young people's songs and talk are often full of ideas about death. Games of 'chicken' in cars and on motor-cycles also seem to be playing with personal death.

Ideas about mortality come quicker to some than others. Certainly the immediate experience of death around one is the most convincing teacher. Nurses, doctors, and soldiers in wartime probably mature in this way sooner than others. However, many adults of mature years keep up their denial of mortality even after many experiences of danger. The behaviour of some drivers on the roads shows us this by the way they place themselves in absurdly dangerous positions. Perhaps being encased in the familiar shell of their car fosters an illusion of invulnerability.

Even in a country at peace, the evidence for personal mortality is inexorably placed before the individual in his own dangers and the deaths of friends and relatives. By the twenties and thirties the idea of personal death has usually taken firm root in the conception of oneself. As we have just mentioned, this is an intrinsic component of a realistic sense of one's identity. In it the individual recognizes that he is finite, and is a humble being like all others. It is frightening but refreshing, because a long-standing denial has been thrown off.

With the sense of mortality included in his awareness, an individual is often spurred to clarify the things he would like to do in his life, and also to divest himself of dreams that mean little to him or are impossible.

By the age of forty or so, awareness of mortality develops into the sense that life is half over and there is not much time left.

Naturally people vary in the quality and time of life of this recognition, but it is sufficiently widespread to be discussed as a general phenomenon in both men and women. It is at heart a *depressive* experience with much attendant anxiety. This is because it is concerned with loss, not necessarily real losses but lost hopes. With a long future in front of him the young man can assuage the sense of his own defeats by dreams of the future. But by the forties a person's contribution to adult life has been delimited by his work and family. His future is restricted both by these and by the physical reality of an ageing body. The old methods of looking to the future to assuage anxiety no longer suffice; a new equilibrium has to be found. This internal situation is often referred to as the *mid-life crisis* (Caplan, 1964. Wallis, 1962). We shall discuss it again later, after we have separately considered middle age in men and women.

5. Middle age in men[1]

The situation of a man in mid-life will largely depend upon his work commitment when young. A young man who has found his identity in an occupation that involves fast physical co-ordination has little to look forward to in middle age unless he can develop to new functioning; he must change large areas of his identity. Such changes are inevitable for footballers, athletes, racing drivers, soldiers, sailors and airmen. The fast co-ordination upon which their callings depend deteriorates noticeably from the late twenties onwards.

Most young men who take up these careers are well aware that the centre of their lives must be transformed in their thirties or forties, and prepare themselves for a two-career life. The second career may grow out of the first, just as a middle-aged team manager must have been a footballer first. The second cannot be as personally glamorous as the first career. The youthful occupations we have mentioned all give the individual satisfaction from the beauty of skill in physical performance. Glamour seems to be essentially linked with this. By the forties, apart from exceptional circumstances, self-gratifying beauty is on the wane. In the transition from one career to another the individual perhaps mourns the loss of his old skill, and at the same time finds new investments. If later careers are self-satisfying, they are often essentially parental rather than glamorous in nature, using past experience to contribute to others. This can be seen, for instance, in management, organizing or education.

[1] Wallis, 1962.

On the whole, a person who has a highly developed intellect is less likely to be faced by such an acute career crisis as is the physical performer. These functions deteriorate more slowly than speed of body movement. However, the swift manipulation of concepts falls off in a way which is rather similar to that of physical dexterity. Thus where speed of thought counts, young men and women are at an advantage. For instance, one usually finds that mathematicians have done much of their original creative work by the age of forty. The same can be observed in chess masters; world champions are nearly always under forty. But where speed is less important than the balanced assimilation and organization of large bodies of information, the individual probably does not reach his prime until he is forty or more.

Men who have committed themselves to work that requires depth and breadth of experience may hardly start being independently productive until they are forty. The same applies to other less intellectual occupations which require steadiness of judgement. A racing driver for instance is old at forty, but a bus driver is least accident prone between forty and fifty-five.

Something rather similar happens in literature. Poets often blossom young and continue into old age, but many novelists and playwrights only reach mastery of their craft by middle age. One can detect development, for instance, in Shakespeare's style as he grew older. His later plays show enormously more flexibility and originality in the use of language than his earlier ones.

It is often thought by young people that the vesting of authority in older people is an outworn quirk of our social system. The considerations we have just made suggest that this is not the only reason. All balanced judgement must rest on the assimilation of relevant information. In many spheres this can be gathered when young. But in others it may take many years to amass. This is particularly so where knowledge of people is concerned, for it requires face-to-face interaction with many different individuals. Thus physicians, psychiatrists, social workers, administrators and statesmen probably only reach their prime in middle age. However, the temptation to fall into stereotyped behaviour and attitudes also sets in with greater experience and age. A young person has his future in front of him, and thus is ready to welcome change. The older person will have vested his self-esteem in ways of life which are necessarily limited. Changes threaten not only his future, but also the valuation of the contributions he has made in the past.

In a traditional form of culture where changes are imperceptible, the middle-aged man is unlikely to find his settled identity being threatened, but in our society customs and techniques are perhaps changing faster than at any time in history. The older person is thus prey to fears that habits which have served him well will be out-moded. He is then prone to withdraw into an enclosed world in which he can be his own ruler and feel safe, while ignoring or rejecting what is happening outside it.

Young people, only too willing to spot the weaknesses in others to assuage their own doubts, are prone to pounce on this element, which is incipient in most older people, and dismiss them with contempt. Such attitudes then seem to confirm the older person's horror of youth. This is one aspect of the familiar war between the generations.

It is likely that a middle-aged person's inability to learn new skills and modes of thought is as much due to emotional investment in old modes as to the actual physical deterioration of the ageing process. For instance, mature students in such courses as teaching or social work often prove, to their own surprise, to be faster learn-ers than young students. This is not, needless to say, likely to be the case where rapid conceptual manipulation is required as in learning mathematics.

When learning anything with freedom and zest, the individual is humble and romantic. To do this it is necessary to allow childlike parts of the self to emerge. An older person often finds this frighten-ing and humiliating, for his self-esteem has developed out of the things he has mastered and about which he need no longer feel childlike. When an older person can still show this eagerness and use it, he seems to take on an ageless quality. It is just as noticeable in some very old people as it is in the young. People having this facility seem to have little difficulty in communicating with any generation. This is readily understandable when we recognize that real communication between people is concerned with mutual learn-ing. When an older person has kept the child alive in himself, he can not only empathize with younger people but also learns from them, and in this way is also naturally acceptable.

6. Middle age in women[1]
The problems for a single woman have perhaps some similarities to those of men. Not many will be faced with exactly the same

[1] Deutsch, 1944.

situation as the ageing male footballer or athlete, except perhaps actresses and dancers. However, just as with a footballer, the days of an ordinary woman's attractiveness are passing, and if she has invested a great deal of self-love in this she is faced with the necessity of internal change or of becoming depressed and helpless. The menopause also impresses upon her that she must give up hope of bearing children herself. Probably by the age of forty-five or so, when the menopause actually occurs, many single women have attuned themselves to this idea anyway so that the actual change, although physically embarrassing may not be too depressing. Even so, the change of life is just what it says. A profound redistribution in body metabolism takes place. With this must come subtle differences in relating to and thinking about the self and people (Deutsch, 1944. Neugarten, 1968. Malleson, 1948).

Very often in the mid-years, single women find themselves burdened with the responsibility of caring for their own ageing parents. This is perhaps one of the most unjust customs in our society. There are no doubt certain neurotic satisfactions in turning the tables on one's parents and having them dependent on oneself rather than vice versa. But very many single women feel it to be a nearly intolerable duty which their conscience tells them they must perform, but which restricts their freedom and has little reward. They often hate their more fortunate brothers and sisters, who because they have children, find it easy to opt out. Only afterwards, perhaps, are they glad that they faced an unpleasant burden instead of avoiding the issue.

A married woman has probably committed a major part of her adult life to rearing children, particularly if she is middle-class and suburban. And, as we have seen, this almost inevitably means 'losing herself' in them. She has vested her life in her children's achievements rather than her own. What is more, she will probably have withdrawn a great deal of interest from the outside world and focused upon domesticity. By her mid-forties the children will have largely gone, leaving a more or less empty house. At about the same time the menopause impresses that she can bear no more children to replace the ones that have gone. With the loss of the old ways of relating and without having new hopes for the future, a married woman is very prone to become anxious and depressed. Such a time is often particularly difficult for a woman who married young and committed herself to motherhood without having found independent ways of living first in young adulthood. She will have no assurance in her identity as an adult other than as a mother, so that turning to other activities is likely to be frightening and she is often reluctant to try them.

One way of avoiding this depressive experience is to attempt to continue one's children's dependence. In some traditional extended family networks this tends to be the normal practice. But with a mobile society, a middle-aged woman has to let her young go. This was perhaps especially difficult a few years ago when the nuclear family had become established as normal, but a married woman's style of life had not changed at the same pace. Married women, especially in the middle classes, were not expected to work, so that if their children left home their lives were likely to be empty. In very recent years two-career life has become more common in the middle classes. This follows a working-class pattern where women have often expected to work.

With children gone, a wife and husband find themselves alone together perhaps for the first time for years. This provides an opportunity for a privacy and freedom which may have been denied them for a quarter of a life-time. Many couples report what a pleasure and relief this is. It can also provide the ground for an unbridgeable gap. The husband may have maintained his outside interests, but it is likely that his wife will have not, so that she is left with emptiness all round. This is probably a most common circumstance and may contribute to menopausal depression. The reader will probably have seen this occurring in some women he knows, if not in overt depressive states then in generalized irritability, grumbling or shrewish behaviour.

7. The mid-life crisis[1]

We can now draw together various strands that have appeared in this discussion. The organization of an adult sense of identity is, among other things, dependent upon the development of the conception of mortality. This has origins early in childhood, but is unlikely to be integrated into the self to become an active agent in coherent thought until adulthood. When active, although frightening in itself, it can provide a spur to effort and creativity.

By mid-life the individual is assailed by recognition of his own ageing processes, the growth of younger generations and awareness of his life's end. Such recognition may be defended against and denied, but signals of age weaken such defences as time progresses.

[1] Caplan, 1964. Erikson, 1950. Wallis, 1962. Kaufman, 1963.

With this weakening comes a psychological crisis or era of change. It must be stressed that this, like adolescence, is a normal crisis. It may be acute, with depression and anxiety, but it is more likely to be quiet. It may even be enjoyable, for change means variety and the opportunity for exploration. An individual is not likely to pinpoint the crisis, for it probably occurs in stages over a period of years. It may be linked with external circumstances like change in work, but is more likely to be private and internal.

One common aspect of this phase of life is *discontent*. The individual, knowing that half his life is over, becomes aware of parts of himself which have remained unfulfilled. He often feels the urge to reject allegiances in the search for satisfaction of neglected yearnings. This may take the form of boredom with wife or husband, who inevitably leave parts of any individual unsatisfied. More frequently, perhaps, it takes the form of disillusionment with work, beliefs, ideals and with the self.

By mid-life few individuals are in a position to change their lives to encompass these unfulfilled desires. Some ignore their limitations and impulsively act upon their yearnings in a way which is often self-destructive, because they ignore other fruitful aspects of their lives. Other people tend to shrink into their own worlds, clinging to what satisfaction they have. For all individuals such a crisis must mean *renunciation* of some dreams, while at the same time investing passion in modes of life which are really possible and available.

It seems that the acceptance of limitation is only one aspect of middle age, though it is the one most commonly noticed. The recognition of mid-life makes for awareness that time is short. This drives some individuals to a sense of urgency. Desires which have hitherto been vague must be brought to fruition. Thus middle and later life may be a time of great creative energy and sense of purpose.

It is a common assumption that the impatient innovators of change are all young. This may be true when considering people in the mass. But the organizing centres of innovation and change, either socially or in ideas, are very frequently individuals in their later life. Taking extreme examples, the major political revolutionaries of history have mostly been middle-aged at the time of fruition. Lenin is a case in point. Britain's major revolutionary organizer, Oliver Cromwell, is also an outstanding example. He was probably fired with nonconformist zeal as a boy by his schoolmaster. But it was not till he was in his late twenties that he became deeply committed to religious puritanism. In his thirties he became politically active. He was over forty before he moulded himself into a military leader and vital political organizer.

The reader will probably find it easier to sympathize with a more peaceful but poignant example of the recognition of mortality as a spur to self-organization. It comes from the life of Guiseppe di Lampedusa. He was an Italian nobleman who, though well known as an intellectual, had written nothing of note until his late sixties, when he was told that he was incurably ill. At this news he set about writing a novel which had been planned for many years. It was published after he died some years ago entitled *The Leopard*, and was immediately recognized as a modern classic.

18

OLD AGE[1]

1. Respect for the old

In our hypothetical static society we might expect the old to be respected. Having lived longest, they can act as the most assured carriers of techniques and beliefs which may be passed on virtually unchanged from one generation to the next. This reverence for the old certainly occurs in many traditional societies, especially if they have both tight family organizations needing an old person's authority, and a plentiful food supply for those who are too old to be producers themselves. In societies, however traditional, where food is scarce and living conditions are hard, as for instance with the Eskimo, the old become a burden upon the young and may be given short shrift.

The conditions of our present society bear some resemblance to both these forms. With a prolonged expectation of life and a highly developed economy, a large proportion of the population is aged and unproductive yet can be supported. At the same time, old people are not seen as essential carriers of culture. Their contributions are indeterminate, so that very many of them have the appearance of being useless and unwanted.

The ageing person is perhaps presented with threats to his well-being from two directions, firstly from the deterioration of his bodily functions and secondly from social expectations that he will become useless on account of his age, irrespective of his real capacities. Many people are compulsorily retired at a fixed age, not just for their own benefit but more for the younger generations to step into their shoes. There are also vague but widely influential attitudes which match this compulsory retirement; for instance, an old person's ideas tend to be dismissed by the young as silly and old-fashioned simply because they come from an aged mind. He may be physically cared for, but is not reverenced and frequently not even respected.

[1] See Bromley, 1966. Townsend, 1957.

2. Depression and ageing[1]

The common feature of ageing is of course shrinkage of body functions. Cell tissue is not replaced as in youth, so that hair thins, skin and muscles lose their vibrance, blood circulation malfunctions and brain cells die. In the last chapter we discussed how, from childhood onwards, there is an impact upon awareness when body parts become diseased. With ageing 'small deaths' become widespread, and moods of depression arise; this happens at any time of life whenever there is a loss of enjoyable functioning. With old age there is less opportunity than before to hope for the future, so that a valuable defence against depression is no longer effective. Coupled with physical deterioration comes the loss of friends and loved ones who will also be ageing and dying, and this also brings depression.

Many individuals accept the shrinkage of their lives with resigned equanimity. Perhaps one factor in this is that loss of vitality can act as a release from guilt. The inner commands of 'ought, must and should' may lose their grip now that it is no longer physically possible to carry them out. The old person is in the position to relax into unambitious contentment. Perhaps those people who have been forced on many previous occasions to accept their fate in a passive way find this contentment of old age most easily. On the other hand, those who have characteristically dealt with uncertainty by self-assertive activity may feel the losses of age more acutely. But, no matter how it is received, ageing seems to be inevitably attended by deep and widespread depressive feelings. These can vary from utter misery to quiet peacefulness, but are never very enjoyable.

Here are a few examples:

(i) A year after suffering a stroke which left her partially paralysed Mrs E. said, 'I wish I could write a book to tell people about it. It was terrible, terrible. I wish I could hurry up and get myself moving again. I just sit and my garden grows weeds. People come and go and are nice, but I just sit.'

(ii) Mrs F. went on working in a pub until she was over seventy, when she slipped and bruised herself one day. She lost her job through being off sick. She recovered quite quickly, but never went back to work. Her husband remained lively and

[1] See Bromley, 1966. Berezin, 1963. Kaufman, 1963.

full of jokes, but she slowly became quiet and apathetic. She complained of aches and pains, but managed the housework and cooking. Then she began to lose weight and looked drawn, giving up doing her hair or using make-up. She usually shuffled about the house in boots and several layers of clothing.

(iii) Mr G. had been a pig-farmer for most of his life. He never gave a thought to retiring. By the time he was over seventy there was a noticeable deterioration in the farm. Roofs were leaking and fences broken. Mrs G. realized her husband could no longer keep up, and suggested he employ a farm-hand. But he was too stubborn to admit his declining abilities and would not listen to his wife. Finally he became acutely ill and was taken to hospital, where he was overcome by despair as he lay in bed. For many years he had dreamt of his family buying up the land around and continuing in his traditions of farming. But he had no sons, and his daughters had all married townsmen. When he dies he will be the last of a long line of farmers.

3. Persecutory and paranoid feelings in old age[1]

Physical deterioration means that there is a concomitant depletion in ego-functioning and shrinkage of the sense of self. The individual feels smaller and more helpless, so that the outside world is consequently larger and less controllable. Events in the external world tend to be experienced passively, and hence may become more persecutory and threatening. This is manifest in an old person's natural fears of roads, trains and whirl and bustle generally.

As ego-functioning and the sense of self tend to shrink, so we would expect primitive, less integrated patterns of thought and feeling to emerge. This regression is manifest not only in an old person's generalized fearfulness, but also in his tendencies to use projective mechanisms in thought. We have noted on many occasions that the individual is prone to attribute unwanted aspects of the self to the outside world both as a child and in adulthood. In the prime of life, this is usually held in check or elaborately covered by rationalizations. With ageing these defences often fall away so that projective mechanisms emerge more nakedly. This is most evident in senility, which will be discussed at the end of this chapter.

[1] Bromley, 1966. Berezin, 1963. Kaufman, 1963.

But a person in full command of his faculties can slowly subside into cantankerousness, which is usually a manifestation of projective mechanisms. For instance:

A widow had had a very active life. She reared a large family, and was also respected throughout her town for being generally interested in people and helpful. As her body slowed up, so she began to become bitter and suspicious. The first sign was an argument with neighbours over a dilapidated fence. This grew into bitter resentment, which spread to anger at all the people she had helped in the past and who now seemed callous towards her. She would however let no one near her to help, because she was convinced that they would make matters worse. Perhaps when young this woman had overcome her passive feelings of being helpless and uncared for by developing a very active and helping character. When this activity was no longer possible, her sense of persecution emerged and consumed her whole attitude to life.

Another instance of projection is commonly seen with regard to awareness of physical deterioration. Thus the sense of body mal-functioning, 'little deaths' as we have called it, is often projected on to the external world, so that dreadful things are felt to be happening outside rather than inside the individual. For instance:

An old countryman was looking at the thatched roof of a cottage and said, 'That thatch is good for another ten years. I'm eighty and never had a day of illness in my life, but the thatch will outlive me, no doubt.' He then lapsed into projection and said, 'But then such terrible things are happening in the world now that it will all be over for everyone on this earth before then, that's for sure.'

Such collapses into awareness of persecution are common but not universal. They are most marked when physical functions have deteriorated and little activity is possible. There is much more to old age than this, but we have introduced the chapter by discussing deterioration, depression and persecutory anxiety because these provide underlying background feelings in ageing. They have to be dealt with by every individual as he grows older, however fit and active he may be.

4. The crisis of retirement[1]

Just as middle age was perhaps epitomized by withdrawal from intimate parenthood, so for many people old age is marked by retirement from money-earning work. This is a crisis of life when changes inevitably occur. New integrations of functions must develop for life to continue fruitfully and in contentment. Retirement from work is only one facet of ageing, but it is clear-cut and easy to recognize. Similar smaller retirements and withdrawals are occurring throughout old age, and likewise call for internal development and reorganization. We shall stress retirement from work here simply because it epitomizes much about this time of life.

A wage-earning man or woman's identity or sense of self will have been largely orientated around working capacity. He may or may not have invested much of himself and his imagination in it, but will inevitably know himself by the work he does. With retirement this identity is taken away from him. So also is a good part of his income. Here are a few examples of how this crisis is managed.

(i) Mr H. said he had mixed feelings when retirement approached. He looked forward to not having to work, but wondered what he was going to do with himself. His wife said she didn't want him hanging around the house all the time. On the actual day, he went to work as usual and wished his friends good-bye at the end of it. Four days later they set off on an extended holiday to relatives in Australia. They returned home loaded with presents and memories and then settled down to being pensioners. The greatest readjustment was living on a reduced income, but the first ten years proved to be happy. They were both healthy, Mr H. took an allotment, so they never had to buy vegetables. They lived close to their children and helped look after the grandchildren. In the summer Mr H. returned to work part-time but in the winter they could relax with their friends and social activities.

(ii) Mr I. says he enjoyed every minute of his life as a mechanic. But he looked forward to retirement and, although offered a number of part-time jobs, turned them all down because he felt he needed a complete break. During the first months Mr and Mrs I. had a series of holidays visiting children and grandchildren and two weeks away on their own.

    After this Mr I. turned into a Jack-of-all-trades. He moved

[1] Bromley, 1966. Townsend, 1957.

around on a bicycle doing gardening, decorating and small repair jobs. His evenings were taken up with committee work. His health has been good, but he notices that there is not so much spring in his legs, and now needs a rest after two or three hours' work. His memory is also not so good, and it takes a little longer to think things out. He may not do as much as he used to, but the quality of his work remains satisfyingly high. He also has a freedom which was denied him when in employment.

In contrast to these men who met the crisis of retirement by developing new functions, the reader will remember Mrs F., and Mr G., the pig-farmer quoted a few paragraphs back. In these cases the crisis was not met by developing new patterns of living, and despair set in.

Let us now consider some of the functions that come into play in this crisis. We have already noted the losses from physical deterioration and attendant depressive feelings. As with any loss, this usually sets in train a process of *mourning*. Here fear, rage and regret may be followed by finding substitute satisfactions and then peaceful sadness at the change. We will say more about this in the next chapter.

On the positive side, the crisis involves finding new investments. One particular psychological quality seems to be important here. We saw how children approach new activities with awe and enthusiastic romanticism. If a person has kept this childlike quality as part of his functioning identity, he is likely to be able to use it late in life to discover and develop new investments.

However, such internal changes as these at the crisis of old age can only take place when the external situation presents opportunities for new investment. For instance, Mr I. the mechanic lived in a fairly built-up area, so that his leaning towards becoming a general handyman met a local need. Mr G. the pig-farmer, on the other hand, could not have turned to this even if he had wanted to, because there were few houses in his rural neighbourhood.

The enjoyment of old age seems to rest, as it does throughout life, upon fusing the satisfaction of personal selfish urges with contributions to others. The environmental situation delimits both of those aspects as much as does an individual's psychological character.

A great pleasure of old age is that few responsibilities are now expected of a person, and self-centred pursuits can be enjoyed

without recrimination. This absolution from guilt must lie at the
heart of many old people's enjoyment of their lives, which seem
sparse in other ways. Perhaps the most common handicaps to this
carefreeness are lack of money and health, or fear of this lack in the
future. Anyone acquainted with old people will have encountered
real poverty as well as ill health.

Just as vital to many individuals, especially in early old age, is the
desire to continue contributing to others. Our present social situation is such that people are tending to lead longer lives around single
careers, so that the last quarter-century of a life may be economically
unfertile. This is slowly being recognized, and agencies for employment in part-time work are being set up. Perhaps in the future a life
of several different careers each attuned to age, will become a
normal part of our social order.

The break-up of extended families living in close proximity to
each other has lessened the opportunity for old people to be used in
child-rearing. But this loss of opportunity does not mean that the
need for such help has disappeared. It is a great strain, even impossible, for a mother to bring up more than two or three children
without assistance either from grandparents or paid help. A mother
who has no grandparents or aunts to fall back on when needed is
often chronically worried about exhaustion or illness. The illustrations given earlier in this chapter show how both old men and
women may turn to being auxiliary parents. It is often noticeable
that particularly affectionate bonds grow up between children and
their grandparents. Grandparents are not burdened with anxiety and
responsibility as are parents, so that they can be both more patient
and have more time to relax and play in a childlike way with children. Communication and a sense of equality often grows between
the old and young which makes them very fond of each other.

Many other activities readily spring to mind to which old people
may contribute. We have already mentioned paid work, odd jobs
and committee organization. The more subtle functions arising
from ordinary informal conversations seem none the less important.
For instance, old people are the living *historians* of a society. By
personal reminiscence they tell younger people how things were in
the past, both from their own lives and those of their parents and
grandparents. Thus their span of personal memory may bridge a
century or more. The young individual may not be called upon to
copy their ways as in a traditional society, but historical conversations help to impress the reality of his place in time. He is made

aware that he has grown out of people before him, and that others will come and take over from him in his turn.

More generally, an old person having experienced many things and being close to death can often express himself about living with a cool, dispassionate clarity devoid of the grandiose illusions to which younger people are prone. With this natural wisdom they can broaden our minds and make us humble. For instance:

> An ex-bank manager of seventy took on a part-time job as book-keeper. The work was dull in itself, but had rewarding side-effects. He had never worked with young mechanics before, and they had never talked informally with a bank manager. The old man said, 'They are gay and witty, but never think about anything beyond their noses.' By conversation, banter and argument, all in the garage were in some degree enriched.

The capacity to make conversational contributions depends upon the old person's own capacity to change his own ideas. Where he can learn from and appreciate the young, then a fruitful to-and-fro dialectic between generations can take place. When, on the other hand, he is frozen in fear of new things, his efforts will be directed solely towards resistance and defending his own ideological position. Conversation then turns to unpleasant and fruitless antipathy.

5. *Dependency upon others*[1]

We have so far been considering the position of old people who still retain their vigour. So long as a person can think and move, he maintains his independence of judgement and hence his individuality. But the progress of shrinkage is inevitable, and the old person has to sink into dependence upon others. This cannot but be painful for all concerned and is often bitterly resisted.

Dependence provides the ground for neurotic satisfactions for both old and young. This is often evident between old parents and their children. For instance, an old person losing his independence of action can gain malicious pleasure in being a ruthless baby who will never be satisfied. The impulse to behave in infantile ways may have been grudgingly held in check for many decades from the days of the old person's own childhood, and only now given vent. The younger person on the other hand may be prone to take pleasure in holding a parent helplessly at his mercy. Perhaps, having felt

[1] Townsend, 1957. Zinberg, 1963.

Q

subservient all his life, he can only now both wreak revenge and also appear virtuous in taking up a succouring stance. The reader will be able to recall other compulsive role play between old and young. No doubt phantasies like these play through the minds of everyone. However, they only become compulsive or neurotic when phantasy invades and blots out each person's recognition of the other's individuality. It may also be noted that compulsive games are not confined to parent–child relationships. They are readily detectable in some professionals working with the aged.

Where mutual recognition of each other's dignity is maintained, underlying phantasies will inevitably still be active. But they will be held in check and used as a spur to activity rather than being a dominating force. When this occurs, care of the aged may still be painful and sad but also deeply rewarding, for both old and young are together close to the elements of life and death.

6. Senility[1]

The progression into muscular incapacity is bitter and deeply depressing, but deterioration of brain function is perhaps worse because communication then becomes transient and difficult. With brain deterioration the usual modes of conversation disappear, so that helpers are left embarrassed and confused. With the lapse of highly integrated thought process, more primitive mental functions emerge unfettered. In particular, the paranoid projective mechanisms mentioned earlier in the chapter often dominate a senile person's thoughts and speech. These are often directed at helpers who can be made to feel hurt and confused.

Bitter paranoia does not occur with every senile person, but all seem to revert to primitive modes of symbolic thought and communication. This regression is disturbing to helpers who are naturally attuned to ordinary objective speech. The primitive symbolism of a senile person can often however be deciphered by a listener. When this is achieved, the contact between him and the old person can be very moving for both.

The code of this primitive symbolism can be roughly described as one where generalized abstract ideas are expressed in terms of specific body functions, and conversely body functions are expressed in terms of generalized or external events. If the listener knows the old person well he can often carry out the necessary translation, so that he understands what is being said.

[1] Bromley, 1966.

Here is an example of an abstract idea being expressed in terms of body functions.

An old man was clouded and wandering in his mind. His son came to ask for his signature for a power of attorney to manage affairs, and was worried whether his father would understand and comply. The old man seemed to wander off to another subject when he said, 'I must now climb up on to your shoulders. I hope I won't be too heavy.' The son, realizing what he meant, said, 'Oh no, everything is in order and we shall be able to manage things quite well,' and then handed him the pen and paper. His father signed it and with a sigh said, 'That's much more comfortable now, but then you always were a broad-shouldered boy.'

Here is an example of a body function being expressed in terms of an external event. An old woman was found crawling in the corridor whimpering, 'There has been an earthquake.' The nurse looked and found that she had soiled herself.

We can see here how external and internal reality have become confused, as happens to all of us when waking up from a dream, or like a person in psychosis. A young baby has also probably not yet made the differentiation between external and internal reality. Such differentiation is one great task of early childhood. In adult life we use our inner phantasy to feed our creative imagination in relation to the outside world. Then with senility the differentiation breaks down, and we can communicate only through concrete symbolic language very like the imagery of dreams. Perhaps as people become more sensitive to primitive symbolic communications, the loneliness of old and senile people will be somewhat alleviated.

19

DYING, GRIEF AND MOURNING

1. Background[1]

We have suggested throughout this book how our modern industrial and mobile society has enhanced the possibilities of individuality. We have also noted how a price may be paid for this in
loneliness, particularly for the parent of young children, and also in
old age isolation. Dying, too, tends to be a hidden and solitary
event.

In a close-knit traditional community we would expect a dying
person to be surrounded by people who knew him, so that death
will be a more or less public event with many participants both old
and young. This is common, not only abroad but also in certain
parts of Britain today, though it is probably dying out. For instance
it is still common, particularly in Wales, Ireland and rural areas, for
many local people to help in nursing a dying person. After death, it
is also expected that any acquaintances, old or young, should pay
their last respects to the body laid out in a bedroom or front
parlour.

In areas of social mobility such public intimacy does not occur. It
would be unthinkable in a suburb for all the inhabitants of a road to
crowd in to view a body. Most would be strangers and hence have
no personal respects to give. Furthermore, modern medicine means
that many people die in hospital alone amongst strangers much of
the time.

The dying and dead have come to be kept hidden from all but
close relatives, doctors and nurses. Death is disturbing to everyone,
and the facility with which it can be hidden gives the opportunity for
its presence to be denied. Just as with other disturbing events, it
tends to be tabooed. It arouses awe and dread, so that its manifestations may be swept away like dirt or excrement. As a consequence,
younger people have little direct experience of real death and the

[1] See Gorer, 1965. Hinton, 1967.

sense of personal humility that this can bring. The old and dying for their part tend to be left alone and isolated.

2. Terminal illness[1]

As many readers will have had little acquaintance with this, here is a brief account of the last weeks of an old man. He was not known to me, and the description is not mine. As you will see, the old man was very much an individual, so his way of growing old and dying was his own. But many features are common experiences, and something of the feeling of a dying person emerges from the account. (For this I am indebted to Barry Palmer.)

For four years Mr J. had been partially paralysed and was unable to move outside his home except in a wheelchair. Even so, although eighty-seven years old, he was very alert and able to converse on many subjects through his daily reading. His favourite topic of conversation was, nevertheless, his past career as a soldier. He was very proud of being an active man.

He had steadily deteriorated in physical health, and on many occasions it was thought that he might die. But he was never willing to admit that his health was declining and, when asked how he was, would say that he was better, and even demonstrate this by getting out of his chair and walking across the room. Each step might take upwards of ten seconds, but it would satisfy him that he had convinced the onlookers that he was not dead yet. His will to live was extraordinarily great.

Mr J. was afraid of being forcibly admitted to hospital. On many occasions it was advisable for the sake of his wife's health that he should leave home for a couple of weeks. He refused on every occasion, and one felt that this was because he had the fear that entry to hospital would be the end of him. On one occasion his wife had to go into hospital, and in spite of the fact that he was most uncomfortable and not properly cared for, he would not leave the house. Mr J. was always conscious of death. He was very fond of his children, but if they called without warning he would get very heated and suggest that they had been sent for. I do not know whether he was afraid of death, but he was of losing command of his life situation. It was always clear that he wished to be the boss of the house and in command of every aspect of his life. The thought of losing his independence,

[1] Hinton, 1967. Saunders, 1959. Kübler-Ross, 1970.

which he had largely done but would not admit it, was very apparent.

Three weeks before he died Mr J. was walking to the toilet when he began to slip, and eventually sat helplessly on the floor. Normally he would claim that he was all right, though someone would have to help him to his feet. On this occasion he said, 'Joan, I'm going.' He did not say much more, except that he wanted to see his children. From this point on he was no longer the man who wished to appear in command, but allowed himself to be cared for. A few days later, having seen his children, he became unconscious much of the time. The one thing which differed from his former collapse was that, though it appeared much the same to the onlookers, he knew that this time he was going to die.

This was one man's way of dying. On the whole only doctors, and nurses more particularly, have a wide experience of the last weeks of life. Hinton (1967) has given us a moving summary of the varieties of experience during this period. It is essential reading for every student.

Death occurs when one or more of the vital systems of the body become so damaged as to prevent functioning. This can occur by sudden catastrophe as in an accident, or by slower disease processes. Ageing of the body tissue makes individual organs prone to specific diseases, so that old people die through the action of these rather than from old age itself.

Death is essentially a physical process and, as far as we know, no one dies solely from a psychological cause. However, depression, and lack of will to live do often mean that an individual's body is undernourished and malfunctions in other ways as well, so that he becomes prone to lethal diseases. Direct death from shock is also known where the automatic nervous system becomes so disorganized that the heart is prevented from functioning. Thus, although the process of death itself must be regarded simply as a physical matter, the emotional life of an individual may predispose his body to physical malfunction and hence death.

Most old people suffer a series of illnesses and growing infirmity before a disease takes such a gross hold that no recovery is possible. The terminal phase of life then sets in. It was heralded in Mr J.'s case by his collapse three weeks before death. He seemed to be aware of its coming.

The terminal phase may last only a few minutes or hours as in the case of an acute coronary thrombosis, it may be several months in the case of cancer and other slow-working diseases. All of us will wonder what it is like for the individual during this period. Perhaps our greatest dread is that of pain. Many dying people do experience pain as a direct result of their disease. For some it is repeated and long-lasting. This on the whole can be alleviated by doses of morphine derivatives. Doctors will usually take care to relieve a person's pain in this way if they can. They are, however, loath to administer these drugs in the early stages of an illness because, although effective, they are also addictive, so that if there is hope for a person's life they will rarely be used.

The degree of pain seems to depend not only upon the nature of the illness, but also upon anxiety. The greater the anxiety the worse the pain tends to be. Perhaps because of this the old tend to feel less pain than a younger person dying. The young person, whose life span is being cut short and who may have uncompleted responsibilities to his family is inevitably more distraught than a person who has lived his life span (Hinton, 1967).

Perhaps as serious a problem as pain is continuing and chronic discomfort both from disease itself and from continued immobility. With chronic discomfort without hope for the future, many dying people become acutely depressed. These experiences of depression naturally occur most often when they suffer acute pain. With the relief of the pain, the depression often lifts.

A very ill person may feel great shame at being a nuisance, or because of incontinence in front of others. But as the illness progresses he usually ceases to worry about such things. Towards the end, a person's consciousness often becomes clouded for long periods. Then perhaps a day or so before the end, he seems to give up interest and lets death take him. Many people lapse into unconsciousness; others may remain aware but simply withdraw; a subtle change takes place so that those around usually recognize that death is very close.

3. Awareness of dying[1]
Let us now turn from immediate and physical sensations to a dying person's general awareness. We have already discussed the individual's developing conception of his mortality. Now we come to

[1] Hinton, 1967. Kübler-Ross, 1970.

consider its recognition when it is close. People seem to be as various in this as they are in their styles of living.

Many cultures hold individual life as of little consequence, and perhaps people in such circumstances give their lives up more easily than in our society, where we have grown to feel ourselves as precious. But even here in some circumstances people can feel elation at the thought of their death. This is particularly noticeable in the contemplation of suicide. The idea of divesting oneself of the torments of living guilt and anxiety seems to bring a sense of delightful freedom. Old people may not be suicidal, but they also can welcome death as a relief from pain, particularly when they feel they have had their time. On the whole, however, elements of dread and fear are present both in the dying as well as the living.

It seems likely that most people are quite aware, at least transiently, of their dying (Hinton, 1967). The individual is internally informed of his own lethal processes without being told about them. However, during the last months his ideas may fluctuate, so that he often loses his recognition and behaves as if he were getting better.

Some people are terrified by this awareness; others accept it with calmness. A person's sense of guilt about unfinished business often plays a strong part in distress. Thus young people who feel they are deserting their dependants can be distraught, particularly if they are parents of young children. People who feel they have wasted their lives can also be tormented by remorse. Guilt seems to play a part as well as where religious feelings are involved. Convinced believers and also thorough-going atheists and agnostics do not seem to suffer such anxieties as those who were vague believers but indolent in their religious practices.

With painful feelings such as these coming beside awareness of death, its denial in hopes of getting better is a blessed relief. However, many old people accept death with a calmness that is awe-inspiring and almost incomprehensible to a younger person. They will steadfastly see that their affairs are tidied up so that relatives can carry on after their death. For instance:

(i) An old man in considerable pain said to his son, 'When this nonsense is over you will find the will in the desk downstairs.' He then proceeded to give instructions about his affairs.

(ii) An old man said to his niece, 'I think I shall be gone by the time you visit me again next week-end, so I think we had better say good-bye now.'

(iii) An old woman in Nigeria was nearly ninety when she fell ill. However, she said to her children, 'Don't waste your money preparing for a funeral now, because I am not going to die yet.' She did not die, but one day some months later she got up and began to make her preparations by walking round to all her friends saying good-bye. The next morning her daughter was due to go out shopping and the old lady said, 'I think you had better say good-bye now before you go.' A few hours later she died.

If, as has been suggested, most people are, if only dimly, aware of their impending death, why is it that the British at least are reticent about mentioning it to them? It very often happens that everyone around talks about it but excludes the dying person, yet he probably also knows from his own inner awareness. The answer usually given is that it would distress him too much. Yet many patients say they are glad to have known the truth and been able to discuss it. There is no doubt that for many people the truth would be too hard to bear. But the ease and relief many patients gain from knowing suggests the taboo on discussion is motivated more to save the living from embarrassment than by thought for the dying. Those who do break through this barrier of silence and talk to dying people rarely regret it. They feel they have contributed something to a person in his last days that is very intimate, and have been enriched themselves by the unforgettable, humbling experience of being with a person who has forsaken defences and illusions. Obviously it would be dogmatic cruelty to insist on telling everyone the truth, come what may. Furthermore, no layman can be justified in telling a patient without a doctor's opinion, for he is the only person who can say with reasonable certainty that a disease process has become irreversible. But after this there are many people – doctors, nurses, relatives, social workers and priests – with whom a person may wish to talk about his death. It would seem cowardice on our parts to be unwilling to be honest in return.

By the time the last hours come, a person has usually given himself up to death and no longer wishes to communicate much. He is often unconscious. Then he dies and the living person that was changes into inert, shrunken mortal remains. All that is left alive of him on this earth now lies in other people. His relatives, children, friends and acquaintances, all those who have experienced him in some measure have learnt from him and have something of him inside themselves. We shall now turn to these survivors, for they have the task of transforming their experience of the dead person as someone outside themselves to an internal living and usable memory.

4. Grief and mourning[1]

Most acquaintances of a dead person feel some shock and depression on hearing the news. It often reminds them of their own death. But such ideas are usually transient, and they move on about their business. It is very different for those who have loved and whose identities have been entwined with the dead person. The acute phase of loss of a deeply loved person is usually referred to as *grief*. The longer-term process of stabilization without the loved person is termed *mourning*.

As an illustration of grief, here is the sequel to Mr J.'s death, described earlier in this chapter.

Before her husband's death Mrs J. was always preoccupied with her own health, so that before a visitor had finished asking Mr J. about how he was, she would be saying how ill she felt. When I spoke to her four days after her husband's death, she only very briefly mentioned herself. She was very preoccupied with thoughts about Mr J. She was relieved that he was gone, saying, 'He was no good to himself,' 'He suffered a lot, I don't think I could have looked after him much longer.' Mingled with this was a feeling of guilt that she had not done enough for him. She constantly said how hard she had worked for him, inviting me to confirm that she had done all she could. In fact she had cared for him well, but regularly complained about his demands, irritability and unfairness to her. Much of this was true, but I sensed she felt guilty that she had complained so much.

Mrs J. used to walk about the room 'doing things' all the time, and I cannot remember a time when she sat still for more than a couple of minutes. But now she did not move from her chair, and appeared to be stunned by her husband's death. She said such things as, 'I feel he's in the next room,' 'I can't believe he's dead,' 'It's just as if he will come in, in a minute.' The finality of the situation had not reached her.

[1] Hinton, 1967. Gorer, 1965.

'Everyone has been so kind and considerate.' This was probably true, but I was very struck by Mrs J. speaking so well of
everyone. She seemed unable to say anything uncomplimentary,
and remarked even how quiet the dustman had been that morning. He had been a regular victim of her complaining tongue in
the past.

There was a compelling quietness about the place. Every
movement was made gently, speech was hushed. There were many
topics of conversation, but all revolved round the dead man.
Only superficially were plans made for the future. It was almost
as if the family's lives had stopped with his.

Everything that the old man would have wished was strictly
adhered to. None of the family wanted to see the body, but all
agreed that he should lie in the front room with the coffin lid off
for twenty-four hours prior to the funeral, because this was what
he would have wished.

In spite of former feelings that he was a tyrant, they all felt
proud of him. I was shown a letter of tribute from his old com-
rades' association, and an insertion that was to be put in the local
press and which told about tributes that the neighbours, the G.P.
and local clergyman had made.

Perhaps the most striking thing of all was attention to detail.
Very precise accounts of the exact place and time that he died were
insisted upon, together with information about where everyone
else was and what they were doing then. The minutest details of
the funeral were explained several times.

We see here how Mrs J.'s ways of relating to her husband, grown
over many years together, could not be cut off overnight. This is
commonly felt and can be very frightening, as it often reaches the
intensity of hallucination. It is perhaps one of the reasons why
kindly relatives feel it necessary to stay with a grieving person. To
experience inner emptiness together with illusions of the continued
presence of a loved person when alone is quite terrifying, and the
opportunity for communication with somebody who is not so disturbed is invaluable as a check upon reality. Soon, when these
chaotic near-hallucinations are not taking place, one often feels
numb, shocked and dead. The severity of such experiences will
depend both upon the suddenness of the death and upon the depth
of investment in a dead person.

Within a little while, perhaps a few days later, a person usually begins to feel things again, if only in patches. Very often this is extremely painful. He may find himself weeping uncontrollably like a child. With this comes a welter of conflicting emotions: pleading with the dead person to come back, interspersed with periods of agonized remorse with self-accusations about failures and sins. Raging anger at the dead person for their desertion often emerges, only to be followed by greater remorse over such unworthy anger at a poor, loved, dead one. With this, perhaps, the phase of acute grief has begun to be transformed into mourning.

Such violence of reaction is nearly universal, though more muted for some than others, and often less intense when it is an old person who has died. Being common does not mean that such experiences can be taken lightly or disregarded. The process of grief and mourning is a serious crisis for an individual. He will never be quite the same again after it. There is plenty of evidence to suggest that although it happens to nearly everyone, it can literally be dangerous and may be lethal. Thus widows and widowers are statistically at rather greater risk in the year after their spouse's death than other married people of the same age. Widowers are more prone than widows, rising to a forty per cent increase in mortality rate in the first six months of bereavement. It also seems that the younger person is at greater risk after the death of a spouse. One study showed that the mortality rate for widows in their thirties was twice the normal for married women, whereas for widowers of the same age there was a fourfold increase (see Hinton, 1967).

Even though the period of mourning is infrequently lethal, it is extremely distressing and critical, for out of it the bereaved person must redirect his life. If left alone he may make irreversible self-deleterious decisions. Yet, just as with the dying, there is something of a British taboo upon conversation about the subject. People tend to avoid becoming too involved with a bereaved person, often through fear of an uncontrolled explosion of feeling or of their own embarrassment.

Here is a description by a woman, Mrs K., of her experiences of death, which not only highlights grief and mourning but also emphasizes the stiff-upper-lip taboo upon feelings about death.

My first experience of the death of a known person came at the age of five, when my aunt died. I did not know what this meant. I only knew that we didn't talk about her any more. Something very frightening and mysterious had happened to her. As far as I knew this 'something' could well happen to me at any moment.

When I was thirteen my grandmother died. She was a much-loved, very elegant lady, with long black skirts down to her ankles, and button boots. I thought as a very young child that she must be a close friend of the Queen. One Saturday she decorated my bedroom, putting on wallpaper that I had been allowed to choose myself for the first time. She sat eating her tea with my new puppy playing in and out of her skirts and trying to bite the buttons off her boots. She was laughing and happy. I slept in my newly-decorated bedroom, smelling of the new wallpaper. That night I was very conscious of how much my grandmother loved me. On Monday morning an aunt came round to our house, just as I was leaving for school. It was the day I was due to take an English examination. My mother and aunt tried to make me go to school, but something in their faces terrified me, and I refused to go. Eventually they told me that my grandmother was dead. She had died very suddenly the previous night. I then went to school, sat the examination and did not think about my grandmother. I did not think about her again until the funeral, when I sat in the carriage with the hearse and the coffin covered in flowers, surrounded by relatives, dressed in black, and I had a black coat too. I did not think about my grandmother herself, because I was too busy trying not to laugh and laugh, and I knew that if I did nobody would understand why, and my mother would be ashamed. When the results of the examinations came out I was top of my class. It seemed as though this was the most shameful thing I had ever done.

A year later my school-friend died. She had pneumonia. I had seen her and she was getting better. The next day my mother told me when I came home from school that she was dead. I did not believe her. I went to see her mother, who told me that my friend died because the doctor would not waken her up to give her medicine. I was very afraid. I dare not go to sleep that night in case I should see my friend. I had loved her, but her death had turned into a terrifying horror.

When I was fifteen my grandfather died. He was ill for a long time, and we knew for a week that he was doing to die any day. Perhaps he wanted to die because my grandmother was dead. We had an end-of-term school dance on the Friday, and all I could think of was that I hoped he wouldn't die until that was over, or

I should not be able to go. He died on Friday night whilst I was enjoying myself at the dance. I hated him for dying then, and became even more afraid of death.

My next experience was years later, when my own daughter was fifteen. Normally she returned home from school with three friends, two boys and a girl. This particular day she was delayed at school and they left without her. A thunderstorm broke as they came across the common. They sheltered under a tree with their bicycles, lightning struck them and all were killed. I could not find words to console my daughter. I could only be thankful that she was alive.

A little later my father died, driving his car home from a foot-ball match. My mother did not ring me up to tell me until two hours after his death, because she 'wanted me to have my tea first'. I was kept very busy looking after her during the next two weeks, and hardly thought about him.

When I was forty-four my mother died. She insisted on living alone. She was very independent and had enough money to do so comfortably. I was always afraid she would have an accident and lie unable to get help. She had a minor stroke and lay unconscious for a whole day before she was found. Nobody told me she was ill – she died before I could get there. I did not say good-bye to her. My aunt said she didn't tell me that she was ill. She thought I might be upset and I 'couldn't do anything anyway'.

A few months later my dearly loved father-in-law died. He died of cancer and we knew that the end was near. We received a telephone call to go to the hospital. Our car was caught in a traffic jam and we arrived at the hospital five minutes after he died. We never talked of any of these people and their deaths.

The last one was my husband and he died after three long-drawn-out months of torture. He had cancer and refused an operation, which would have been useless anyway. I used to pray that he would hurry up and die, and was glad when he did.

After they had taken him away his dog ripped up his bed and his pillows and scattered the feathers all over the stairs. I changed all the furniture around the day he died, and then I carried on doing all the same things that I had done before. I used to pretend he was at work.

I couldn't stop buying the foods he liked from the grocers. I didn't know when to go to bed or when to get up. My son drove his father's car, and the dog nearly went mad every day when the car came down the drive. We sold the car. Eventually we had to find a new home for the dog, who would have died of misery if we hadn't. My friends were all very kind. They kept me very busy with empty business. I was lonelier with people than without them. Nobody could talk about my husband. Christmas was hell. We always wound up our special clock on Christmas day. I let it stop. My birthday, our wedding anniversary, his birthday and his children's birthdays were hell, but we never spoke about him. After a few months people started to say how brave I'd been, and what a wonderful new life I'd made. There was relief in their voices. They could look me in the eye again and didn't need to be embarrassed. I remember the relief that he was dead and couldn't suffer any more, or was it that I didn't have to watch him suffer? I never talked about him.

More recently I have thought about the cruelties of our culture, that demands a 'stiff upper lip' and no embarrassing show of emotion. I think I have learnt how to say good-bye, and that through sorrow and conscious weeping that the horror of pain and disease-riddled bodies can be allowed to sink into the background and mourning becomes more joyful. When this happens, memories can be of happiness known of a loving mother, warm and alive, of a husband walking in the sunshine across the paddock, his pipe in his mouth, his dog by his side, coming in to tea.

Mrs K. is here both informing us of her experiences, and making a plea for greater openness about death and mourning. It is the same conclusion as that drawn by Gorer (1965) and Hinton (1967) in their books. Perhaps with recognition of the problem, this aspect of British culture will slowly change.

It may well be asked why it seems important that a mourner should have the opportunity for conversation. The person in mourning has lost his old ways of feeling and relating to an external person. He has nowhere to place his passion. Without a recipient the lonely person can well find relief only in bitter resentment of an alien and unnoticing world. This experience of hatred is very disturbing. Furthermore the solitary mourner becomes entangled within his own feelings. He turns into phantasy, loving and hating imagined objects instead of real things and people in the outside world. Reality discrimination may therefore be threatened. We have seen how a bereaved person is swept by violent ideas and feelings, weeping with remorse, love, bitterness and anger which are alien to our everyday practices. If a sympathetic companion realizes that such feelings naturally emerge in grief, then he can act as a check to the mourner. The bereaved can experience his ideas being recognized, but sees that they do not contain the same implications to another person as they seem in his own fevered mind. With such an opportunity in conversation, the individual often feels safer with his ideas. They can come to belong simply to himself and not to a chaotic sense of the whole of reality. He can keep his psychological boundaries intact, and the processes of redistribution of personal investment can continue quietly within himself.

5. Grief in childhood

A young child's inner representations of his world and loved people are less stable than an adult's. He cannot explicitly recognize or manifest his sense of loss. He rarely weeps at a loved person's death. His mental organization is not sufficiently coherent for him to do so. This raises the question as to whether children who have lost a parent should be told about it or not and, if so, how. Very many people avoid the issue by saying they are too young to understand. And the young child, usually thunderstruck by his loss and by the depression of others in the family, rarely asks questions about it spontaneously. He has not developed the integrative capacity to put his ideas into words. From his silence, adults then often make the assumption that grief means nothing to him.

Some people will go to remarkable lengths to prevent a child knowing about a parent's death. For example:

The mother of three young children died after a long illness. Their father decided it was best to pretend that mother was still in hospital and would be home again one day. He asked the children's teacher to keep the news from them. The teacher, trying to be considerate and helpful, asked all the others in the children's classes and their parents not to talk about the death. However, the school was large and many children in other classes knew what had happened and naturally talked about it. Throughout the neighbourhood children were baffled and ill at ease, some having been told not to talk about it, but not knowing why, while others felt guilty for talking quite freely, having had instructions to the contrary. Eventually matters were sorted out by someone mentioning the problem to the teacher, who got someone to talk things over with the father.

The father cannot be condemned for the confusion. He was distraught after the death of his wife, with three young children to look after. The teacher too was trying to help him. But a lie arose which caused more trouble to his children than it was worth, for not only were they surrounded by grief at home but also by embarrassment, secretiveness and confusion among their school friends.

We can see from this that not to tell a child about the death of a parent is to withhold the truth about an important reality. Naturally enough this does not matter if the child is too young to attach meaning to the spoken word. It would, for instance, be absurd to tell a young baby of his parent's death. So the question arises first as to how much children understand about what has happened and secondly, how much of verbal explanation is helpful (Anthony, 1940).

It seems that children dimly realize at a very early age that something terrible has happened. What is more, even if they do not feel much at the time, the death of a parent soon becomes evident, for they never see him again. This is the main meaning of a death to a young child. A parent has disappeared and never returns. As we saw in earlier chapters, loss and separation can have far-reaching effects upon the child's capacity to feel and think.

The situation is made more complex by the fact that a young child cannot yet communicate his grief coherently. He may *act* in a disturbed way, but he has not yet organized his ideas in order to speak or openly weep about it as an older mourner does. A helping adult cannot wait until the child is openly ready to talk, because he may never be able to verbalize his grief coherently. It seems that it is best for adults to give an explanation which is within the comprehension of the child, and then to leave it to the child to ask what questions he can as the time goes by. Answers can then be simple and truthful, confined to what is understandable to the child. Over and above this, the adult must expect anxiety and disturbed behaviour from a little child about ideas and feelings which he cannot yet put into words. Sensitive people find their own ways intuitively about how to respond in these circumstances. Specific rules and procedures are out of place. Without understanding the child is left with his own grief in an alien, uncommunicative world.

This alienation will remain if his adults do not feel for his anxiety and loss, however kind they may be in other ways.

6. Disturbances in mourning

We have mentioned how young children are unlikely to be able to weep about the loss of a parent. The full meaning of the loss cannot impinge itself upon a child's comprehension as it does for an adult. We often find that adults also feel unable to cry, and this is often extremely distressing. Weeping seems to bring the greatest relief to a mourner. One often sees relatives helping a mourner to cry at a funeral by holding them while they weep uncontrollably. As Mrs K. described, the process of weeping allows the loss of a loved one to become more recognizable and tolerable.

Some people weep silently, but others cannot weep at all and seem to go cold inside. Or, on the other hand, their weeping may become chronically uncontrolled. When either of these happens it is likely that something has gone wrong with the mourning process, and professional help may be called for (Parkes, 1965). In ordinary circumstances relatives and friends provide sufficient company and sympathy to allow normal mourning to take its own course.

7. Completion of mourning

The stage of acute distress may last for only a few weeks, but critical changes inside the individual go on less dramatically for many months and more quietly for years.

Slowly the grieving person finds a new distribution for his energies, and new objects to love and hate. And yet if mourning is successful, awareness of the dead person is not lost. The immediate experience of the person as dead loses force and gives way to living memory of the person as he was when alive. The mourner in doing this has not necessarily 'become' the dead person, though this sometimes happens, but rather he has internalized him, and has his experience of him from the past ready to use in present and future situations.

After months and perhaps years, the mourners slowly come alive again. The dead person has gained a certain immortality in the memory of his loved ones. They themselves are then perhaps ready to carry on living, and are a little more prepared to die themselves one day, for other generations to carry them on also to the future.

REFERENCES

Starred titles are of detailed technical texts; all others are for general reading.

Aberle, D. F. and Noegele, K. D. (1968), 'Middle Class Fathers, Occupational Roles and Attitudes to Children', in Bell, E. W. and Vogel, N., *A Modern Introduction to the Family*. London, Collier-Macmillan (188–98).

Abraham, K. (1927), *Selected Papers*. London, Hogarth.
Theory of anal character (370–92). Influence of oral eroticism (393–406).

Alexander, F. (1952), *Psychosomatic Medicine*. London, Allen & Unwin.
General principles (54–82), emotional factors in disease (82–215).

Anthony, S. (1940), *The Child's Discovery of Death*. London, Kegan Paul.

Bell, E. W. and Vogel, N. (1968), *A Modern Introduction to the Family*. London, Collier-Macmillan.
The family over the world (37–112).

Benedek, T. (1952), *'The Functions of the Sexual Apparatus and their Disturbances', in Alexander, F., *Psychosomatic Medicine*. London, Allen & Unwin (216–39).

Berezin, M. A. (1963), 'Intrapsychic Aspects of Ageing', in Zinberg, N., *Normal Psychology of the Ageing Process*. New York, I.U.P. (92–117).

Berne, E. (1964), *Games People Play*. Harmondsworth, Penguin.

Bernstein, B. (1970), 'A Sociolinguistic Approach to Socialisation', in Rubinstein, D. and Stoneman, C., *Education and Democracy*. Harmondsworth, Penguin.

Bibring, G. (1961), *'A Study of the Psychological Processes in Pregnancy', *Psychoanalytic Study of the Child*. London, Hogarth.
Vol. 16 (9–72).

Blanck, R. and Blanck, G. (1968), *Marriage and Personal Development*. New York and London, Columbia University Press.

Blos, P. (1962), *On Adolescence*. London, Collier-Macmillan.
Puberty (75–87), mid-adolescence (87–128), late adolescence (128–58), masturbation (159–69).

Bowlby, J. (1953), *Child Care and the Growth of Love*. Abridged by Fry, M. Harmondsworth, Penguin.

Boyle, D. G. (1969), *A Student's Guide to Piaget*. Oxford, Pergamon.
Sensori-motor phase (30–51), summary of developmental periods (89–94), language (125–38).

Brecher, R. and E. (1966), *An Analysis of the Human Sexual Response*. London, Panther.

Brody, S. (1956), *Patterns of Mothering*. New York, I.U.P.
Maternal attitudes (269–79), patterns in feeding (286–321).

Bromley, D. B. (1966), *The Psychology of Human Ageing*. Harmondsworth, Penguin.
Biological aspects (32–66), social aspects (67–92), adjustment in old age (104–14), psychopathology (115–48), skill and age (172–206).

Brown, J. A. C. (1954), *The Social Psychology of Industry*. Harmondsworth, Penguin.
Work, its nature, conditions and motivation (186–218).

Butcher, H. J. (1968), *Human Intelligence, its Nature and Assessment*. London, Methuen.

Cameron, N. (1963), **Personality Development and Psychopathology*. Boston, Houghton Miflin.
Infancy and oral phase (25–58), self-assertion and anal phase (59–66), oedipal phase (67–77), latency (77–97), adolescence (99–114), self, ego, id and super-ego (115–99), anxiety and defences (200–45).

Caplan, G. (1961), *An approach to Community Mental Health*. London, Tavistock.
Pregnancy (65–96), early mother–child relationship (97–132).

Caplan, G. (1964), *Principles of Preventive Psychiatry*. London, Tavistock.
Crisis concept (3–112).

Carmichael, L. (1954), *Manual of Child Psychology*. New York, Wiley.
Onset and early development of behaviour (60–185).

Carter, C. O. (1962), *Human Heredity*. Harmondsworth, Penguin.

Carter, M. (1966), *Into Work*. Harmondsworth, Penguin.
Approaching work (39–106), work satisfaction (164–78).

Chamberlain, G. (1969), *The Safety of the Unborn Child*. Harmondsworth, Penguin.
Development of embryo (26–49), congenital abnormalities (69–134), intra-uterine hazards (135–72).

Davis, N. (ed.) (1963), *The Paston Letters*. London, Oxford University Press.

Deutsch, H. (1944), *The Psychology of Women. London, Research Books.
Vol. I. Girlhood, prepuberty (1–18), puberty (19–145), Vol. II. Motherhood, conception and pregnancy (93–177), delivery and confinement
(178–258), mother–child (259–92), menopause (402–30).

Dicks, H. V. (1967), Marital Tensions. London, Routledge & Kegan
Paul.
Social and individual setting of marriage (13–44), splitting in marriage
(68–84).

Douglas, J. W. B. and Blomfield, J. M. (1958), Children under Five.
London, Allen & Unwin.

Erikson, E. H. (1950), Childhood and Society. Harmondsworth, Penguin.
Comparison of development in different cultures (105–82), trust (239–43),
autonomy and shame (243–46), industry (250–2), identity (252–4),
intimacy (255–8), male identity (269–392).

Erikson, E. H. (1964), Insight and Responsibility. New York, W. W.
Norton.
Identity and uprootedness (81–108).

Erikson, E. H. (1968), Identity, Youth and Crisis. London, Faber and
Faber.
Mutuality of recognition (96–106), will to be oneself (107–14), industry
(122–7), adolescence (128–34), youth (232–60), womanhood and the
inner space (201–94).

Fleming, C. M. (1967), Adolescence, Its Social Psychology. London,
Routledge & Kegan Paul.
Bodily changes (5–20), adolescent at home (5–86), at school (87–186).

Flugel, J. C. (1945), Man, Morals and Society. Harmondsworth, Penguin.

Fraiberg, S. H. (1959), The Magic Years. London, Methuen.
First months (35–67), feeding (72–5), separation anxiety (76–83), bowel
training (91–101), conscience (146–58), oedipus complex (202–9).

Frazer, R. (ed.) (1967), Work, Twenty Personal Accounts. Harmondsworth, Penguin.

Freud, A. (1937), The Ego and the Mechanisms of Defence. London,
Hogarth.

Freud, A. (1949), *'Aggression in Relation to Emotional Development',
Psychoanalytic Study of the Child III/IV. London, Hogarth (37–42).

Freud, A. (1952), *'The Role of Bodily Illness in the Mental Life of
Children', Psychoanalytic Study of the Child VII. London, Hogarth
(69–81).

Freud, A. (1953), *'Some Remarks on Infant Observation', Psychoanalytic
Study of the Child VIII. London, Hogarth (9–19).

R

Freud, A. (1965), *Normality and Pathology in Childhood*. London and New York, I.U.P.
Developmental lines (62–8), sucking to eating (69–71), wetting and soiling to control (72–4), body management (75–7), egocentricity to companionship (78–83).

Freud, S. (1905), *Three Essays on the Theory of Sexuality*, Standard Edition Vol. VII. London, Hogarth.
Infantile sexuality (173–200), puberty (207–30).

Freud, S. (1913), *Totem and Taboo*, Standard Edition Vol. XIII. London, Hogarth (1–164).

Freud, S. (1915), *Instincts and their Vicissitudes*, Standard Edition Vol. XIV. London, Hogarth.

Freud, S. (1916), *Introductory Lectures on Psychoanalysis*, Standard Edition XV and XVI. London, Hogarth.
Evidence for unconscious processes (15–82), dreams (83–241), sexual development (303–39).

Freud, S. (1923), *The Ego and The Id*, Standard Edition XIX. London, Hogarth.

Gavron, H. (1966), *The Captive Wife*. Harmondsworth, Penguin.

Gesell, A. (1940), *The First Five Years of Life*. New York, Harper.

Goldberg, E. M. (1958), *Family Influences & Psychosomatic Illness*. London, Tavistock.

Gorer, G. (1955), *Exploring English Character*. London, Cresset.
People and homes (34–50), growing up and ideas about sex (77–124), marriage (125–61).

Gorer, G. (1965), *Death, Grief and Mourning in Contemporary Britain*. London, Cresset.

Green, J. H. (1969), *Basic Clinical Physiology*. Oxford, O.U.P.

Green, L. (1968), *Parents and Teachers, Partners or Rivals*. London, Allen & Unwin.

Griffiths, R. (1954), *The Abilities of Babies*. London, University of London Press.

Haley, J. (1968), 'The Family of the Schizophrenic', in Hendel, G. (ed.), *The Psychosocial Interior of the Family*. London, Allen & Unwin (251–75).

Harris, C. (1969), *The Family*. London, Allen & Unwin.
Kinship and Family (19–92), Family in society (93–148), nuclear family (149–84).

Hebb, D. O. (1949), *The Organisation of Behaviour*. New York, Wiley.

Hinton, J. (1967), *Dying*. Harmondsworth, Penguin.
Attitudes to death (21–52), dying (53–110), mourning (167–93).

Hoffer, W. (1949), *'Mouth, Hand and Ego Integration', *Psychoanalytic Study of the Child* III/IV. London, Hogarth (49–56).

Isaacs, S. (1930), *The Intellectual Development of Young Children*. London, Routledge.

Isaacs, S. (1933), *The Social Development of Young Children*. London, Routledge.

Isaacs, S. (1952), *'The Nature and Function of Phantasy', in Klein, M. et al., *Developments in Psychoanalysis*. London, Hogarth (67–121).

Jaques, E. (1970), *Work, Creativity & Social Justice*. New York, International Universities Press, Inc.

Kaufman, I. (1963), *'Psychodynamic Considerations in Normal Ageing', in Zinberg, N. (ed.), *The Normal Psychology of the Ageing Process* (188–224). New York, I.U.P.

Klein, J. (1965), *Samples of English Cultures*. London, Routledge & Kegan Paul.
Vol. I, Working class families (121–218), middle class families (303–429).
Vol. II, Attitudes to conception (439–42), early feeding (443–7), early discipline (448–56), later parental discipline (464–551).

Klein, M. (1947), *Contributions to Psychoanalysis*. London, Hogarth.
Oedipus complex in light of early anxieties (339–90), early development of conscience (267–77).

Klein, M. and Riviere, J. (1953), *Love, Hate and Reparation*. London, Hogarth.
Aggression (4–10), projection (11–15), envy (25), hate (28–9), conscience (45–50).

Klein, M. (1960), *Our Adult World and its Roots in Infancy*. London, Tavistock Pamphlet.

Kübler-Ross, E. (1970), *On Death and Dying*. London, Tavistock.

Laing, R. D. and Esterson, A. (1964), *Sanity, Madness and the Family*. Harmondsworth, Penguin.

Lewis, M. M. (1963), *Language, Thought and Personality*. London, Harrap.

Lidz, T. (1963), *The Family and Human Adaptation*. London, Hogarth.

Lidz, T. (1968), *The Person*. London, Basic Books.

Lomas, P. (1967) (ed.), *The Predicament of the Family*. London, Hogarth.
Family relationships (9–25), puerperal breakdown (126–39).

Luce, G. G. and Segal, J. (1966), *Sleep*. London, Heinemann.
Dreams (149–213).

Lynd, H. M. (1958), *Shame and the Search for Identity*. London, Routledge & Kegan Paul.
Shame and guilt (20–6), search for identity (183–200).

Malleson, J. (1948), *Change of Life*. Harmondsworth, Penguin.

Mayer-Gross *et al.* (1960), *Clinical Psychiatry*.
Anxiety (125–30), paranoid reaction (166–72), depressive reaction (217–21).

Masters, W. H. and Johnson, V. E. (1966), *The Human Sexual Response*. London, Churchill.
Female response (27–170), male response (171–222).

McCarthy, D. (1954), 'Language Development', in Carmichael, L. (ed.), *Manual of Child Psychology*. New York, Wiley (492–630).

Mead, M. (1928), *Coming of Age in Samoa*. Harmondsworth, Penguin.

Mead, M. (1950), *Male and Female*. Harmondsworth, Penguin.
Ways of the body (67–176), fatherhood (177–91).

Mead, M. (1963), *Growing up in New Guinea*. Harmondsworth, Penguin.

Millar, S. (1968), *The Psychology of Play*. Harmondsworth, Penguin.
Theory (23–58), exploration (103–35), make-belief and phantasy (136–57), imitation (158–77), social play (178–90).

Morrison, A. and McIntyre, D. (1969), *Teachers and Teaching*. Harmondsworth, Penguin.

Newson, J. and E. (1963), *Infant Care in an Urban Community*, Harmondsworth, Penguin.
Childbirth (17–31), feeding (32–79), discipline (115–132), fathering (133–50).

Neugarten, B. C. (1968), *Middle Age and Ageing*. Chicago, University of Chicago Press.

Opie, I. and P. (1959), *The Lore and Language of School Children*. Oxford, O.U.P.
Unpopular children (175–205), friendships (323–42), authority (361–76), pranks (377–92).

Opie, I. and P. (1969), *Children's Games in Streets and Playground.* Oxford, O.U.P.

Parkes, C. M. (1965), 'Bereavement and Mental Illness', *Brit. J. Med. Psych.* Vol. 38 (1–16).

Piaget, J. (1932), **The Language and Thought of the Child.* London, Routledge & Kegan Paul.

Piaget, J. (1953), **The Origins of Intelligence.* London, Routledge & Kegan Paul.
First stage (21–46), acquired (47–121), circular reactions (153–209), reactions applied to new situations (210–62).

Piaget, J. (1955), **The Child's Construction of Reality.* London, Routledge & Kegan Paul.
Development of object concept (3–96).

Reisman, D. (1950), *The Lonely Crowd.* Yale, Yale University Press.

Rycroft, C. H. (1968) a., *A Critical Dictionary of Psychoanalysis.* London, Nelson.

Rycroft, C. H. (1968) b., *Anxiety and Neurosis.* Harmondsworth, Allen Lane, The Penguin Press.

Sandler, J. and Rosenblatt, B. (1962), **'The Concept of the Representational World',* *Psycho Analytic Study of the Child* XVII. London, Hogarth (181–202).

Saunders, C. (1959), *Care of the Dying.* London, Macmillan.

Schofield, M. (1968), *The Sexual Life of Young People.* Harmondsworth, Penguin.

Segal, H. (1964), **Introduction to the Work of Melanie Klein.* London, Heinemann.
Phantasy (1–10), splitting and paranoid anxiety (11–25), depressive anxiety (54–68), oedipus complex (90–103).

Sheridan, M. (1968), *The Developmental Progress of Infants and Young Children.* London, H.M.S.O. pamphlet.

Spitz, R. (1965), *The First Year of Life.* New York, I.U.P.
Objectless stage (35–52), perception and learning (53–83), mother–child relationship (122–47), good object and bad object (167–73), communication (180–94), deprivation (267–77).

Sluckin, W. (1970), *Early Learning in Man and Animals.* London, Allen & Unwin.
Conditioning (26–35), imprinting (36–57), imitation (77–85), language (86–96).

Spock, B. (1957), *Baby and Child Care.* New York, Pocket Books, Inc.

Stone, J. C. and Church, J. (1957), *Childhood and Adolescence.* New York, Random House.

Storr, A. (1960), *The Integrity of the Personality.* Harmondsworth, Penguin.
Self (22–39), identification (76–87), defensive mechanisms (88–114), heterosexuality (115–26).

Storr, A. (1968), *Human Aggression.* Harmondsworth, Allen Lane, The Penguin Press.
Territory and ritual (31–7), aggression in child development (38–49), aggression between the sexes (59–71).

Townsend, P. (1963), *The Family Life of Old People.* Harmondsworth, Penguin.

Wallis, J. H. (1962), *The Challenge of Middle Age.* London, Routledge & Kegan Paul (74–92).

Werner, H. (1957), *Comparative Psychology of Mental Development.* New York, I.U.P.
First year (59–103), sensori-motor organization (104–42), imagery (143–66), notions of space and time (167–81), primitive thought (213–98).

West, D. J. (1960), *Homosexuality.* Harmondsworth, Penguin (40–56).

Westermarck, E. (1926), *A Short History of Marriage.* London, Macmillan.
Origin of marriage (1–30).

Winnicott, D. W. (1958), **Collected Papers.* London, Tavistock.
Primitive emotional development (145–56), aggression in relation to development (204–18), transitional objects (229–42), depressive position (255–61), primary maternal preoccupation (300–5).

Winnicott, D. W. (1964), *The Child, the Family and the Outside World.* Harmondsworth, Penguin.
Mother–baby (19–102), father (113–18).

Winnicott, D. W. (1965) a., *The Family and Individual Development.* London, Tavistock.
First year (3–14), mother and baby (15–20), five-year-old (34–9), adolescence (79–87).

Winnicott, D. W. (1965) b., **The Maturational Process and Facilitating Environment.* London, Hogarth.
Guilt (15–28), capacity to be alone (29–36), holding (44–60), self (56–60), contributing and concern (73–82), good enough mother (145–6).

Wiseman, S. (1967), *Intelligence and Ability.* Harmondsworth, Penguin.

Young, P. and Wilmott, P. (1957), *Family and Kinship in East London.* Harmondsworth, Penguin.

Zinberg, N. A., 'The Relationship of Regressive Phenomena to the Ageing Process', in Zinberg N. (ed.), *Normal Psychology of the Ageing Process.* New York, I.U.P. (143–59),

INDEX

Abstraction, 15, 51–2, 75, 90–1
Adolescence
  crisis, 157
  identification with parents, 150–2
  and identity, 152–9
  puberty, 140–9
Ageing, 223, 234–6
Aggression
  towards children, 33, 50, 65, 66, 83
  and control, 78–80
  and frustration, 61–5
  in marriage, 191
  towards parents, 138, 148, 151, 155–6
  and reality, 60–1
  and sexuality, 111–14
Ambivalence, 65, 107
Anal functions, 80–5, 97
Anger, 50, 61, 65, 86
Anxiety
  and ageing, 229
  defences against, 65–6, 122–7, 165
  and parents, 109
  persecutory, 65, 79
  and play, 92–4
  in pregnancy, 31
  primitive, 64–5
  at school, 128–33
  separation, 67–70
  and siblings, 37
  and splitting, 65
Auto-eroticism, 142

Basic trust – mistrust, 47, 67–70, 79–80, 85, 190
Berne, E., 165
Birth, 38–41
Body
  fascination with parts of, 154
  image, 143–5
  at puberty, 141, 144
  support for infant, 41
Bowel and bladder control, 80–5
Bowlby, J., 48, 67
Brain as control system, 53
Breast and bottle feeding, 43, 49, 55
Bullying, 129, 135–6

Childbirth, 38–41
Circular reactions, 45
Communication
  and anxiety, 64
  in infancy, 62–5
  and negation, 63
  and language, 74–7, 89, 100
Compulsive role play, 164–6
Concept formation, 76, 88, 90–1, 101–3
Conception, 26
Concern, 84, 86, 114, 163–4, 199
Conflict, 78, 111–13, 120–2, 139, 164
Conformity, 78, 80, 169, 194
Confusion in child, 65, 73, 78, 79, 90, 109
Conscience, 118–22, 136, 163–4

Conscious – Unconscious, 20, 53, 122–7
Contribution to others
  of child to parents, 37
  of child to teachers, 133–5
  in old age, 234
  in work, 160–4
Control
  bowel and bladder, 80–5
  by parents, 78
  self, 78, 117
  systems, 58
Courtship, 171–85
Creativity, 75, 88, 101, 105, 161–6, 232
Crisis
  adolescent, 150–7
  mid-life, 231–3
  retirement, 238–41
Criticism, self, 85, 119, 148
Cross-gender identification, 194, 218
Cruelty, 112, 129, 135–6
Cuddling, 44, 49, 62, 203
Cultural differences, 13
  adolescence, 140–1, 145–7, 150
  ageing, 235, 240
  courtship, 171–5, 184
  dying, 244
  marriage, 186–90, 193
  mourning, 252–6
  parents, 200–1, 206–11, 231

Death
  awareness of, 223–7
  dying, 244–50
Defence mechanisms, 122–7, 161, 165
Depression
  and ageing, 227, 235–6
  in childhood, 67, 79, 84, 224
  and dying, 247
  and melancholia, 123
  and menopause, 230–1
  puerperal, 48

Depressive guilt and concern, 84, 86, 113–14, 199
Deprivation, 44, 48, 67, 70
Deterioration, 223
Development, 12
  of awareness of mortality, 223–7, 252–5
  of awareness of people, 64
  determinants of, 22–4
  of ego, 139
  of feelings, 42, 86
  of guilt, 84
  identity, 150–1, 157–9
  intellectual, 44–6, 75–7, 87–91, 101–3
  language, 74–7, 88, 102
  of love, 175–80
  of meaning, 21, 46, 56–7
  of motor activity, 44–7, 55, 72, 87
  schedules, 45, 56
  of self-control, 78, 104, 116–20
  of sociability, 100, 103–6
Dichotomization, 66, 194, 198
Discipline, 78–85, 104, 109, 133
Disillusionment, 203
Displacement, 222
Distress, 42, 60–1, 64–5, 69
Dominance skew, 193–4
Dreaming, 58, 60, 98, 243
Drugs, 153
Eating phantasies, 97; see also feeding
Ecstasies, 59
Egocentrism
  in play, 100, 104
  sacrifice of, 104, 159
Ego-functions, 54, 85–6, 115–22, 138–9, 156–7, 236
Empathy, 20–2, 49, 102, 114
Environment and inheritance, 22–3
Envy and jealousy, 37, 107, 108, 112, 178–80
Erikson, E. H., 47, 95, 127, 158, 179

Esteem, self-, 31, 63
Experience
  as a focus of study, 21
  its function in learning, 15
Exploration, 45, 62, 153

Family
  and the aged, 240–2
  and courtship, 183–5
  and culture, 186–8, 200–1, 206–11
  and defences, 125–7
  environment for child, 23
  nuclear and extended, 24
Father, 208–19
  with child, 107–9, 214–18
  with infant, 50–1
  and mother, 205, 212–14, 218–19
  phantasy and responsibility, 210
  and pregnancy, 29–30, 35–6
  and sexuality, 109–14
  and work, 210–12
Feeding
  breast, bottle and solids, 43, 49, 55
  and ecstasy, 59
Feelings
  development of, about objects, 70–1
  good and bad, 61, 65–7
  and physiology, 70
Fixation, 38, 42
Freud, S., 3, 97, 111, 112, 113, 118, 171
Friendship
  adolescent, 145
  childhood, 100, 103–6, 135–8
  and loving, 175
  mother – child, 205
Frustration, 61

Gender
  differentiation, 94–6, 108
  skew, 194–5
Generation differences, 148–9

Genitals
  in childhood, 59, 94–8, 111–14, 117
  and imagination, 98
  in intercourse, 192–3
  at puberty, 141–9
Grandparents, 240
Grief, 155, 250–7
Guilt, 50, 79, 82–5, 118–22, 130, 235
Hallucination, 58, 91
Hatred, 62, 64–6, 83
Helplessness, 61–2, 107
Holding and support
  of infant, 41–3, 44
  between husband and wife, 51, 213
Homeostasis, 52
Homosexuality, 154
Hypothesis-testing, 18, 21

Id-functions, 53–4, 99, 120–2
Idealization, 83, 154, 176, 178, 180, 182
Idealism, 152–3
Ideas; see mental representations
Identification
  with other adults, 20
  with baby, 49–50
  with careers, 31
  with other children, 139
  cross-gender, 218
  with gender, 95, 139, 151, 155
  with lover, 179
  with parents, 73, 115–22
  with teachers, 133, 139
Identity
  adolescent, 157
  adult, 158–70
  in ageing, 231, 239
  compromise in, 169–70
  definition, 157
  and love, 180
  and work, 159–61
Illness, physical and mental, 71

Illusion, 142, 153, 154
Imagination; *see* concept forma-
    tion *and also* phantasy
Imitation, 56, 73, 75, 95, 119
Incest, 171
Industriousness, 137
Inheritance and environment, 22
Inhibition, normal, 116–20
Internal
    conflict, 120
    objects, 71
    space, 96, 101
    world, 70, 86, 102, 112
Internalization, 80, 118–20
Introjection, 123

Jealousy and envy, 37, 107, 108, 112

Klein, M., 44, 64–5, 84, 97, 112

Labour, 38
Language development, 74–7, 88,
    89, 102
Latency, 118, 175
Learning
    in adult, 164
    in childhood, 73, 87–9, 200
    in infancy, 45–6
    in mid-life, 229
    in old age, 239
Love
    and courtship, 171–85
    in marriage, 188–93
    of parents, 59, 63, 86
    and sexuality in children, 110–14

Make-believe, 91–4, 98–9
Marriage, 189–99
    choice, 171–85
    arranged, 171
Married couple
    in discord, 183, 191, 195–99
    and pregnancy, 29–30
    and sexual intercourse, 190–3
    as team, 188–90, 206

Masturbation
    in childhood, 97, 148
    and homosexuality, 154
    after puberty, 142–5, 162
Maternal preoccupation, 28, 43,
    201
Maturity, 164
Meaning
    and concept formation, 90–1
    in infancy, 41–6, 50–7
    and language, 74–6
Memory, 46
Menopause, 229–31
Mental representations, 17–18, 57–
    59, 70–1, 90–1, 102, 139
Middle Age, 220–33
Mid-life crisis, 221, 231–3
Milestones, 45, 56, 81
Mistrust, 47, 79–80
Mortality, awareness of, 224–7,
    245–50
Mother, 200–7
    and father, 205, 212–14
    and guilt of child, 83
    and hatred to child, 62, 65, 66,
        83
    with infant, 42–50, 62–4
    as integrating agent, 65
    and language, 176–7
    as loved and hated, 42–50, 60,
        65, 107
    and multiple responsibility, 203–
        5
    in pregnancy, 26–35, 37–8
    and separation anxiety, 67–70
    and socializing, 79–80
Motor development, 44–6, 55, 73,
    87
Mourning, 155, 239, 250–8
Mouth, in infancy, 43–4, 57

Negation, 63, 68
Negative feelings, 63

Objects, psychological

Objects—*cont.*
　inanimate, 64, 70
　internal and external, 70–1
　other people, 64
　parents, 62, 65, 70, 114
Object relations, 70–1
Oedipus complex, 109–14, 175
Omnipotence, 61–2
Oral functions, 44, 57–8, 97–8
Orgasm, 59–60, 143
Paranoid ideas, 83–4, 123, 198–9,
　236–7
Parents
　and adolescence, 148, 155–6
　attacked by child, 138, 148, 150–
　3, 155–6
　confusing the child, 65, 73, 90,
　109, 203
　controlling child, 77–80
　as couple to child, 109–14, 205
　cultural differences, 200–1, 206–
　11, 231
　explaining to child, 89–90
　and identification, 107–9, 118–22
　and infant separation, 67–70
　integrating feelings, 65–6
　loved and hated, 62, 65, 114
　in old age, 240
　phantasies about children, 203
　and sexuality, 110–14
Part and whole person, 20, 178–9
Persecutory anxiety, 64, 78, 83, 84,
　111–14, 135–6, 236–7
Phantasy
　and body function, 96–9
　and concepts, 90
　and gender, 95
　in grief, 255
　and guilt, 84
　in marriage, 195
　and masturbation, 143, 145, 148
　and parents, 38, 201–3, 210
　in play, 91–9
　in pregnancy, 30–5
　and reality, 57–62

　in senility, 243
　and sexuality, 109–14, 176
Piaget, J., 43, 45, 76, 100
Play
　and anxiety, 92
　compulsive, 164–6
　and discipline, 104
　egocentric, 100
　and gender, 95–6
　in infancy, 56
　make-believe, 91–4, 98–9
　and phantasy, 91–5
　sensory and manipulative, 72
　social, 100, 135–6
　wish-fulfilment, 94
Pregnancy, 25–39
Prejudice, 66, 84
Pride, 82
Primary maternal preoccupation,
　28, 43, 201
Privacy, 148, 179, 181
Problem-solving, 11–13, 161–4,
　187–8, 210
Projection, 122–3, 236–7
Psychodynamics, 11, 93
Psychosis, 58, 60–1, 84
Puberty, 140–9
Punishment, 80–136
Puzzlement, 90, 103

Rage, 61, 65
Reality
　representation of, 57–9, 60–1
　testing in courtship, 182–3
Rebellion, 138, 125–7
Reciprocal appreciation, 177–9
Reciprocity, 103–6, 135–6
Reflexes, 40–1, 43
Regression, 198, 220
Representations, mental, 18, 70
Repression, 124
Residues of childhood, 166–9
Responsibility, 125–7, 140, 161–6,
　203–6, 210–19
Retirement, 238–41

Revenge, 78, 86
Role play, compulsive, 164–6
Romance
   in learning, 164, 229, 239
   in love, 171–5

Sadness, 155
Scapegoating, 123, 138, 148
School, 128–33, 145, 160
Self
   in adolescence, 152–4
   attacks on, 151, 232
   awareness, 22
   control, 78, 104, 117
   criticism, 85, 117–22, 148
   efficacy, 137
   and ego, 54
   esteem, 31, 63, 86, 135, 139
   and guilt, 83, 118–22
   and identity, 158–9
   and masturbation, 142
   parts of, 176–8
   public image, 150–1, 157
   and reality, 60–1, 68, 70
   responsibility, 140
Senility, 242
Separation
   anxiety, 67–70
   from parents, 117, 138
Sex and gender, 94–6
Sexuality
   adolescent, 140–9, 154
   in childhood, 94–8, 109–14, 117
   in courtship, 171–85
   in marriage, 190–3
Shame, 82–5, 129, 130
Siblings, 106–7
Single people, 220–3

Sleep, 41, 55
Social background; see cultural differences
Social relations in childhood, 100, 103–6, 135–6
Socialization, 77–80, 133–6
Space, inner and outer, 53, 96, 101
Spitz, R., 63, 67
Splitting, 65, 85, 112, 122, 148–9, 189, 198
Sublimation, 222
Super-ego, 85–6, 118–22
Support; see holding
Symbolism, 91–9, 243

Taboo
   on death, 245, 249, 252–5
   on sexuality, 97–8, 111, 171
Terminal illness, 245–7
Theory construction, 15, 18, 51
Trauma, 48, 69, 92
Trust – mistrust, 47, 67–70, 79–80, 85, 190

Unconscious mental processes, 20, 53, 80, 123
Understanding
   empathetic mode, 21–2
   other individuals, 15–22
   physical mode, 19–21
Unintegration, 115–16

Violence
   in adolescence, 153
   and sexuality, 109–14

Winnicott, D. W., 28, 37, 43, 49
Wish-fulfilment, 58–9, 94, 98
Work, 159–64, 227–9